JOYFUL NOISE

An Anthology of American Spiritual Poetry

JOYFUL NOISE

edited by
Robert Strong

PITTSBURGH

Autumn House Press Staff
Executive Director: Michael Simms
Community Outreach Director: Michael Wurster
Co-Director: Eva Simms
Managing Editor: Christina Clark
Editorial Consultant: Ziggy Edwards
Technology Consultant: Matthew Hamman
Media Consultant: Jan Beatty
Tech Crew Chief: Michael Milberger
Special Events Coordinator: Joshua Storey
Contributing Editor: Mike James

ISBN: 978-1-932870-12-1
Library of Congress Control Number: 2006932673

All Autumn House books are printed on acid-free paper and meet the international standards of permanent books intended for purchase by libraries.

A Noiseless Patient Spider

A noiseless patient spider,
I mark'd where on a little promontory it stood isolated,
Mark'd how to explore the vacant vast surrounding,
It launch'd forth filament, filament, filament, out of itself,
Ever unreeling them, ever tirelessly speeding them.

And you O my soul where you stand,
Surrounded, detached, in measureless oceans of space,
Ceaselessly musing, venturing, throwing, seeking the spheres to connect them,
Till the bridge you will need be form'd, till the ductile anchor hold,
Till the gossamer thread you fling catch somewhere, O my soul.

Walt Whitman

The Autumn House Poetry Series

Michael Simms, General Editor

OneOnOne by Jack Myers
Snow White Horses, Selected Poems 1973-1988 by Ed Ochester
The Leaving, New and Selected Poems by Sue Ellen Thompson
Dirt by Jo McDougall
Fire in the Orchard by Gary Margolis
Just Once, New and Previous Poems by Samuel Hazo
The White Calf Kicks by Deborah Slicer / • / *2003, selected by Naomi Shihab Nye*
The Divine Salt by Peter Blair
The Dark Takes Aim by Julie Suk
Satisfied with Havoc by Jo McDougall
Half Lives by Richard Jackson
Not God After All by Gerald Stern
(with drawings by Sheba Sharrow)
Dear Good Naked Morning by Ruth L. Schwartz / • / *2004, selected by Alicia Ostriker*
A Flight to Elsewhere by Samuel Hazo
Collected Poems by Patricia Dobler
The Autumn House Anthology of Contemporary American Poetry,
edited by Sue Ellen Thompson
Déjà Vu Diner by Leonard Gontarek
Lucky Wreck by Ada Limón / • / *2005, selected by Jean Valentine*
The Golden Hour by Sue Ellen Thompson
Woman in the Painting by Andrea Hollander Budy
Joyful Noise: An Anthology of American Spiritual Poetry, edited by Robert Strong
No Sweeter Fat by Nancy Pagh / • / *2006, selected by Tim Seibles*

• Winner of the Autumn House Poetry Prize

Contents

Introduction

"God himself does not speak prose"
—*Ralph Waldo Emerson*

All poetry is spiritual. As I worked on this anthology, I heard this sentiment again and again, from poets and readers alike. The spiritual, after all, is what our existence soaks in; it is both everywhere and ineffable, always right here and just out of reach. We see it in blades of grass, sense it in love and the cry of a newborn, in the eyes of the dying, in volcanos and choirs. The question arises: are all spiritual things poetry? The following pages seem to answer that spiritual things give us templates of extra-ordinary perception that cannot be explained, unless by poetry.

American verse was born from three traditions grounded in direct experience of the spiritual in everyday life: Native, African, and Puritan. These cultures were at a radical remove from the "literary" traditions of Europe and the empires beyond. The men and women we call our earliest poets did not, in fact, consider themselves to be "poets" – they were only human beings struggling to make meaning of their existence. These struggles were spiritual ones, and they made writers of people who understood no distinction between spirituality and poetry, nor, for that matter, between the world and God. As the native song that opens this anthology declares, "I, the song, I walk here!" And on this our three merging tribes agreed: the song that walks here is God and, to the extent that any of us attempt to sing, we pray. When Emerson wrote that God does not speak prose, he was not describing the deity but explaining our own imperfect struggle to apply language to life – he was explaining our impulse for poetry. In the confluence of two disparate oral traditions and one bookish band of radical Protestants who believed that nothing, least of all men's words, can stand between us and the natural world that is God's book, American poetry emerges. It springs from an instinct to sing God's book and praises; it will grow into a great country's own scripture.

Readers will discover, in the more than four centuries represented here, nothing less than the construction of a national consciousness and conscience. If our earliest writers considered their poetry a natural extension of their spiritual engagement, our contemporary poets are returning along the same path: while most are without announced sectarian affiliations, the living poets in this collection find their spiritual awareness to be a natural and necessary foundation for their writing. That foundation has grown with America over the centuries to include multiple traditions – Jewish, Catholic, Muslim, Buddhist, Skeptic, and more are included here. Across generations and leanings, we discover a constant poetic-spiritual dilemma: a central observer overwhelmed by the eternal realization that he or she is not, after all, the center. From our false human center, poets cast out language, as Walt Whitman's spider-like soul does, "Ceaselessly musing, venturing . . . Till the goassamer thread you fling catch somewhere."

Many thanks to the contemporary poets included in this anthology, all of whom made the preliminary selections of the more "spiritual" among their work. These pieces represent, therefore, not this one editor's conception of spiritual poetry, but the idea as created by some of our most important and vibrant poets. Readers will find not only work dealing directly with life, death, and faith, but also with such divergent concerns as weapons systems, yoga, atheism, art, and frogs, in an expansive variety of poetic forms. Of the earlier works included here, many were not written originally as "poems"– some were not originally written down at all. There are songs that have been sung since before recorded time, spirituals grown from community practice, sermons delivered, and letters sent. There are a handful of hymns (such as "Amazing Grace") that, while their authors never ventured to America, have lived on our tongues so comfortably as to become an indelible part of our culture. What these pieces all share are the language and intent that makes them American spiritual poems indeed.

Readers will gather for themselves the many strains that emerge and persist in our common experience, but I should comment here on two of the more striking ones. First, the nature poem emerges as a dominant mode of American spiritual writing: present before time in Native song, recentralized by the great poets of the American Renaissance during the industrial nineteenth century, and desperately conserved in verse today as our (lost) paradise. Second, the original sin of slavery provides – sadly, hopefully – another major poetic-spiritual metaphor in our national library. As muse, America is not only the template of paradise and all the good we hope to accomplish there, but also the direct and very real result of our worst human behavior. While the rest of the world has its myths and fables to use as source material, America sings from the grit of our own lush and tragic soil.

It is my hope to provide readers with a comprehensive introduction to the rich tradition, and dynamic evolution, of American spiritual poetry. But it is also my hope to introduce readers to as many authors as possible, all of whom deserve further attention. The devoted reader will want to read not only all of

Whitman and Dickinson, but also Edward Taylor, Phillis Wheatley, and Jones Very; not only T.S. Eliot, but H.D.; not only the canonized names of our own generations, but newer ones like G.C. Waldrep, Brenda Hillman, and Brigit Pegeen Kelly. With that mission in mind, I bring to the page here as many names as possible, keeping the selections from many writers (and every living poet) to a single poem. I hope you will take each one as the starting point for an enriched reading of American spiritual poetry.

My grateful acknowledgment to Michael Simms and the entire Autumn House family, along with the librarians at Southworth and Owen D. Young libraries, the Humanities Department at SUNY Canton, and the Canton College Foundation, without whom this anthology would have been impossible.

Robert Strong

Ancient Native Songs

Modoc

I,
the song,
I walk here!

Potawatomi

1. Everybody sings,
Sings with this world,
With the wind, with the water.
You can hear the water roar.
I sing in the wind, sing to be heard.
I strike my drum. It sings in this world.
I shake my gourd. It sings too.
2. We all sing and dance,
Dance thanksgiving that we have lived so long.
So I sing in the water, sing in the air,
Sing with my drum, sing with my gourd.
We all sing in this roaring water,
As we hear it roar, roar, roar.
3. The Great Manido will help us
Singing, singing, singing!
Singing in this world!

Inuit

Delightful, the animals,
There is no song about them.
Words for a song are hard to find –
Seals on the ice, down here –
When I found a few words
I fit them to music –
The seals left for their breathing holes.

Delightful, the animals,
There is no song about them.
Words hard to catch –
Antlered caribou on the land, down here –
When I found a few words
I fit them to music –
When they crossed the plains.
Delightful, the animals,
There is no song about it.
Words hard to catch –
Bearded seals on the ice down here –
When I found a few words
I fit them to music –
When they left for their breathing holes.

Hamakhav / Mohave

This is the water, my water.
This is the river, my river.
  We love its water.
  We love its driftwood,
  Its foam wood.
It shall flow forever,
When the weather grows hot,
It will rise and overflow its banks,
It shall flow forever.

Yuki

This rock did not come here by itself.
This tree did not stand here of itself.
There is one who made all this,
Who shows us everything.

A'nish'inabeg / Chippewa / Ojibwa

An overhanging cloud
Repeats my words pleasingly!

•

In the middle of the sea,
  The vast sea,
  There I sit!

•

The receding sound
Of the nest,
  I listen to it!

•

Sometime I go about pitying myself
As I am carried across the sky.

•

What are you saying to me?
"I am arrayed like the roses,
And beautiful as they."

•

In the center of the earth,
  Wherever he may be,
  Or under earth.

Wazhazhe / Osage

Amid the earth,
Renewed in green plants,
Amid the rising smoke,
I see my grandfather's footprints as I wander from place to place.
I see the rising smoke as I wander.
Amid all forms visible, I see the rising smoke as I move from place to place.
Amid all forms visible, I see the little hills in rows as I move from place to place.
Amid all forms visible, I see the spreading blades as I move from place to place.
Amid all forms visible, I see the light of day as I move from place to place.

Salish

From now on,
You will be the fire drill,
For those who will be people
From now on.

Kwatsan / Yuma

  Howling Coyote took up common dirt
And scattered it toward the sky!
He caused the dirt to become
  Stars and rainbow.

Nuxalk / Bellacoola

My child perished like the sky when it broke.
Go to S'qlwalo'sem of the sky, my child!
Gladden my heart, my child,
Sit down in the mouth of the sky, my child!

Kwagutl / Kwakiutl

I am the Thunder of my people,
I am the Sea Monster of my people,
I am the earthquake of my people,
  When I start to fly
Thunder resounds through the world.
  When I rage
The voice of the Sea Bear
Rumbles through the world.

•

Slowly we race each other through the world.
Slowly we race, walking through this world.
Ha, I make the clouds!
  I come to you
From the north end of the world.

Ha, I bring the fog.
  I come to you
From the north end of the world.
Ha, I bring the red sky in the morning.
  When I come to you
From the Great Copper Bringer,
Ha, I bring the warmth.
  When I come to you
From the Great World Brightener.
Ha, and he will dance the Tongass Dance,
Your Chief's son,
Whom we praise.

Chahiksichahiks / Pawnee

Let us see, is this real,
This life I am living?
You Holy Ones who dwell everywhere,
Let us see, is this real,
This life I am living?

•

I am like a Bear.
I hold up my hands.
Waiting for the sun to rise.

Hopitu / Hopi

Your beautiful rays, may they color our faces;
Being dyed in them, somewhere at an old age,
  We shall fall asleep,
  Old women.

Hotcangara / Winnebago

I am ready.
I do not want to be put in chains.
Let me be free.
I have given away my life.
It is gone like that dust!
I would not take it back.
It is gone!

Mascoutens

Charcoal, Charcoal! Charcoal
Taught me how to follow the Great Spirit.
Power lies in the Charcoal!
The Charcoal lies in the fire,
And ashes come from the fire.
So my body will be, so will we all be!
We go down the same path.
We go down the Charcoal Way.
We go down to dust.

Dakota / Sioux

It was a protection predicted for me!
A lightning wears me!
Behold it!
It is Sacred!

Thomas Morton (b. 1575)

from *New English Canaan*

In the month of June, anno salutis 1622, it was my chance to arrive in the parts of New England . . . I did endeavor to take a survey of the country. The more I looked, the more I liked it. And when I had more seriously considered of the beauty of the place, with all her fair endowments, I did not think that in all the known world it could be paralleled, of so many goodly groves of trees, dainty fine round rising hillocks, delicate fair large plains, sweet crystal fountains, and clear running streams that twine in fine meanders through the meads, making so sweet a murmuring noise to hear as would even lull the senses with delight asleep – so pleasantly do they glide upon the pebble stones, jetting most jocundly where they do meet, and hand in hand run down to Neptune's court, to pay the yearly tribute which they owe to him as sovereign lord of all springs. Contained within the volume of the land are fowls in abundance, fish in multitude; and I discovered, besides, millions of turtledoves in the green boughs, which sat pecking of the full ripe pleasant grapes that were supported by the lusty trees, whose fruitful load did cause the arms to bend; among which here and there dispersed, you might see lilies and of the daphnean tree, which made the land to me seem paradise; for in mine eye 'twas nature's masterpiece; her chiefest magazine of all where lives her store. If this land be not rich, then the whole world is poor...

John Rolfe (b. 1585)

from *To Sir Thomas Dale Seeking Approval to Marry Pocahontas*

Let therefore this, my well-advised protestation, which here I make between God and my own conscience, be a sufficient witness at the dreadful Day of Judgement (when the secret of all men's hearts shall be opened) to condemn me herein, if my chiefest intent and purpose be not to strive with all my power of body and mind in the undertaking of so mighty a matter – in no way led (so far forth as man's weakness may permit) with the unbridled desire of carnal affection, but striving for the good of this plantation, for the honor of our country, for the glory of God, for my own salvation, and for the converting to the true knowledge of God and Jesus Christ of an unbelieving creature, namely Pocahontas, to whom my hearty and best thoughts are, and have for a long time been, so entangled, and enthralled in so intricate a labyrinth, that I was ever wearied to unwind myself thereout. But Almighty God, who never faileth His followers that truly invoke His Holy Name, hath opened the gate and led me by the hand so that I might plainly see and discern the safe paths wherein to tread.

Jonathan Winthrop (b. 1588)

from *A Model of Christian Charity, Written Onboard the Arabella, on the Atlantic Ocean, Anno 1630.*

We must delight in each other, make others' Conditions our own, rejoice together, mourn together, labour, and suffer together, always having before our eyes our Commission and Community in the work, our Community as members of the same body . . . that men shall say of succeeding plantations: the lord make it like that of New England: for we must Consider that we shall be as a City upon a Hill, the eyes of all people are upon us; so that if we shall deal falsely with our god in this work we have undertaken and so cause him to withdraw his present help from us, we shall be made a story and a by-word through the world...

Edward Johnson (b. 1598)

from *Good News from New-England*

With hearts revived in conceit, new land and trees they eye,
Scenting the Cedars and sweet fern from heats reflection dry,

Much like the bird from dolsome Romes enclosed in cage or wire,
  Set forth in fragrant fields doth skip in hope of her desire.
So leap the hearts of these mixed men by straights o'er seas inured,
  To following hard-ships wilderness, doth force to be endured.
In clipping arms of out-stretched Capes, there ships now gliding enter,
  In bay where many little Isles do stand in waters Center.
Where Sea-calves with their hairy heads gaze 'bove the water's brim,
  Wondring to see such uncouth sights their sporting place to swim.
The sea's vast length makes welcome shores unto this wandring race,
  Who now found footing freely for, Christ's Church his resting place.
.....
Unlevel'd lies this land new found with hills and valleys low,
With many mixtures of such mold where fruits do fertile grow.
Well watered with the pleasant springs that from the hills arise,
The waters run with warbling tunes, with stones that in them lies.
To welcome weary travellers, resting unneath the shade,
Of lofty banks, where lowly boughs, for them fresh harbour made.
.....
Bespread with Roses Summer 'gins take place with hasty speed,
  Whose parching heat Strawberries cool doth moderation breed.
Ayre darkening sholes of pigeons pick their berries sweet and good,
  The lovely cherries birds entice to feast themselves in woods.
The Turkeys, Partridge, Heath-hens and their young ones tracing pass,
  The woods and meadows, Acorns eat, and hoppers in the grass.
.....
Good wholesome and delightful food, variety and store,
  The Husbandman rejoicing keeps, with fruit the earth's womb bore.
Peas plenty, Barley, Oats and Wheat, Rye richly stocking stands,
  Such store the ploughman late hath found, that they feed foreign lands.
Cucumbers, melons, apples, pears, and plums do flourish fair,
  Yea what delight and profit would, they still are adding there.
.....
Yet unto God this people feeling says,
  Not unto us, but to thy name be praise.
Now must I mind what hindrances remain,
Some would none should endeavor unity,
  Tyrants (say they) do hinder liberty:
Why truth's but one, and Christ will make you free,
  Come to the Word, let that your touch-stone be.

William Bradford (b. 1590)

[untitled]

How greatly things here began to grow...
As wheat and rye, barley, oats, beans and pease.
Here all thrive, and they profit from them raise;
All sorts of roots and herbs in gardens grow,
Parsnips, carrots, turnips, or what you'll sow,
Onions, melons, cucumbers, radishes,
Skirrets, beets, coleworts, and fair cabbages...
Pears, apples, cherries, plums, quince, and peach,
Are now no dainties; you may have of each.

Roger Williams (b. 1603)

from *A Key into the Language of America: or, An Help to the Language of the Natives in That Part of America, called New-England.*

CHAP. XXI.
Of Religion, the soul, &c.

Manìt, mannittówock. *God, Gods.*

Obs. He that questions whether God made the World, the *Indians* will teach him. I must acknowledge I have received in my converse with them many Confirmations of those two great points, Heb. 11.6 *viz:*

1. That God is.
2. That he is a rewarder of all them that diligently seek him.

They will generally confess that God made all: but then in special, although they deny not that *English-mans* God made *English* Men, and the Heavens and Earth there! yet their Gods made them, and the Heaven and Earth where they dwell.

Nummusquaunamúckqun manìt. *God is angry with me.*

Obs. I have heard a poor *Indian* lamenting the loss of a child at break of day, call up his Wife and children, and all about him to Lamentation, and with abundance of tears cry out! O God thou has taken away my child! thou art angry with me: O turn thine anger from me, and spare the rest of my children.

If they receive any good in hunting, fishing, Harvests &c. they acknowledge God in it.

Yea, if it be but an ordinary accident, a fall, &c. they will say God was angry and did it.

musquàntum manit God is angry. But herein is their Misery.

First they branch their God-head into many Gods.

Secondly, attribute it to Creatures.

.....

More particular:

Two sorts of men shall naked stand
Before the burning ire 2 Thes. 1.8
Of him that shortly shall appear,
In dreadful flaming fire.

First, millions know not God, nor for
His knowledge care to seek:
Millions have knowledge store, but in
Obedience are not meek.

If woe to Indians, Where shall Turk,
Where shall appear the Jew?
O, where shall stand the Christian false?
O blessed then the True.

[Coarse Bread and Water's Most Their Fare]

Coarse bread and water's most their fare;
O England's diet fine;
Thy cup runs o'er with plenteous store
Of wholesome beer and wine.

Sometimes God gives them Fish or Flesh,
Yet they're content without;
And what comes in, they part to friends
and strangers round about.

God's providence is rich to his.
Let none distrustful be;
In wilderness, in great distress,
These Ravens have fed me.

[God Gives Them Sleep on Ground, on Straw]

God gives them sleep on Ground, on Straw,
on Sedgie Mats or Board:
When English softest Beds of Down,
sometimes no sleep afford.

I have known them leave their House and Mat
to lodge a Friend or stranger,
When Jews and Christians oft have sent
Christ Jesus to the Manger.

'Fore day they invocate their Gods,
though Many, False and New:
O how should that God worshipped be,
who is but One and True?

Anne Bradstreet (b. 1612)

from *Contemplations*

1
Some time now past in the Autumnal Tide,
When *Phoebus* wanted but one hour to bed,
The trees all richly clad, yet void of pride,

Where gilded o're by his rich golden head.
Their leaves and fruits seem'd painted, but was true
Of green, of red, of yellow, mixed hew,
Rapt were my senses at this delectable view.

2

I wist not what to wish, yet sure thought I,
If so much excellence abide below;
How excellent is he that dwells on high?
Whose power and beauty by his works we know.
Sure he is goodness, wisdom, glory, light,
That hath this under world so richly dight:
More Heaven than Earth was here, no winter and no night.

3

Then on a stately Oak I cast mine Eye,
Whose ruffling top the Clouds seem'd to aspire;
How long since thou was in thine Infancy?
Thy strength, and stature, more thy years admire,
Hath hundred winters past since thou wast born?
Or thousand since thou brakest thy shell of horn,
If so, all these as nought, Eternity doth scorn.

4

Then higher on the glistering Sun I gaz'd,
Whose beams was shaded by the leafy Tree,
The more I look'd, the more I grew amaz'd,
And softly said, what glory's like to thee?
Soul of this world, this Universe's Eye,
No wonder, some made thee a Deity:
Had I not better known, (alas) the same had I.

5

Thou as a Bridegroom from thy Chamber rushes,
And as a strong man, joys to run a race,
The morn doth usher thee, with smiles and blushes,
The Earth reflects her glances in thy face.
Birds, insects, Animals with Vegative,
Thy heat from death and dullness doth revive,
And in the darksome womb of fruitful nature dive.

6
The swift Annual, and diurnal Course,
Thy daily straight, and yearly oblique path;
Thy pleasing fervor, and thy scorching force,
All mortals here the feeling knowledge hath.
Thy presence makes it day, thy absence night,
Quaternal Seasons caused by thy might:
Hail Creature, full of sweetness, beauty and delight.

7
Art thou so full of glory, that no Eye
Hath strength, thy shining Rays once to behold?
And is thy splendid Throne erect so high?
As to approach it, can no earthly mould.
How full of glory then must thy Creator be?
Who gave this bright light luster unto thee:
Admir'd, ador'd for ever, be that Majesty.

8
Silent alone, where none or saw, or heard,
In pathless paths I lead my wandring feet,
My humble Eyes to lofty Skyes I rear'd
To sing some Song, my mazed Muse thought meet.
My Creator I would magnify,
That nature had, thus decked liberally:
But Ah, and Ah, again, my imbecility!

Thomas Tillam (c. 1620)

Upon the First Sight of New-England, June 29, 1638

Hail holy-land wherein our holy lord
Hath planted his most true and holy word
Hail happy people who have dispossest
Your selves of friends, and means, to find some rest
For your poor wearied souls, opprest of late
For Jesus-sake, with Envy, spite, and hate

To you that blessed promise truly's given
Of sure reward, which you'll receive in heaven
Methinks I hear the Lamb of God thus speak
Come my dear little flock, who for my sake
Have left your Country, dearest friends, and goods
And hazarded your lives o'th raging floods
Possess this Country; free from all annoy
Here I'll be with you, here you shall Enjoy
My sabbaths, sacraments, my ministry
And ordinances in their purity
But yet beware of Satan's wily baits
He lurks amonst you, Cunningly he waits
To Catch you from me; live not then secure
But fight 'gainst sin, and let your lives be pure
Prepare to hear your sentence thus expressed
Come ye my servants of my father Blessed

William Adams (c. 1620)

from *An Account of His Experiences Transcribed from His Own Handwriting*

I was born of Godly Parents who brought me up in the fear of God whereby I was restrained from many sins, yet my heart was very corrupt sinful and often breaking out in sinful ways and courses as occasion was offered unto me. In Old England I had many notions in my heart about Heaven and Hell and was sometimes thinking how I might know whether I should be saved or no. When I was between 14 & 15 years of age, I came over to New England and here living first under the ministry of Master Hooker and hearing of the misery of all men by Nature and of a work of conversion and believing in Christ, which I had heard little of before. I began to have some stirrings in my heart about my condition and began to think of setting upon seeking of God by prayer for the getting out of my Natural Condition, but was for a while kept from it by my own wretched sinful heart, being loath to take pains and making many excuses for want of convenient time and place. That I could not do it so secretly, as I would have done.

....

After this [the minister] preaching out of Eph 1:13 concerning the sealing of the spirit and coming to encourage the people of God to come up to assurance, to look to those signatures of the spirit of God and those Impressions of the grace of God upon the soul, which are given to be a seal and testimony, which stand firm. Though there may be decays in the sense and power of it and that we should hold it and not suspend our faith upon the sense of these testimonies, he farther directed us to look to the manner of our sealing. That it is after believing much work done before to melt and mould the soul and fit it for Christ. The marks of the seal, an agreement with the word of God, the heart turned to the will of God, with consent, submission, and conformity, though with Difficulty of performance, this stamp beats out the old stamp, though not perfectly and at once, yet that the heart is under the subduing work of the spirit and though he may be overcome. Yet it is that which we would not but would out with all, and that that is a bent of hearts and inclination Godward. He showed that these impressions of God upon the soul are seals and pledges that we are God's own, though never so small yet they were tokens between God and us and therefore we should not lose the comfort of them.

Samuel Danforth (b. 1626)

from *A Brief Recognition of New England's Errand into the Wilderness*

"What went ye out into the wilderness to see? A reed shaken with the wind?

But what went ye out for to see? A man clothed in soft raiment? Behold, they that wear soft clothing are in kings' houses.

But what went ye out for to see? A prophet? Yea, I say unto you, and more than a prophet" (Matt. 11.7-9).

These words are our Savior's proem to his illustrious encomium of John the Baptist. John began his ministry not in Jerusalem nor in any famous city of Judea, but in the wilderness, i.e., in a woody, retired, and solitary place, thereby withdrawing himself from the envy and preposterous zeal of such as were addicted to their old traditions and also taking the people aside from the noise and tumult of their secular occasions and businesses, which might have obstructed their ready and cheerful attendance unto his doctrine.

.....

The general question is, "What went ye out into the wilderness to see?" He saith not, "Whom went ye out to hear," but "What went ye out to see?" The phrase agrees to shows and stage plays, plainly arguing that many of those who seemed well affected to John and flocked after him were theatrical hearers, spectators rather than auditors; they went not to "hear," but to "see"; they went to gaze upon a new and strange spectacle.

.....

Doctrine: *Such as have sometime left their pleasant cities and habitations to enjoy the pure worship of God in a wilderness are apt in time to abate and cool in their affection thereunto; but then the Lord calls upon them seriously and thoroughly to examine themselves, what is it was that drew them into the wilderness, and to consider that it was not the expectation of ludicrous levity nor courtly pomp and delicacy, but of the free and clear dispensation of the Gospel and kingdom of God.*

Michael Wigglesworth (b. 1631)

"Meditation X" from *Meat Out of the Eater*

Although Affliction tanne the Skin,
Such Saints are Beautiful within.

1

How amiable is
The face of suffering Saints,
Where God thus quieteth their hearts
And stilleth their complaint!
Where 'tis their daily care,
And earnest heart's desire,
To love, and bless, and honour God
In middest of the fire.

2

Where nothing grieves them more
Than what their God doth grieve:
Where nothing pleaseth them like that
Which make them sin to leave.

Where though they have a will
And wishes of their own:
Yet at the foot of Jesus Christ
They meekly lay them down.

3
These are the happy men,
Judge of them what thou please
Vain world, amongst thy Darlings all
Thou hast not one like these.
As God is dear to them,
So they to him are dear,
And he to all the world ere long
Will make it to appear.

4
The Daughter of the King,
All glorious is within,
How Black soever and Sun-Burnt,
May seem her outward Skin.
Because I Blackish am
Upon me – look not ye,
Because that with his Beams the Sun
Hath looked down on me.

5
A patient suffering Saint
Is a right comely one:
Though black as *Kedar's* Tents, and as
Curtains of *Solomon*.
Thus beautify my soul
Dear Saviour; thus adorn it.
As for the Trappings of the world,
And Bravery, I can scorn it.

6
Some deck the outside fair;
But are like Graves within:
Some sweep and wash their houses clean;

Whose hearts most nasty been.
Some bodies fat and fair
Have Souls both foul and lean:
But howsoe'er my Body fare,
Lord make my soul more clean.

John Stansby (c. 1636)

from *Shepard's Confessions*

Tis a mercy I have long begged and waited for, and then I bless God for this I know I came in the world a child of hell, and if ever any a child of devil, I. . . . I sought a match for my lust; and herein I have been like the devil not only to hell myself but enticing and hailing others to sink rejoicing when I could make others drink and sin. And for aught I know, others in hell for them. And the Lord might have given me my portion, but when I lay in my blood, love came to me in Cambridge. . . . I knew my condition naught, yet my heart was so naught that I would have my haunts. . . . I would have my lusts and haunts . . . And here I found mercy of the Lord breaking my heart . . . And I saw as soon as ever I committed sin, I was condemned, and if pardoned, it must cost the heart blood of Christ, and that I did as much as in me lie to drag Christ to the cross.

Edward Taylor (b.1642)

Meditation 1.11 (Isai. 25.6)

A deity of Love Incorporate
My Lord, lies in thy Flesh, in Dishes stable
Ten thousand times more rich than golden Plate
In golden Services upon thy Table,
To feast thy People with. What Feast is this!
Where richest Love lies Cookt in e'ry Dish?

A Feast, a Feast, a Feast of Spiced Wine
Of Wines upon the Lees, refined well
Of Fat things full of Marrow, things Divine
Of Heavens blest Cookery which doth excell.
The Smell of Lebanon, and Carmell sweet
Are Earthly damps unto this Heavenly reech.

This Shew-Bread Table all of Gold with white
Fine Table Linen of Pure Love, 's ore spred
And Courses in Smaragdine Chargers bright
Of Choicest Dainties Paradise e're bred.
Where in each Grace like Dainty Sippits lie
Oh! brave Embroderies of sweetest joy!

Oh! what a Feast is here? This Table might
Make brightest Angells blush to sit before.
Then pain my Soule! Why wantst thou appetite?
Oh! blush to thinke thou hunger dost no more.
There never was a feast more rich than this:
The Guests that Come hereto shall swim in bliss.

Hunger, and Thirst my Soule, goe Fasting Pray,
Untill thou hast an Appetite afresh:
And then come here; here is a feast will pay
Thee for the same with all Deliciousness.
Untap Loves Golden Cask, Love run apace:
And o're this Feast Continually say Grace.

Meditation 1.34 (1Cor. 3.22)

My Lord I fain would Praise thee Well but finde
    Impossibilities blocke up my pass.
My tongue Wants Words to tell my thoughts, my Minde
    Wants thoughts to Comprehend thy Worth, alas!
    Thy Glory far Surmounts my thoughts, my thoughts
    Surmount my Words: Hence little Praise is brought.

But seeing Non-Sense very pleasant is
    To parents, flowing from the Lisping Child,
I Conjue to thee, hoping thou in this
    Will finde some hearty Praise of mine Enfoild,
    But though my pen drop'd golden Words, yet would
    Thy Glory far out shine my Praise in Gold.

Poor wretched man Death's Captive stood full Chuffe
    But thou my Gracious Lord didst finde reliefe,
Thou King of Glory didst, to handy cuff
    With King of Terrours, and dasht out his Teeth,
    Plucktst out his sting, his Poyson quelst, his head
    To pieces brakest. Hence Cruell Death lies Dead.

And still thou by thy gracious Chymistry
    Dost of his Carkass Cordialls make rich, High,
To free from Death makst Death a remedy:
    A Curb to Sin, a Spur to Piety.
    Heavens brightsom Light shines out in Death's Dark Cave.
    The Golden Dore of Glory in the Grave.

The Painter lies who pensills death's Face grim
    With White bare butter Teeth, bare staring bones,
With Empty Eyeholes, Ghostly Lookes which fling
    Such Dread to see as raiseth Deadly groans,
    For thou hast farely Washt Death's grim face
    And made his Chilly finger-Ends drop grace.

Death Tamed, Subdude, Washt fair by thee! Oh Grace!
    Made Usefull thus! thou unto thine dost say

Now Death is yours, and all it doth in't brace.
The Grave's a Down bed now made for your clay.
Oh! Happiness! How should our Bells hereby
Ring Changes, Lord, and praises trust with joy.

Say I am thine, My Lord: Make me thy bell
To ring thy Praise. Then Death is mine indeed
A Hift to Grace, a Spur to Duty; Spell
To Fear; a Frost to nip each naughty Weede.
A Golden doore to Glory. Oh I'le sing
This Triumph o're the Grave! Death where's thy Sting?

Meditation 1.32. (1Cor. 3.22.)

Thy Grace, Dear Lord's my golden Wrack, I finde
Screwing my Fancy into ragged Rhymes,
Tuning thy Praises in my feeble mind
Until I come to strike them on my Chimes.
Were I an Angel bright, and borrow could
King David's Harp, I would them play on gold.

But plung'd I am, my mind is puzzled,
When I would spin my Fancy thus unspun,
In finest Twine of Praise I'm muzzled.
My tazzled Thoughts twirled into Snick-Snarls run.
Thy Grace, My Lord, is such a glorious thing,
It doth confound me when I would it sing.

Eternall Love an Object mean did smite
Which by the Prince of Darkness was beguiled,
That from this Love it ran and swelled with spite
And in the way with filth was all defiled
Yet must be reconciled, cleansed, and begraced
Or from the fruits of God's first Love displaced.

Then Grace, my Lord, wrought in thy Heart a vent,
Thy Soft Soft hand to this hard work did go,
And to the Milk White Throne of Justice went
And entered bond that Grace might overflow.
Hence did thy Person to my Nature tie
And bleed through human Veins to satisfy.

Oh! Grace, Grace, Grace! this Wealthy Grace doth lay
  Her Golden Channels from thy Father's throne,
Into our Earthen Pitchers to Convey
  Heaven's Aqua Vitae to us for our own.
  O! let thy Golden Gutters run into
  My Cup this Liquor till it overflow.

Thine Ordinances, Graces Wine-fats where
  Thy Spirits Walks, and Graces runs doe ly
And Angels waiting stand with holy Cheer
  From Graces Conduite Head, with all Supply.
  These Vessels full of Grace are, and Bowls
  In which their Taps do run, are precious Souls.

Thou to the Cups dost say (that Catch this Wine,)
  This Liquor, Golden Pipes, and Wine-fats plain,
Whether Paul, Apollos, Cephas, all are thine.
  Oh Golden Word! Lord speak it o'er again.
  My Bells shall then thy Praises bravely chime.

Meditation 1.3. (Can. 1.3)

How sweet a Lord is mine? If any should
    Guarded, Engarden'd, nay, Enbossomed be
In reechs of Odours, Gales of Spices, Folds
    Of Aromatics, Oh! how sweet was he?
    He would be sweet, and yet his sweetest Wave
    Compared to thee my Lord, no Sweet would have.

A box of Ointments, broke; sweetness most sweet.
    A surge of spices: Odours Common Wealth,
A Pillar of Perfume: as steaming Reech
    Of Aromatic Clouds: All Saving Health.
    Sweetness itself thou art: And I presume
    In Calling of thee Sweet, who art Perfume.

But Woe is me! who have so quick a Scent
    To Catch perfumes puffed out from Pincks, and Roses
And other Muscadalls, as they get Vent,
    Out of their Mother's Wombs to bob our noses.

And yet thy sweet perfume doth seldom latch
My Lord, within my Mammulary Catch.

Am I de-nosed? or doth the Worlds ill scents
Engarrison my nostrils narrow bore?
Or is my smell lost in these Damps it Vents?
And shall I never find it any more?
Or is it like the Hawks, or Hounds whose breed
Take stinking Carrion for Perfume indeed?

This is my Case. All things smell sweet to me:
Except thy sweetness, Lord. Expell these damps.
Break up this Garrison: and let me see
Thy Aromatics pitching in these Camps.
Oh! let the Clouds of thy sweet Vapours rise,
And both my Mammularies Circumcise.

Shall Spirits thus my Mammularies suck?
(As Witch's Elves their teats,) and draw from thee
My Dear, Dear Spirit after fumes of muck?
Be Dunghill Damps more sweet than Graces be?
Lord, clear these Caves. These Passes take, and keep.
And in these Quarters lodge thy Odours sweet.

Lord, break thy Box of Ointment on my Head;
Let thy sweet Powder powder all my hair:
My Spirits let with thy perfumes be fed
And make thy Odours, Lord, my nostrils fare.
My Soul shall in thy sweets then soar to thee:
I'll be thy Love, thou my sweet Lord shalt be.

Meditation 1.7. (Ps. 45.2)

Thy Human Frame, My Glorious Lord, I spy,
A Golden Still with Heavenly Choice drugs filled;
Thy Holy Love, the Glowing heat whereby,
The Spirit of Grace is graciously distilled.
Thy Mouth the Neck through which these spirits still.
My Soul thy Vial make, and therewith fill.

Thy Speech the Liquour in thy Vessel stands,
Well tinged with Grace a blessed Tincture, Lo,
Thy Words distilled, Grace in thy lips poured, and,
Give Graces Tincture in them where they go.
The words in graces tincture stilled, Lord, may
The Tincture of thy Grace in me Convey.

That Golden Mint of Words, thy Mouth Divine,
Doth tip these Words, which by my Fall were spoiled;
And Dub with Gold dug out of Graces mine
That they thine Image might have in them foiled.
Grace in thy Lips poured out's as Liquid Gold.
Thy Bottle make my Soul, Lord, it to hold.

Christopher Noyes (b. 1647)

A Prefatory Poem

The *Fire* of *Meditation* burns
What *Sense* into the *Fancy* turns.
And all is Grist that comes to Mill
Where *thinking* is with *grace* and *skill*
For all men know the busy mind
Into one Object not confined.
The touch, the taste, Eye, Ear and Smell,
Invention, Judgement, Memory.
And Conscience have a faculty,
To make *all* praise him that made *all:*
The *Sanctified thus bless Him shall.*
There is a *Stone* (as I am told)
That turns *all Metals* into *Gold:*
But I believe, that there is none,
Save pious *Meditation*.

Francis Daniel Pastorius (b. 1651)

[Thy Garden, Orchard, Fields]

Thy Garden, Orchard, Fields,
And Vineyard being planted
With what good Nature yields,
Brave things to thee are granted;
Besides the Gifts of Grace,
Therefore go on and gather,
Use each kind in its place,
And Bless our God and Father,
Who gives so liberally,
What's needful for our Living.
And would us have Reply
In bowed-down Thanks-giving
To him, to whom belongs
All Praise in Prose and Songs.

[Most Weeds, Whilst Young]

Most weeds, whilst young,
An easy hand can pluck;
But when grown strong,
Men then must pull and tuck.
This thus apply, Friend
To thine Inward State,
What thoughts should die,
With speed eradicate:
Make no Delay
That Quick grass to destroy,
Before it may
The best of Plants annoy;
When once it sets
Its running Strings about,
And deep ground gets,
'Tis hard to Root it out.

Samuel Sewall (b. 1652)

Upon the Springs Issuing Out from the Foot of Plymouth Beach, and Running Out into the Ocean

The humble Springs of stately Plymouth Beach,
To all Inferiors, due Observance teach.
Perpetually Good Humor'd they concur,
Praying the Sea, Accept our Duty, Sir!
He, mild severe, I've now no need and When...
As you are come, Go back, and come again.

Cotton Mather (b. 1663)

The Sons of God, Singing Among the Trees of God

A Barren Tree! O, Why, My Lord,
  This Cumberer of the Ground;
Why has it not yet heard the Word,
  The Just Word, Cut it down!

'Tis owing, O my SAVIOUR, to
  thy Intercession still,
That I am sav'd and standing so,
  And not thrown down to Hell.

But from this Time, Oh, let me be
  A Tree of Righteousness:
Fill'd with the Fruits of it; A Tree
  Which thou wilt own and Bless.

A Tree planted and prun'd by GOD;
  Fix'd by His Water-side:
The Fruits thereof Rich, Sweet, and Good;
  And Thou thence Glorified.

From the Forbidden Tree I am,
  How Poison'd and Undone!
From thence, how dismal Mischiefs came,
  And Deaths, in which I groan!

But, O my SAVIOUR, By thy Death
  Upon a Tree, thou art
The Tree of Life, to which my Faith
  Flies with a Joyful Heart.

On Thee, O Tree of Life, I must
  Rejoicing Feed and Live;
Thou'lt me, when fell'd and laid in Dust,
  A Resurrection give.

Yea, When below to Mortal Eyes
  I must no more appear,
Transplanted to thy Paradise,
  I shall still flourish there.

Jonathan Edwards (b. 1703)

from *Images and Shadows of Divine Things*

147. The changing of the course of trade and the supplying of the world with its treasures from America is a type and forerunner of what is approaching in spiritual things, when the world shall be supplied with spiritual treasures from America.

156. The Book of Scripture is the interpreter of the book of nature two ways: viz. by declaring to use those spiritual mysteries that are indeed signified or typified in the constitution of the natural world; and secondly, in actually making application of the signs and types in the book of nature as representations of those spiritual mysteries in many instances.

Jupiter Hammon (c. 1711)

A Dialogue; Entitled, The Kind Master and the Dutiful Servant

1. Master.
According to thy place;
And surely God will be with thee,
And send thee heav'nly grace.

2. Servant.
Dear Master, I will follow thee,
According to thy word,
And pray that God may be with me,
And save thee in the Lord.

3. Master.
My Servant, lovely is the Lord,
And blessed those servants be,
That truly love his holy word,
And thus will follow me.

4. Servant.
Dear Master, that's my whole delight,
Thy pleasure for to do;
As far as grace and truth's in sight,
Thus far I'll surely go.

5. Master.
My Servant, grace proceeds from God,
And truth should be with thee;
Whence e'er you find it in his word,
Thus far come follow me.

6. Servant.
Dear Master, now without control,
I quickly follow thee;
And pray that God would bless thy soul,
His heav'nly place to see.

7. Master.
My Servant, Heaven is high above,
Yea, higher than the sky:
I pray that God would grant his love,
Come follow me thereby.

8. Servant.
Dear Master, now I'll follow thee,
And trust upon the Lord;
The only safety that I see,
Is Jesus's holy word.

9. Master.
My Servant, follow Jesus now,
Our great victorious King;
Who governs all both high and low,
And searches things within.

10. Servant.
Dear Master I will follow thee,
When praying to our King;
It is the Lamb I plainly see,
Invites the sinner in.

11. Master.
My Servant, we are sinners all,
But follow after grace;
I pray that God would bless thy soul,
And fill thy heart with grace.

12. Servant.
Dear Master I shall follow then,
The voice of my great King;
As standing on some distant land,
Inviting sinners in...

19. Master.
We pray that God would give us grace,
And make us humble too;
Let ev'ry nation seek for peace,
And virtue make a show.

20. Servant.
Then we shall see the happy day,
That virtue is in power;
Each holy act shall have its sway,
Extend from shore to shore.

21. Master.
This is the work of God's own hand,
We see by precepts given;
To relieve distress and save the land,
Must be the pow'r of heav'n.

22. Servant.
Now glory be unto our God,
Let ev'ry nation sing;
Strive to obey his holy word,
That Christ may take them in.

23. Master.
Where endless joys shall never cease,
Blessed Angels constant sing;
The glory of their God increase,
Hallelujahs to their King.

24. Servant.
Thus the Dialogue shall end,
Strive to obey the word;
When ev'ry nation act like friends,
Shall be the sons of God.

25.
Believe me now my Christian friends,
Believe your friend called HAMMON:
You cannot to your God attend,
And serve the God of Mammon.

26.
If God is pleased by his own hand
To relieve distresses here;
And grant a peace throughout the land,
'Twill be a happy year.

27.
'Tis God alone can give us peace;
It's not the pow'r of man:
When virtuous pow'r shall increase,
'Twill beautify the land.

28.
Then shall we rejoice and sing
By pow'r of virtues word,
Come sweet Jesus, heav'nly King,
Thou art the Son of God.

29.
When virtue comes in bright array,
Discovers ev'ry sin;
We see the dangers of the day,
And fly unto our King.

30.
Now glory be unto our God,
All praise be justly given;
Let ev'ry soul obey his word,
And seek the joy of heav'n.

Samson Occom (b. 1723)

Wak'd by the Gospel's Joyful Sound

Wak'd by the gospel's joyful sound,
My soul in guilt and thrall I found,
Exposed to endless woe:
Eternal truth aloud proclaim'd
The sinner must be born again,
Or else to ruin go.

Surpris'd I was, but could not tell
Which way to shun the gates of hell,
    For they were drawing near:
I strove indeed, but all in vain –
The sinner must be born again,
    Still sounded in my ear.

Then to the law I flew for help;
But still the weight of guilt I felt,
    And no relief I found:
While death eternal gave me pain,
The sinner must be born again,
    Did loud as thunder sound.

God's justice now I did behold,
And guilt lay heavy on my soul –
    It was a heavy load!
I read my Bible; it was plain
The sinner must be born again,
    Or feel the wrath of God.

I heard some tell how Christ did give
His life, to let the sinner live;
    But him I could not see:
This solemn truth did still remain –
The sinner must be born again,
    Or dwell in misery.

But as my soul, with dying breath,
Was gasping in eternal death,
    Christ Jesus did I spy:
Free grace and pardon he proclaim'd;
The sinner then was born again,
    With raptures I did cry.

The Angels in the world above,
And saints can witness to the love,
    Which then my soul enjoy'd.
My soul did mount on faith, its wind,
And glory, glory, did I sing,
    To Jesus Christ my Lord.

Come, needy sinners, hear me tell
What boundless love in Jesus dwell,
How Mercy doth abound;
Let none of mercy doubting stand,
Since I the chief of sinners am,
Yet I have mercy found.

John Newton (b. 1725)

Amazing Grace

Amazing grace! How sweet the sound
That saved a wretch like me!
I once was lost, but now am found;
Was blind, but now I see.
'Twas grace that taught my heart to fear,
And grace my fears relieved;
How precious did that grace appear
The hour I first believed!
Through many dangers, toils and snares,
I have already come;
'Tis grace hath brought me safe thus far,
And grace will lead me home.
The Lord has promised good to me,
His Word my hope secures;
He will my Shield and Portion be,
As long as life endures.
Yea, when this flesh and heart shall fail,
And mortal life shall cease,
I shall possess, within the veil,
A life of joy and peace.
The earth shall soon dissolve like snow,
The sun forbear to shine;
But God, Who called me here below,
Will be forever mine.

When we've been there ten thousand years,
Bright shining as the sun,
We've no less days to sing God's praise
Than when we'd first begun.

Traditional African American Spirituals

The Downward Road Is Crowded

Oh, the downward road is crowded, crowded, crowded,
Oh, the downward road is crowded,
with unbelieving souls.

Come, all ye wayward travellers,
And let us all join and sing,
The everlasting praises,
Of Jesus Christ our King.
Old Satan's mighty busy,
He follows me night and day,
And everywhere I'm appointed,
There's something in my way.

When I was a sinner
I loved my distance well,
But when I came to find myself,
I was hanging over Hell.

Oh, the downward road is crowded, crowded, crowded,
Oh, the downward road is crowded,
with unbelieving souls.

Hear the Lambs A-Crying

You hear the lambs a-crying,
Hear the lambs a-crying,
Hear the lambs a-crying,
Oh, shepherd, feed-a my sheep.

Our Savior spoke these words so sweet:
"Oh, shepherd, feed-a my sheep,"
Said, "Peter if you love me, feed my sheep."
Oh, shepherd, feed-a my sheep.
Oh, Lord, I love Thee, Thou dost know;
Oh, shepherd, feed-a my sheep.
Oh, give me grace to love Thee more;
Oh, shepherd, feed-a my sheep.

I don't know what you want to stay here for,
For this vain world's no friend to grace;
If I only had wings like Noah's dove,
I'd fly away to the heavens above.
When I am in an agony,
When you see me, pity me,
For I am a pilgrim travelling on
The lonesome road where Jesus gone.

Oh, see my Jesus hanging high,
He looked so pale and bled so free;
Oh, don't you think it was a shame,
He hung three hours in dreadful pain.

You hear the lambs a-crying,
Hear the lambs a-crying,
Hear the lambs a-crying,
Oh, shepherd, feed-a my sheep.

The Enlisted Soldiers

Hark! listen to the trumpeters,
They call for volunteers,
On Zion's bright and flowery mount,
Behold the officers.

They look like men, they look like men,
They look like men of war,
All armed and dressed in uniform,
They look like men of war.

Their horses, white with their armor bright,
With courage bold they stand,
Enlisting soldiers for their King,
They march to Canaan's land.
They look like men, they look like men,
They look like men of war,
All armed and dressed in uniform,
They look like men of war.

It set my heart in quite a flame,
A soldier thus to be,
I will enlist, gird on my arms,
And fight for liberty.
They look like men, they look like men,
They look like men of war,
All armed and dressed in uniform,
They look like men of war.

We want no cowards in our band,
That will their colors fly;
We call for valiant-hearted men,
Who're not afraid to die.
They look like men, they look like men,
They look like men of war,
All armed and dressed in uniform,
They look like men of war.

To see our armies on parade,
How martial they appear,
All armed and dressed in uniform.
They look like men, they look like men,
They look like men of war,
All armed and dressed in uniform,
They look like men of war.

They follow their great General,
The great Eternal Lamb,
His garment stained in His own blood,
King Jesus is his name.
They look like men, they look like men,
They look like men of war,
All armed and dressed in uniform,
They look like men of war.

The trumpets sound, the armies shout,
They drive the host of Hell,
How dreadful is our God to adore,
The great Immanuel.
They look like men, they look like men,
They look like men of war,
All armed and dressed in uniform,
They look like men of war.

I and Satan Had a Race

I and Satan had a race,
Hallelujah, hallelujah,
I and Satan had a race,
Hallelujah, hallelujah.

Win the race against the course,
Satan tells me to my face,
He will bring my kingdom down;
Jesus whispers in my heart,
He will build it up again.

Satan mounts the iron-grey,
Rides half way to Pilot-Bar;
Jesus mounts the milk-white horse,
Says you cheat my Father's children,
Says you cheat them out of glory;
Trouble like a gloomy cloud
Gathers thick and thunders loud.

I and Satan had a race,
Hallelujah, hallelujah,
I and Satan had a race,
Hallelujah, hallelujah.

Fare Ye Well

O, fare ye well, my brother,
Fare ye well by the grace of God,
For I'm going home;
I'm going home, my Lord,
I'm going home.
Master Jesus gave me a little broom,
To sweep my heart clean,
Sweep it clean by the grace of God,
And glory in my soul.

Dum-A-Lum

I was way down a-yonder a-by my self,
I was hunting a-for some bosom a-friend.
Away down yonder a-by my self-o,
Dum a la dum a lum a dum a lum.

An angel of the Lord done change my name,
  my brother,
An' I don't know where my leader's gone;

Good Lord, my Jesus done died one time,
  my brother,
An' he never 'tends to die no mo'.

'Twas a Mary and a Martha an' a James
  and a John,
An' all of them prophets are dead an' gone.

'Twas like a flower a-in a-bloom
That made Jericho for to fall so soon.

Good Lord, my Jesus done died one time,
    my brother,
An' he never 'tends to die no mo'.

Ezekiel Saw the Wheel

Ezekiel saw the wheel,
Away up in the middle of the air,
Ezekiel saw the wheel,
Away up in the middle of the air;
And the little wheel runs by faith,
And the big wheel runs by the grace of God,
'Tis a wheel in a wheel,
Away up in the middle of the air.

Some go to church for to sing and shout,
Before six months they are all turned out;
Let me tell you what a hypocrite'll do,
He'll talk about me and he'll talk about you;
One of these days about twelve o'clock,
This old world's going to reel and rock.

Ezekiel saw the wheel,
Away up in the middle of the air.

Ottiwell Heginbothom (b. 1744)

Fillmore

Great God, let all my tuneful pow'rs
  Awake, and sing Thy mighty name;
Thy hand revolves my circling hours,
  Thy hand from whence my being came.
Thus will I sing till nature cease,
  Till sense and language are no more;
And after death Thy boundless grace
  Through everlasting years adore.

Olaudah Equiano (Gustavus Vassa) (c. 1745)

From *Miscellaneous Verses; or, reflections on the state of my mind during my first convictions of the necessity of believing the truth, and of experiencing the inestimable benefits of Christianity*

Well may I say my life has been
One scene of sorrow and of pain;
From early days I griefs have known,
And as I grew my griefs have grown:

Dangers were always in my path;
And fear of wrath, and sometimes death;
While pale dejection in me reigned
I often wept, by grief constrained.

When taken from my native land,
By an unjust and cruel band,
How did uncommon dread prevail!
My sighs no more I could conceal.

To ease my mind I often strove,
And tried my trouble to remove:
I sung, and uttered sighs between –
Assayed to stifle guilt with sin.

But O! Not all that I could do
Would stop the current of my woe;
Conviction still my vileness showed;
How great my guilt – how lost from God!
.....
Yet here, 'midst blackest clouds confined,
A beam from Christ, the day-star, shined;
Surely, thought I, if Jesus please,
He can at once sign my release.

I, ignorant of his righteousness,
Set up my labours in its place,
Forgot why his blood was shed,
And prayed and fasted in its stead.

He died for sinners – I am one!
Might not his blood for me atone?
Tho' I am nothing else but sin,
Yet surely he can make me clean!

Thus light came in and I believed;
Myself forgot, and help received!
My Saviour then I know I found,
For, eased from guilt, no more I groaned.

O happy hour, in which I ceased
To mourn, for then I found a rest!
My soul and Christ were now as one –
Thy light, O Jesus, in me shone!

Bless'd by thy name, for now I know
I and my works can nothing do;
The Lord alone can ransom man –
For this the spotless Lamb was slain!

When sacrifices, works, and prayer,
Proved vain, and ineffectual were,
"Lo, then I come!" the Saviour cried,
And, bleeding, bowed his head and died!

He died for all who ever saw
No help in them, nor by the law: –
I this have seen; and gladly own
"Salvation is by Christ alone!"

Jane Dunlap *(c. 1745)*

from *[untitled]*

Shall his due praise be so loudly sung
By a young Afric damsel's virgin tongue?
And I be silent! No mention make
Of his blessed name, who did so often speak.

To us, the words of life,
Fetched from the fountain pure,
Of God's most holy sacred truths;
Which ever shall endure.

William Billings (b. 1746)

Chester

Let tyrants shake their iron rod,
And slavery clank her galling chains.
We fear them not; we trust in God;
New England's God forever reigns.

When God inspired us for the fight
Their ranks were broke, their lines were forced;
Their ships were shattered in our sight
Or swiftly driven from our coast.

The foe comes on with haughty stride;
Our troops advance with martial noise.
Their veterans flee before our youth,
And generals yield to beardless boys.

What gratefull offerings shall we bring?
What shall we render to the Lord?
Loud hallelujahs let us sing.
And praise his name on every chord.

Philip Freneau (b. 1752)

On the Uniformity and Perfection of Nature

On one fix'd point all nature moves,
Nor deviates from the track she loves;
Her system, drawn from reason's source,
She scorns to change her wonted course.

Could she descend from that great plan
To work unusual things for man,
To suit the insect of an hour –
This would betray a want of power,

Unsettled in its first design
And erring, when it did combine
The parts that form the vast machine,
The figures sketch'd on nature's scene.

Perfections of the great first cause
Submit to no contracted laws,
But all-sufficient, all-supreme,
Include no trivial views in them.

Who looks through nature with an eye
That would be the scheme of heaven descry,
Observes her constant, still the same,
I all her laws, through all her frame.

No imperfection can be found
In all that is, above, around –
All, nature made, in reason's sight
Is order all, and *all is right.*

Phillis Wheatley (b. 1753)

On Being Brought from Africa to America

'Twas mercy brought me from my pagan land,
Taught my benighted soul to understand
That there's a God, that there's a Savior too:
Once I redemption neither sought nor knew.
Some view our sable race with scornful eye.
"Their color is a diabolic dye."
Remember, Christians, Negroes, black as Cain,
May be refined, and join the angelic train.

from *Thoughts on the Works of Providence*

Arise, my soul, on wings enraptured, rise
To praise the monarch of the earth and skies,
Whose goodness and beneficence appear
As round its center moves the rolling year,
Or when the morning glows with rosy charms,
Or the sun slumbers in the ocean's arms:
Of light divine by a rich portion lent
To guide my soul, and favor my intent.
Celestial muse, my arduous flight sustain,
And raise my mind to a seraphic strain!

Adored forever be the God unseen,
Which round the sun revolves this vast machine,
Though to His eye its mass a point appears:
Adored the God that whirls surrounding spheres,
Which first ordained that mighty Sol should reign
The peerless monarch of the ethereal train:
Of miles twice forty millions is his height,
And yet his radiance dazzles mortal sight
So far beneath – from him the extended earth
Vigor derives, and every flowery birth:
Vast through her orb she moves with easy grace
Around her Phoebus in unbounded space;
True to her course in the impetuous storm derides
Triumphant o'er the winds, and surging tides.

Almighty, in these wond'rous works of Thine,
What Power, what Wisdom, and what Goodness shine!
And are Thy wonders, Lord, by men explored,
And yet creating glory unadored!

.....

Among the mental powers a question rose,
"What most the image of the Eternal shows?"
When thus to Reason (so let Fancy rove)
Her great companion spoke, immortal Love.

"Say, mighty power, how long shall strife prevail,
And with its murmurs load the whispering gale?
Refer the cause to Recollection's shrine,

Who loud proclaims my origin divine,
The cause whence heaven and earth began to be,
And is not man immortalized by me?
Reason let this most causeless strife subside."
Thus Love pronounced, and Reason thus replied.

"Thy birth, celestial queen! 'tis mine to own,
In thee resplendent is the Godhead shown;
Thy words persuade, my soul enraptured feels
Resistless beauty which thy smile reveals."
Ardent she spoke, and, kindling at her charms,
She clasped the blooming goddess in her arms.

Infinite Love wher'er we turn our eyes
Appears: this every creature's wants supplies;
This most is heard in Nature's constant voice,
This makes the morn, and this the eve rejoice;
This bids the fostering rains and dews descend
To nourish all, to serve one general end,
The good of man: yet man ungrateful pays
But little homage, and but little praise.
To Him, whose works arrayed with mercy shine,
What songs should rise, how constant, how divine!

from *On Imagination*

Imagination! who can sing thy force?
Or who describe the swiftness of thy course?
Soaring through air to find the bright abode,
Th' empyreal palace of the thund'ring God,
We on thy pinions can surpass the wind,
And leave the rolling universe behind:
From star to star the mental optics rove,
Measure the skies, and range the realms above.
There in one view we grasp the mighty whole,
Or with new worlds amaze th' unbounded soul.

Daniel Bliss (c. 1753)

[epitaph]

God wills us free; man wills us slaves.
I will as God wills; God's will be done
– Here lies the body of –
– JOHN JACK –
A native of Africa who died
March 1773, aged about 60 years.
Tho' born in a land of slavery
He was born free.
Tho' born in a land of liberty,
He lived a slave.
Till by his honest, tho' stolen labors,
He acquired the source of slavery,
Which gave him his freedom;
Tho' not long before
Death, the grand tyrant,
Gave him his final emancipation,
And set him on a footing with kings.
Tho' a slave to vice,
He practiced those virtues
Without which kings are but slaves.

Joel Barlow (b. 1757)

from *The Vision of Columbus*

from Book I

(Condition and soliloquy of Columbus. Appearance and speech of the Angel. They ascend the Mount of Vision. Continent of America draws into view, and is described by the mountains, rivers, lakes, soil, temperature and some of the natural productions.)

Columbus woke, and to the walls address'd
The deep-felt sorrows of his manly breast.
Here lies the purchase, here the wretched spoil,
Of painful years and persevering toil:
For these dread walks, this hideous haunt of pain,
I traced new regions o'er the pathless main,
Dared all the dangers of the dreary wave,
Hung o'er its clefts and topp'd the surging grave,
Saw billowy seas, in swelling mountains roll,
And bursting thunders rock the reddening pole,
Death rear his front in every dreadful form,
Gape from beneath and blacken in the storm;
Till, soft far onward to the skirts of day,
Where milder suns dispens'd a smiling ray,
Through brighter skies my happier sails descry'd
The golden banks that bound the western tide,
And gave the admiring world that bounteous shore
Their wealth to nations and to kings their power.
O land of transport! dear, delusive coast,
To these fond, aged eyes forever lost!
No more thy gladdening vales I travel o'er,
For me thy mountains rear the head no more,
For me thy rocks no sparkling gems unfold,
Or streams luxuriant wear their paths in gold;
For realms of promised peace forever borne;
I hail dread anguish, and in secret mourn.
.....
Thus mourn'd the hapless chief; a thundering sound
Roll'd round the shuddering walls and shook the ground
O'er all the dome, where solemn arches bend,
The roofs unfold and streams of light descend;
The growing splendor fill'd the astonish'd room,
And gales ethereal breathed a glad perfume;
Mild in the midst a radiant seraph shone,
Robed in the vestments of the rising sun;
Tall rose his stature, youth's primeval grace
Moved o'er his limbs and brighten'd in his face,
His closing wings, in golden plumage dressed,
With gentle sweep came folding o'er his breast,
His locks in rolling ringlets glittering hung,
And sounds melodious moved his heavenly tongue.

Rise, trembling Chief, to scenes of rapture, rise,
This voice awaits thee from the approving skies;
Thy just complaints, in heavenly audience known,
Call mild compassion from the indulgent throne;
Let grief no more awake the piteous strain,
Nor think thy piety or toils are vain.
Tho' faithless men thy injured worth despise,
Depress all virtue and insult the skies,
Yet look thro' nature, Heaven's conduct trace,
What power divine sustains the unthankful race!
From that great Source, that life-inspiring Soul,
Suns drew their light and systems learn'd to roll,
Time walk'd the silent round, and life began,
And God's fair image stamp'd the mind of man.
Down the long vale, where rolling years descend,
To thy own days, behold his care extend;
From one eternal Spring, what love proceeds!
Smiles in the seraph, in the Saviour bleeds,
Shines through all worlds, that fill the bounds of space,
And lives immortal in thy favour'd race.
Yet no return the almighty Power can know,
From earth to heaven no just reward can flow,
Men spread their wants, the all-bounteous hand supplies,
And gives the joys that mortals dare despise.
In these dark vales where blinded faction sways,
Wealth, pride and conquest claim the palm of praise,
Awed into slaves, while groping millions groan,
And blood-stained steps lead upwards to a throne.
Far other wreaths thy virtuous temples claim,
Far nobler honours build thy sacred name,
Thine be the joys the immortal mind that grace
Pleased with toils, that bless thy kindred race.
Now raise thy ravished soul to scenes more bright,
The glorious fruits ascending on thy sight;
For, wing'd with speed, from brighter worlds I came,
To sooth thy grief and show thy distant fame.

.....

Yet hear with reverence what attends thy state,
Nor pass the confines of eternal fate.
Led by this sacred light thy soul shall see,
That half mankind shall owe their bliss to thee,

And joyous empires claim their future birth,
In these fair bounds of sea-encircled earth;
While unborn times, by thine example pressed,
Shall call forth heroes to explore the rest.

Richard Allen (b. 1760)

See! How the Nations Rage Together

See! how the nations rage together,
Seeking of each other's blood;
See how the scriptures are fulfilling!
Sinners awake and turn to God.

We see the fig-tree budding;
You that in open ruin lie,
Behold the leaves almost appearing,
Awake! behold your end is nigh.

We read of wars, and great commotions,
To come before that dreadful day;
Sinners quit your sinful courses,
And trifle not your time away.

Consider now the desolation,
And the shortness of your time;
Since there's none but a dark ocean,
For all that don't repent in time.

Ye ministers that wait on preaching,
Teachers and exhorters too,
Don't you see your harvest wasting,
Arise, there is no rest for you.

O think upon that strict commandment,
God has on his teachers laid:

The sinner's blood that dies unwarned,
Shall fall upon the teacher's head.

Arise dear brethren, let's be doing,
See the nations in distress;
The Lord of hosts forbid their ruin,
Before their day of grace is past.

To see the land lie in confusion,
Looks dreadful in our mortal eye;
But O dear sinners, that is nothing,
To when the day of doom draws nigh.

To see the Lord in clouds descending,
Saints and angels guard him round;
The saints from earth will rise to meet
But sinners speechless at his frown.

To see the mountains a burning,
Mountains and hills must forward fly;
The moon in blood, the stars a falling,
And comets blazing thro' the sky.

O sinners! that's not all that's dreadful,
Before your Judge you must appear;
To answer for your past transactions,
How you ran your courses here.

The book of Conscience will be open'd
And your character read therein;
The sentence is, depart ye cursed,
And every saint will cry, Amen.

O Lord, forbid that this our nation,
That this should be our dreadful case;
O sinners turn and find salvation,
While now he offers you free grace.

'Tis now you have a gospel morning,
And yet the lamp holds out to burn;
'Tis now you have sufficient warning,
O sinners! sinners! will you turn?

John Stephenson (b. 1772)

Milford

If angels sung a Savior's birth,
  On that auspicious morn,
We well may imitate their mirth,
  Now He again is born.

John Jea (b. 1773)

Hymn 252. Works of Creation

Africa nations, great and small,
  Upon this earthly ball,
Give glory to the God above,
  And crown him Lord of all.

'Tis God above, who did in love
  Your souls and bodies free,
By British men with life in hand,
  The gospel did decree.

By God's free grace they run the race,
  And did his glory see,
To preach the gospel to our race,
  The gospel Liberty.

His wisdom did their souls inspire,
  His heavenly riches spread;
And by the Spirit of the Lord,
  They in his footsteps tread.

Hymn 281. Confession of Master and Mistress

Our master and our mistress too,
  To us they did confess,
That we were theirs, and not our own,
  They bought us with a price.

The price of silver and of gold,
  Which they did call their own,
The sons and daughters did the same,
  As their grandfathers did.

They did not think that God well knew
  All they did think and say
Against us poor African slaves,
  As they do every day.

But God who did poor Joseph save,
  Who was in Egypt sold,
So did he unto us poor slaves,
  And he'll redeem the whole.

Then shall we give him all the praise,
  And glory to his name;
Redeeming love shall be our song,
  And end with endless days.

Peter Williams, Jr. (b. 1780)

Hymn I

To the Eternal Lord,
By saints on earth ador'd
  And saints above.
Let us glad honors rear,
In strains of praise and pray'r
His glorious name declare,
  The God of Love.

When the oppressor's hands
Bound us in iron bands
  Thou didst appear.
Thou saw our weeping eyes,
And list'ning to our cries,
In mercy didst arise,
  Our hearts to cheer.

Thou did'st the trade o'erthrow,
The source of boundless woe,
  The world's disgrace,
Which ravag'd Afric's coast,
Enslaved its greatest boast,
A happy num'rous host,
  A harmless race.

In diff'rent parts of earth
Thou called the Humane forth,
  Our rights to plead,
Our griefs to mitigate,
And to improve our state,
An object truly great,
  Noble indeed.

Thou didst their labours bless,
And gave them great success,
  In Freedom's cause.
They prov'd to every sight
By truth's unerring light,
All men are free by right
  Of Nature's laws.

They to insure our bliss,
Taught us that happiness
  Is from above.
That it is only found
On this terrestrial ground,
Where virtuous acts abound,
  And Mutu'l Love.

William Ellery Channing (b. 1780)

from *Discourse at the Ordination of The Rev. Jared Sparks*

Our leading principle in interpreting Scripture is this, that the Bible is a book written for men, in the language of men, and that its meaning is to be sought in the same manner as that of other books. We believe that God, when he speaks to the human race, conforms, if we may so say, to the established rules of speaking and writing. How else would the Scriptures avail us more, than if communicated in an unknown tongue?

.....

We profess not to know a book, which demands a more frequent exercise of reason than the Bible. In addition to the remarks now made on its infinite connections, we may observe, that its style nowhere affects the precision of science, or the accuracy of definition. Its language is singularly glowing, bold, and figurative, demanding more frequent departures form the literal sense, than that of our own age and country, and consequently demanding more continual exercise of judgment . . . We find, too, that some of these books are strongly marked by the genius and character of their respective writers, that the Holy Spirit did not so guide the Apostles as to suspend the peculiarities of their minds.

Anonymous, New Hampshire (1784)

Jesus Christ the Apple Tree

The tree of life my soul hath seen,
Laden with fruit and always green:
The trees of nature fruitless be
Compared with Christ the apple tree.

His beauty doth all things excel:
By faith I know but ne'er can tell
The glory which I now can see
In Jesus Christ the apple tree.

For happiness I long have sought,
And pleasure dearly I have bought:
I missed of all; but now I see
'Tis found in Christ the apple tree.

I'm weary with my former toil,
Here I sit and rest a while:
Under the shadow I will be
Of Jesus Christ the apple tree.

This fruit doth make my soul to thrive,
It keeps my dying faith alive;
Which makes my soul in haste to be
With Jesus Christ the apple tree,
With Jesus Christ the apple tree.

William Cullen Bryant (b. 1794)

Thanatopsis

To him who in the love of nature holds
Communion with her visible forms, she speaks
A various language; for his gayer hours
She has a voice of gladness, and a smile
And eloquence of beauty; and she glides
Into his darker musings, with a mild
And healing sympathy that steals away
Their sharpness ere he is aware. When thoughts
Of the last bitter hour come like a blight
Over thy spirit, and sad images
Of the stern agony, and shroud, and pall,
And breathless darkness, and the narrow house,
Make thee to shudder, and grow sick at heart; –
Go forth, under the open sky, and list
To Nature's teachings, while from all around –
Earth and her waters, and the depths of air –

Comes a still voice. Yet a few days, and thee
The all-beholding sun shall see no more
In all his course; nor yet in the cold ground,
Where thy pale form was laid, with many tears,
Nor in the embrace of ocean, shall exist
Thy image. Earth, that nourished thee, shall claim
Thy growth, to be resolved to earth again,
And, lost each human trace, surrendering up
Thine individual being, shalt thou go
To mix forever with the elements,
To be a brother to the insensible rock
And to the sluggish clod, which the rude swain
Turns with his share, and treads upon. The oak
Shall send his roots abroad, and pierce thy mold.

Yet not to thine eternal resting-place
Shalt thou retire alone, nor couldst thou wish
Couch more magnificent. Thou shalt lie down
With patriarchs of the infant world – with kings,
The powerful of the earth – the wise, the good,
Fair forms, and hoary seers of ages past,
All in one mighty sepulchre. The hills
Rock-ribbed and ancient as the sun, – the vales
Stretching in pensive quietness between;
The venerable woods – rivers that move
In majesty, and the complaining brooks
That make the meadows green; and, poured round all,
Old Ocean's gray and melancholy waste, –
Are but the solemn decorations all
Of the great tomb of man. The golden sun,
The planets, all the infinite host of heaven,
Are shining on the sad abodes of death
Through the still lapse of ages. All that tread
The globe are but a handful to the tribes
That slumber in its bosom. – Take the wings
Of morning, pierce the Barcan wilderness,
Or lose thyself in the continuous woods
Where rolls the Oregon, and hears no sound,
Save his own dashings – yet the dead are there:
And millions in those solitudes, since first
The flight of years began, have laid them down
In their last sleep – the dead reign there alone.

So shalt thou rest – and what if thou withdraw
In silence from the living, and no friend
Take note of thy departure? All that breathe
Will share thy destiny. The gay will laugh
When thou art gone, the solemn brood of care
Plod on, and each one as before will chase
His favorite phantom; yet all these shall leave
Their mirth and their employments, and shall come
And make their bed with thee. As the long train
Of ages glides away, the sons of men –
The youth in life's fresh spring, and he who goes
In the full strength of years, matron and maid,
The speechless babe, and the gray-headed man –
Shall one by one be gathered to thy side,
By those, who in their turn, shall follow them.

So live, that when thy summons comes to join
The innumerable caravan, which moves
To that mysterious realm, where each shall take
His chamber in the silent halls of death,
Thou go not, like the quarry-slave at night,
Scourged to his dungeon, but, sustained and soothed
By an unfaltering trust, approach thy grave
Like one who wraps the drapery of his couch
About him, and lies down to pleasant dreams.

Amos Bronson Alcott (b. 1799)

Matter

Out of the chaos dawns in sight
The globe's full form in orbed light;
Beam kindles beam, kind mirrors kind,
Nature's the eyeball of the Mind;
The fleeting pageant tells for nought
Till shaped in Mind's creative thought.

Man

He omnipresent is,
All round himself he lies,
Osiris spread abroad,
Upstaring in all eyes:
Nature had globed thought,
Without him she were not,
Cosmos from Chaos were not spoken,
And God bereft of visible token.

Approaching God

When thou approachest to the One,
Self from thyself thou first must free,
Thy cloak duplicity cast clean aside,
And in thy Being's being be.

Anonymous (1801)

from *The Negro's Prayer*

Lord if thou dost with equal eye,
See all the sons of Adam die;
Why dost thou hide thy face from slaves,
Consign'd by fate to serve the knaves?
Stolen or sold in Africa,
Imported to America,
Like hogs or sheep, at market sold,
To stem the heat or brook the cold,
To work all day and half the night,
And rise before the morning light,
Sustain the lash, endure the cane,
Expos'd to storms of snow and rain,
Pinch'd with hunger and with cold,
And if we beg we meet a scold,
And after all the tedious round,
At night to stretch upon the ground.
Has Heaven decreed that negroes must,
By cruel men be ever cursed!
For ever drag the galling chain,
And ne'er enjoy themselves as men!
When will *Jehova* hear our cries!
When will the sun of freedom rise,
When will a Moses for us stand,
And free us from Pharaoh's hand?
What tho' our skin be black as jet,
Our hair be curl'd, our noses flat,
Must we, for this no freedom have,
Until we find it in the grave?

William Henry Furness (b. 1802)

The Soul

What is this that stirs within,
Loving goodness, hating sin,
Always craving to be blest,
Finding here below no rest?

Nought that charms the ear or eye
Can its hunger satisfy;
Active, restless, it would pierce
Through the outward universe.

What is it? and whither? and whence?
This unsleeping, secret sense,
Longing for its rest and food
In some hidden, untried good?

'T is the soul! Mysterious name!
Him it seeks from whom it came;
It would, Mighty God, like thee,
Holy, holy, holy be!

Ralph Waldo Emerson (b. 1803)

from *Journals and Letters*

April 18, 1824

I have, or had, a strong imagination, and consequently a keen relish for the beauties of poetry . . . Nor is it strange that with this confession I should choose theology, which is from everlasting to everlasting "debateable ground." For the highest species of reasoning upon divine subjects is rather the fruit of a sort of moral imagination...

August 5, 1835

The human mind seems a lens formed to concentrate the rays of the Divine laws to a focus, which shall be the personality of God. But that focus falls so far into the infinite that the form or person of God is not within the ken of the mind. Yet must that ever be the effort of a good mind, because the avowal of our sincere doubts leaves us in a less favorable mood for action, and the statement of our best thoughts, or those of our convictions that make most for theism, induces new courage and force.

August 1 / September 23, 1826

There are, I take it, in each man's history insignificant passages which he feels to be to him not insignificant; little coincidences in little things, which touch all the springs of wonder, and startle the sleeper conscience in the deepest cell of his repose; the mind standing forth in alarm with all her faculties, suspicious of a Presence which it behoves her deeply to respect . . . These are not the state reasons by which we can enforce the burdensome doctrine of a Deity on the world, but make often, I apprehend, the body of evidence on which private conviction is built . . . it is one of the *feelings* of modern philosophy, that it is wrong to regard ourselves so much in a *historical* light as we do, putting Time between God and us; and that it were fitter to account every moment of the existence of the Universe as a new Creation, and *all* as a revelation proceeding each moment from the Divinity to the mind of the observer...

selections from *Nature*

The foregoing generations beheld God and nature face to face; we, through their eyes. Why should not we also enjoy an original relation to the universe? Why should not we have a poetry and philosophy of insight and not of tradition, and a religion by revelation to us, and not the history of theirs?

In the woods is perpetual youth. Within these plantations of God, a decorum and sanctity reign, a perennial festival is dressed, and the guest sees not how he should tire of them in a thousand years. In the woods, we return to reason and faith. There I feel that nothing can befall me in life, – no disgrace, no calamity (leaving me my eyes), which nature cannot repair.

Standing on the bare ground, – my head bathed by the blithe air and uplifted into infinite space, – all mean egotism vanishes. I become a transparent eyeball; I am nothing; I see all; the currents of the Universal Being circulate through me; I am part or parcel of God.

I see the spectacle of morning from the hilltop over against my house, from daybreak to sunrise, with emotions which an angel might share. The long slender bars of cloud float like fishes in the sea of crimson light. From the earth, as a shore, I look out into that silent sea. I seem to partake its rapid transformations; the active enchantment reaches my dust, and I dilate and conspire with the morning wind. How does Nature deify us with a few and cheap elements! Give me health and a day, and I will make the pomp of emperors ridiculous.

Nature is the vehicle of thought, and in a simple, double, and threefold degree.

1. Words are signs of natural facts.
2. Particular natural facts are symbols of particular spiritual facts.
3. Nature is the symbol of spirit.

As we go back in history, language becomes more picturesque, until its infancy, when it is all poetry; or all spiritual facts are represented by natural symbols. The same symbols are found to make the original elements of all languages. It has moreover been observed, that the idioms of all languages approach each other in passages of the greatest eloquence and power. And as this is the first language, so is it the last. This immediate dependence of language upon nature, this conversion of an outward phenomenon into a type of somewhat in human life, never loses its power to affect us . . . A man's power to connect his thought with its proper symbol, and so to utter it, depends on the simplicity of his character, that is, upon his love of truth and his desire to communicate it without loss. The corruption of man is followed by the corruption of language.

Hence, good writing and brilliant discourse are perpetual allegories. This imagery is spontaneous. It is the blending of the experience with the present action of the mind. It is proper creation. It is the working of the Original Cause through the instruments he has already made.

The relation between the mind and matter is not fancied by some poet, but stands in the will of God, and so is free to be known by all men.

All things are moral; and in their boundless changes have an unceasing reference to spiritual nature. Therefore is nature glorious with form, color, and motion; that every globe is the remotest heaven, every chemical change from the rudest crystal up to the laws of life, every change of vegetation from the first principle of growth in the eye of a leaf, to the tropical forest and antediluvian coal-mine, every animal function from the sponge up to Hercules, shall hint or thunder to man the laws of right and wrong, and echo the Ten Commandments. Therefore is Nature ever the ally of Religion: lends all her pomp and riches to the religious sentiment . . . All things with which we deal, preach to us. What is a farm but a mute gospel?

Nature is made to conspire with spirit to emancipate us. . . . by mechanical means, is suggested the difference between the observer and the spectacle – between man and nature. Hence arises a pleasure mixed with awe; I may say, a low degree of the sublime is felt, from the fact, probably, that man is hereby apprized that whilst the world is a spectacle, something in himself is stable. In a higher manner the poet communicates the same pleasure. By a few strokes he delineates, as on air, the sun, the mountain, the camp, the city, the hero, the maiden, not different from what we know them, but only lifted from the ground and afloat before the eye. He unfixes the land and the sea, makes them revolve around the axis of his primary thought, and disposes them anew. Possessed himself by a heroic passion, he uses matter as symbols of it. The sensual man conforms thoughts to things; the poet conforms things to his thoughts.

selections from *Poetry and Imagination*

Natural objects, if individually described and out of connection, are not yet known, since they are really parts of a symmetrical universe, like words of a sentence; and if their true order is found, the poet can read their divine significance as orderly as in a Bible.

Every correspondence we observe in mind and matter suggests a substance older and deeper than either of these old nobilities. We see the law gleaming through, like the sense of a half-translated ode of Hafiz. The poet who plays with it best justifies himself; is most profound and most devout.

The poet knows the missing link by the joy it gives.

God himself does not speak prose, but communicates with us by hints, omens, inference and dark resemblances in objects lying all around us.

The endless passing of one element into new forms, the incessant metamorphosis, explains the rank which the imagination holds in our catalogue of mental powers. The imagination is the reader of these forms. The poet accounts all productions and changes of Nature as the nouns of language, uses them representatively, too well pleased with their ulterior to value much their primary meaning.

Poetry, if perfected, is the only verity; is the speech of man after the real, and not after the apparent.

He [the poet] observes higher laws than he transgresses.

"What news?" asks man of man everywhere. The only teller of news is the poet. When he sings, the world listens with the assurance that now a secret of God is to be spoken.

For poetry is faith. To the poet the world is virgin soil; all is practicable; the men are ready for virtue; it is always time to do right.

American life storms about us daily, and is slow to find a tongue. This contemporary insight is transubstantiation, the conversion of daily bread into the holiest symbols, and every man would be a poet if his intellectual digestion were perfect.

Poetry must be affirmative. It is the piety of the intellect. "Thus saith the Lord," should begin the song.

O celestial Bacchus! drive them mad, – this multitude of vagabonds, hungry for eloquence, hungry for poetry, starving for symbols, perishing for want of electricity to vitalize this too much pasture, and in the long delay indemnifying themselves with the false wine of alcohol, of politics or of money.

Poetry is inestimable as a lonely faith, a lonely protest in the uproar of atheism.

The Rhodora
On Being Asked, Whence Is the Flower?

In May, when sea-winds pierced our solitudes,
I found the fresh Rhodora in the woods,
Spreading its leafless blooms in a damp nook,

To please the desert and the sluggish brook.
The purple petals, fallen in the pool,
Made the black water with their beauty gay;
Here might the red-bird come his plumes to cool,
And court the flower that cheapens his array.
Rhodora! if the sages ask thee why
This charm is wasted on the earth and sky,
Tell them, dear, that if eyes were made for seeing,
Then Beauty is its own excuse for being:
Why thou wert there, O rival of the rose!
I never thought to ask, I never knew:
But, in my simple ignorance, suppose
That self-same Power that brought me there brought you.

Brahma

If the red slayer think he slays,
  Or if the slain think he is slain,
They know not well the subtle ways
  I keep, and pass, and turn again.

Far or forgot to me is near;
  Shadow and sunlight are the same;
The vanished gods to me appear;
  And one to me are shame and fame.

They reckon ill who leave me out;
  When me they fly, I am the wings;
I am the doubter and the doubt,
  And I the hymn the Brahmin sings.

The strong gods pine for my abode
  And pine in vain the sacred Seven;
But thou, meek lover of the good!
  Find me, and turn thy back on heaven.

Nathaniel Hawthorne (b. 1804)

The Ocean

The Ocean has its silent caves,
Deep, quiet and alone;
Though there be fury on the waves,
Beneath them there is none.
The awful spirits of the deep
Hold their communion there;
And there are those for whom we weep,
The young, the bright, the fair.

Calmly the wearied seamen rest
Beneath their own blue sea.
The ocean solitudes are blessed,
For there is purity.
The earth has guilt, the earth has care,
Unquiet are its graves;
But peaceful sleep is ever there,
Beneath the dark blue waves.

Frederic Henry Hedge (b. 1805)

Questionings

Hath this world, without me wrought,
Other substance than my thought?
Lives it by my sense alone,
Or by essence of its own?
Will its life, with mine begun,
Cease to be when that is done,
Or another consciousness
With the self-same forms impress?

Doth yon fireball, poised in air,
Hang by my permission there?
Are the clouds that wander by,
But the offspring of mine eye,
Born with every glance I cast,
Perishing when that is past?
And those thousand, thousand eyes,
Scattered through the twinkling skies,
Do they draw their life from mine,
Or, of their own beauty shine?

Now I close my eyes, my ears,
And creation disappears;
Yet if I but speak the word,
All creation is restored.
Or – more wonderful – within,
New creations do begin;
Hues more bright and forms more rare,
Than reality doth wear,
Flash across my inward sense,
Born of the mind's omnipotence.

Soul! that all informest, say!
Shall these glories pass away?
Will those planets cease to blaze,
When these eyes no longer gaze?
And the life of things be o'er,
When these pulses beat no more?

Thought! that in me works and lives, –
Life to all things living gives, –
Art thou not thyself, perchance,
But the universe in trance?
A reflection inly flung
By that world thou fanciedst sprung
From thyself; – thyself a dream; –
Of the world's thinking thou the theme.

Be it thus, or be thy birth
From a source above the earth.
Be thou matter, be thou mind,

In thee alone myself I find,
And through thee alone, for me,
Hath this world reality.
Therefore, in thee will I live,
To thee all myself will give,
Losing still, that I may find,
This bounded self in boundless Mind.

Joseph Smith (b. 1805)

from *Pearl of Great Price,* Joseph Smith 2.25

So it was with me. I had actually seen a light, and in the midst of that light I saw two Personages, and they did in reality speak to me; and though I was hated and persecuted for saying that I had seen a vision, yet it was true; and while they were persecuting me, reviling me, and speaking all manner of evil against me falsely or so saying, I was led to say in my heart: Why persecute me for telling the truth? I have actually seen a vision; and who am I that I can withstand God, or why does the world think to make me deny what I have actually seen? For I had seen a vision; I knew it, and I knew that God knew it, and I could not deny it, neither dared I do it; at least I knew that by so doing I would offend God, and come under condemnation.

John Greenleaf Whittier (b. 1807)

All's Well

The clouds, which rise with thunder, slake
  Our thirsty souls with rain;
The blow most dreaded fallst to break
  From off our limbs a chain;

And wrongs of man to man but make
  The love of God more plain.
As through the shadowy lens of even
The eye looks farthest into heaven
On gleams of star and depths of blue
The glaring sunshine never knew!

First-Day Thoughts

In calm and cool and silence, once again,
  I find my old accustomed place among
  My brethren, where, perchance, no human tongue
  Shall utter words; where never hymn is sung,
Nor dim light falling through the pictured pane!
There, syllabled by silence, let me hear
The still small voice which reached the prophet's ear;
Read in my heart a still diviner law
Than Israel's leader on his tables saw!
There let me strive with each besetting sin,
  Recall my wandering fancies, and restrain
  The sore disquiet of a restless brain;
  And, as the path of duty is made plain,
May grace be given that I may walk therein,
  Not like the hireling, for his selfish gain,
With backward glances and reluctant tread,
Making a merit of his coward dread,
  But, cheerful, in the light around me thrown,
  Walking as one to pleasant service led;
  Doing God's will as if it were my own,
Yet trusting not in mine, but in His strength alone!

Giving and Taking

I have attempted to put in English verse a prose translation of a poem by Tinnevaluva, a Hindoo poet of the third century of our era. (Whittier's note)

Who gives and hides the giving hand,
  Nor counts on favor, fame, or praise,
  Shall find his smallest gift outweighs
The burden of the sea and land.

Who gives to whom hath naught been given,
  His gift in need, though small indeed
  As is the grass-blade's wind-blown seed,
Is large as earth and rich as heaven.

Forget it not, O man, to whom
  A gift shall fall, while yet on earth;
  Yeah, even to thy seven-fold birth
Recall it in the lives to come.

Who broods above a wrong in thought
  Sins much; but greater sin is his
  Who, fed and clothed with kindnesses,
Shall count the holy alms as naught.

Who dares to curse the hands that bless
  Shall know of sin the deadliest cost;
  The patience of the heavens is lost
Beholding the man's unthankfulness.

For he who breaks all laws may still
  In Sivam's mercy be forgiven;
  But none can save, in earth or heaven,
The wretch who answers good with ill.

The Word

Voice of the Holy Spirit, make known
  Man to himself, a witness swift and sure,
  Warning, approving, true and wise and pure,
Counsel and guidance that misleadeth none!
By thee the mystery of life is read;
  The picture-writing of the world's gray seers,
  The myths and parables of the primal years,
Whose letter kills, by thee interpreted
Take healthful meanings fitted to our needs,
  And in the soul's vernacular express
  The common law of simple righteousness.
Hatred of cant and doubt of human creeds
May well be felt: the unpardonable sin
Is to deny the Word of God within!

Utterance

But what avail inadequate words to reach
  The innermost of Truth? Who shall essay,
  Blinded and weak, to point and lead the way,
Or solve the mystery in familiar speech?
Yet, if it be that something not thy own,
  Some shadow of the Thought to which our schemes,
  Creeds, cult, and ritual are at best but dreams,
Is even to thy unworthiness made known,
Thou mayst not hide what yet thou shouldst not dare
  To utter lightly, lest on lips of thine
  The real seem false, the beauty undivine.
So, weighing duty in the scale of prayer,
Give what seems given thee. It may prove a seed
Of goodness dropped in fallow-grounds of need.

Henry Wadsworth Longfellow (b. 1807)

A Psalm of Life
What the Heart of the Young Man Said to the Psalmist

Tell me not, in mournful numbers,
  Life is but an empty dream! –
For the soul is dead that slumbers,
  And things are not what they seem.

Life is real! Life is earnest!
  And the grave is not its goal;
Dust thou art, to dust returnest,
  Was not spoken of the soul.

Not enjoyment, and not sorrow,
  Is our destined end or way;
But to act, that each tomorrow
  Find us farther than to-day.

Art is long, and Time is fleeting,
  And our hearts, though stout and brave,
Still, like muffled drums, are beating
  Funeral marches to the grave.

In the world's broad field of cattle,
  In the bivouac of Life,
Be not like dumb, driven cattle!
  Be a hero in the strife!

Trust no Future, howe'er pleasant!
  Let the dead Past bury its dead!
Act, – act in the living Present!
  Heart within, and God o'erhead!

Lives of great men all around us
  We can make our lives sublime,
And, departing, leave behind us
  Footprints on the sands of time;

Footprints, that perhaps another,
  Sailing o'er life's solemn main,
A forlorn and shipwrecked brother,
  Seeing, shall take heart again.

Let us, then, be up and doing,
  With a heart for any fate;
Still achieving, still pursuing,
  Learn to labor and to wait.

The Slave Singing at Midnight

Loud he sang the psalm of David!
He, a Negro and enslavèd,
Sang of Israel's victory,
Sang of Zion, bright and free.

In that hour, when night is calmest,
Sang he from the Hebrew Psalmist,
In a voice so sweet and clear
That I could not choose but hear,

Songs of triumph, and ascriptions,
Such as reached the swart Egyptians,
When upon the Red Sea coast
Perished Pharaoh and his host.

And the voice of his devotion
Filled my soul with strange emotion;
For its tones by turns were glad,
Sweetly solemn, wildly sad.

Paul and Silas, in their prison,
Sang of Christ, the Lord arisen.
And an earthquake's arm of might
Broke their dungeon-gates at night.

But, alas! what holy angel
Brings the Slave this glad evangel?
And what earthquake's arm of might
Breaks his dungeon-gates at night?

Michael Fortune (1808)

New Year's Anthem

To Thee, Almighty, gracious power,
Who sit'st, enthroned, in radiant heaven,
On this bless'd morn, this hallow'd hour,
The homage of the heart be given!

Lift up your soul to God on high,
The fountain of eternal grace,
Who, with a tender father's eye,
Look'd down on Afric's helpless race!

The nations heard His stern commands!
Britannia kindly sets us free;
Columbia tears the galling bands,
And gives the sweets of Liberty.

Then strike the lyre! your voices raise!
Let gratitude inspire your song!
Pursue religion's holy ways,
Shun sinful Pleasure's giddy throng!

From Mercy's seat may grace descend,
To wake contrition's heartfelt sighs!
O! may our pious strains ascend,
Where ne'er the sainted spirit dies!

Then, we our freedom shall retain,
In peace and love, and cheerful toil:
Plenty shall flow from the wide main,
And golden harvest from the soil.

Ye nations that to us restore
The rights which God bestow'd on all;
For you His blessing we implore:
O! listen further to His call!

From one parental stem ye spring,
A kindred blood your bosoms own;
Your kindred tongues God's praises sing,
And beg forgiveness at his throne:

O, then, your mutual wrongs forgive,
Unlock your hearts to social love!
So shall ye safe and happy live,
By grace and blessings from above.

William Hamilton (1808)

Hymn Sung on the Second Anniversary of the Abolition of the Slave Trade

Great God, what wonders have been wrought,
  For us by thy almighty hand,
In cutting off the trade which brought
  Direful confusion in our land.

Its cruel power with dreadful sway,
  On Afric's peaceful, happy shore,
Spread war, confusion and dismay,
  And drench'd its fields with human gore.

Those dwellings where true happiness,
  Did long and constantly reside,
Were robb'd of peace, content, and bliss,
  And every pleasing hope beside.

Those knit of soft conjugal love,
  Were sever'd by a barb'rous stroke;
And doom'd in distant climes to prove
  A tyrant's cruel galling yoke.

Parents from children oft were torn,
  Relations from relations near;
And doom'd forever thence to mourn
  the loss of friends by nature dear.

But in supreme, unbounded love,
  Thou didst behold their suff'ring plight,
And from thy splendid courts above
  Asserted injur'd Afric's right.

Thy powerful arm the host restrain
  Which ravag'd wide its golden shore;
And crowns its spicy, fertile plains,
  With peace and happiness once more.

Let ev'ry heart then join to bless
  And glorify thy holy name,
Let every tongue thy love confess,
  And shout aloud thy matchless name.

Edgar Allan Poe (b. 1809)

Sonnet, Silence

There are some qualities – some incorporate things,
    That have a double life, which thus is made
A type of that twin entity which springs
    From matter and light, evinced in solid and shade.
There is a two-fold *Silence* – sea and shore –
    Body and Soul. One dwells in lonely places,
    Newly with grass o'ergrown; some solemn graces,
Some human memories and tearful lore,
Render him terrorless: his name's "No more."
He is the corporate Silence: dread him not!
    No power hath he of evil in himself;

But should some urgent fate (untimely lot!)
    Bring thee to meet his shadow (nameless elf,
That haunteth the lone regions where hath trod
No foot of man,) commend thyself to God!

Margaret Fuller (b. 1810)

Let Me Gather from the Earth

Let me gather from the Earth, one full grown fragrant flower,
Let it bloom within my bosom through its one blooming hour.
Let it die within my bosom and to its parting breath
Mine shall answer, *having lived,* I shrink not now from death.
It is this niggard halfness that turns my heart to stone,
'Tis the cup seen, not tasted, that makes the infant moan.
Let me for once press firm my lips upon the moment's brow,
Let me for once distinctly feel *I am all happy now,*
And bliss shall seal a blessing upon that moment's brow.

Ellen Sturgis Hooper (b. 1812)

Better a Sin Which Purposed Wrong to None

Better a sin which purposed wrong to none
Than this still wintry coldness at the heart,
A penance might be borne for evil done
And tears of grief and love might ease the smart.
But this self-satisfied and cold respect
To virtue which must be its own reward,
Heaven keep us through this danger still alive,
Lead us not into greatness, heart-abhorred –

Oh God, who framed this stern New-England land,
Its clear cold waters, and its clear, cold soul,
Thou givest tropic climes and youthful hearts
Thou weightest spirits and dost all control –
Teach me to wait for all – to bear the fault
That most I hate because it is my own,
And if I fail through foul conceit of good,
Let me sin deep so I may cast no stone.

Charles Timothy Brooks (b. 1813)

The Great Voices

A voice from the sea to the mountains,
From the mountains again to the sea;
A call from the deep to the fountains:
O spirit! be glad and be free!

A cry from the floods to the fountains,
And torrents repeat the glad song
As they leap from the breast of the mountains:
O spirit! be free and be strong!

The pine forests thrill with emotion
Of praise as the spirit sweeps by;
With the voice like the murmur of ocean
To the soul of the listener they cry.

Oh, sing, human heart, like the fountains,
With joy reverential and free;
Contented and calm as the mountains,
And deep as the woods and the sea.

Christopher Pearse Cranch (b. 1813)

Correspondences

All things in nature are beautiful types to the soul that can read them;
Nothing exists upon earth, but for unspeakable ends,
Every object that speaks to the senses was meant for the spirit;
Nature is but a scroll; God's handwriting thereon.
Ages ago when man was pure, ere the flood overwhelmed him,
While in the image of God every soul yet lived,
Every thing stood as a letter or word of a language familiar,
Telling of truths which now only the angels can read.
Lost to man was the key of those sacred hieroglyphics,
Stolen away by sin, till by heaven restored.
Now with infinite pains we here and there spell out a letter,
Here and there will the sense feebly shine though the dark.
When we perceive the light that breaks through the visible symbol,
What exultation is ours! *We* the discovery have made!
Yet is the meaning the same as when Adam lived sinless in Eden,
Only long hidden it slept, and now again is revealed.
Man unconsciously uses figures of speech every moment,
Little dreaming the cause why to such terms he is prone,
Little dreaming that every thing here has its own correspondence
Folded within its form, as in the body the soul.
Gleams of the mystery fall on us still, though much is forgotten,
And through our commonest speech, illumine the path of our thoughts.

Thus doth the lordly sun shine forth a type of the God-head;
Wisdom and love the beams that stream on a darkened world.
Thus do the sparkling waters flow, giving joy to the desert,
And the fountain of life opens itself to the thirst.
Thus doth the word of God distil like the rain and the dew-drops;
Thus doth the warm wind breathe like to the Spirit of God;
And the green grass and the flowers are signs of the regeneration.

O thou Spirit of Truth, visit our minds once more,
Give us to read in letters of light the language celestial
Written all over the earth, written all over the sky –
Thus may we bring our hearts once more to know our Creator,
Seeing in all things around, types of the Infinite Mind.

Jones Very (b. 1813)

Nature

The bubbling brook doth leap when I come by,
Because my feet find measure with its call;
The birds know when the friend they love is nigh,
For I am known to them both great and small;
The flowers, which on the lovely hill-side grow,
Expect me there, when Spring their bloom has given;
And many a bush and tree my wanderings know,
And e'en the clouds and silent stars of heaven:
For he, who with his Maker walks aright,
Shall be their lord, as Adam was before;
His ear shall catch each sound with new delight,
Each object wear the dress that then it wore;
And he, as when erect in soul he stood,
Hear from his Father's lips that all is good.

The Hand and Foot

The hand and foot that stir not, they shall find
Sooner than all the rightful place to go;
Now in their motion free as roving wind,
Though first no snail more limited and slow;
I mark them full of labor all the day,
Each active motion made in perfect rest;
They cannot from their path mistaken stray,
Though 'tis not theirs, yet in it they are blest;
The bird has not their hidden track found out,
Nor cunning fox, though full of art he be;
It is the way unseen, the certain route,
Where ever bound, yet thou art ever free;
The path of Him, whose perfect law of love
Bids spheres and atoms in just order move.

The Winter Rain

The rain comes down, it comes without our call;
Each pattering drop knows well its destined place,
And soon the fields whereon the blessings fall,
shall change their frosty look for Spring's sweet face;
So fall the words thy Holy Spirit sends,
Upon the heart where Winter's robe is flung;
They shall go forth as certain of their ends,
As the wet drops from out thy vapors wrung;
Spring will not tarry, though more late its rose
Shall bud and bloom upon the sinful heart;
Yet when it buds, forever there it blows,
And hears no Winter bid its bloom depart;
It strengthens with his storms, and grows more bright,
When o'er the earth is cast his mantle white.

The New Birth

'Tis a new life – thoughts move not as they did
With slow uncertain steps across my mind,
In thronging haste fast pressing on they bid
The portals open to the viewless wind;
That comes not, save when in the dust is laid
The crown of pride that gilds each mortal brow,
And from before man's vision melting fade
The heavens and earth – Their walls are falling now –
Fast crowding on each thought claims utterance strong,
Storm-lifted waves swift rushing to the shore
On from the sea they send their shouts along,
Back through the cave-worn rocks their thunders roar,
And I a child of God by Christ made free
Start from death's slumbers to eternity.

The Spirit

I would not breathe, when blows thy mighty wind
O'er desolate hill and winter-blasted plain,
But stand in waiting hope if I may find
Each flower recalled to newer life again;
That now unsightly hide themselves from Thee,
Amid the leaves or rustling grasses dry,
With ice-cased rock and snowy-mantled tree
Ashamed lest Thou their nakedness should spy;
But Thou shalt breathe and every rattling bough
Shall gather leaves; each rock with rivers flow;
And they that hide them from thy presence now
In new found robes along thy path shall glow,
And meadows at thy coming fall and rise,
Their green waves sprinkled with a thousand eyes.

William Ellery Channing II (b. 1817)

Gifts

A dropping shower of spray,
  Filled with a beam of light, –
The breath of some soft day, –
  The groves of wan moonlight, –
    Some rivers flow,
    Some falling snow,
Some bird's swift flight; –

A summer field o'erstrown
  With gay and laughing flowers,
And shepherd's clocks half blown,
  That tell the merry hours, –
    The waving grain,
    The spring soft rain, –
Are these things ours?

Henry David Thoreau (b. 1817)

Within the Circuit of This Plodding Life

Within the circuit of this plodding life
There enter moments of an azure hue,
Untarnished fair as in the violet
Or anemone, when the spring strews them
By some meandering rivulet, which make
The best philosophy untrue that aims
But to console man for his grievances.
I have remembered when the winter came,
High in my chamber in the frosty nights,
When in the still light of the cheerful moon,
On every twig and rail and jutting spout,
The icy spears were adding to their length
Against the arrows of the coming sun,
How in the shimmering noon of summer past
Some unrecorded beam slanted across
The upland pastures where the Johnswort grew;
Or heard, amid the verdure of the mind,
The bee's long smothered hum, on the blue flag
Loitering amidst the mead; or busy rill,
Which now through all its course stands still and dumb
Its own memorial, – purling at its play
Along the slopes, and through the meadows next,
Until its youthful sound was hushed at last
In the staid current of the lowland stream;
Or seen the furrows shine but late upturned,
And where the fieldfare followed in the rear,
When all the fields around lay bound and hoar
Beneath a thick integument of snow.
So by God's cheap economy made rich
To go upon my winter's task again.

I Am a Parcel of Vain Strivings Tied

I am a parcel of vain strivings tied
By a chance bond together,
Dangling this way and that, their links
Were made so loose and wide,
Methinks,
For milder weather.

A bunch of violets without their roots,
And sorrel intermixed,
Encircled by a wisp of straw
Once coiled about their shoots,
The law
By which I'm fixed.

A nosegay which Time clutched from out
Those fair Elysian fields,
With weeds and broken stems, in haste,
Doth make the rabble rout
That waste
The day he yields.

And here I bloom for a short hour unseen,
Drinking my juices up,
With no root in the land
To keep my branches green,
But stand
In a bare cup.

Some tender buds were left upon my stem
In mimicry of life,
But ah! the children will not know,
Till time has withered them,
The woe
With which they're rife.

But now I see I was not plucked for naught,
And after in life's vase
Of glass set while I might survive,
But by a kind hand brought
Alive
To a strange place.

That stock thus thinned will soon redeem its hours,
And by another year,
Such as God knows, with freer air,
More fruits and fairer flowers
Will bear,
While I droop here.

I Make Ye an Offer

I make ye an offer,
Ye gods, hear the scoffer,
The scheme will not hurt you,
If ye will find goodness, I will find virtue.
Though I am your creature,
And child of your nature,
I have pride still unbended,
And blood undescended,
Some free independence,
And my own descendants.
I cannot toil blindly,
Though ye behave kindly,
And I swear by the rood,
I'll be slave to no God.
If ye will deal plainly,
I will strive mainly,
If ye will discover,
Great plans to your lover,
And give him a sphere
Somewhat larger than here.

An Early Unconverted Saint

An early unconverted Saint,
Free from noontide or evening taint,
Heathen without reproach,
That did upon the civil day encroach,
And ever since its birth
Had trod the outskirts of the earth.

Woof of the Sun, Ethereal Gauze

Woof of the sun, ethereal gauze,
Woven of Nature's richest stuffs,
Visible heat, air-water, and dry sea,
Last conquest of the eye;
Toil of the day displayed, sun-dust,
Aerial surf upon the shores of earth,
Ethereal estuary, frith of light,
Breakers of air, billows of heat,
Fine summer spray on inland seas;
Bird of the sun, transparent-winged
Owlet of noon, soft-pinioned,
From heath or stubble rising without song;
Establish thy serenity o'er the fields.

Samuel Gray Ward (b. 1817)

The Consolers

Consolers of the solitary hours
When I, a pilgrim, on a lonely shore
Sought help, and found none, save in those high powers
That then I prayed might never leave me more!
There was the blue, eternal sky above,
There was the ocean silent at my feet,
There was the universe – but nought to love;
The universe did its old tale repeat.
Then came ye to me, with your healing wings,
And said, "Thus bare and branchless must thou be,
Ere thou couldst feel the wind from heaven that springs."
And now again fresh leaves do bud for me, –
Yet let me feel that still the spirit sings
In quiet song, coming from heaven free.

John Weiss (b. 1818)

Method

Central axis, pole of pole,
Central ark and goal of goal,
Worship, to whose sovereign end
All the spirit's uses tend.
Taught of her high mystery,
Perfect will the man-child be.
Not with sorrow, not with moan
Comes the soul unto her own;
Not with sounding steps of thunder,
Not with flaming looks of fire,
But with calm delight and wonder,
Simple hope and sweet desire.
Then, through all the motions stealing
Of the manifold existence,
Ever lifting, soothing, healing,
Love attunes each thought and feeling
Unto patience and persistence.

Charles Anderson Dana (b. 1819)

Eternity

Utter no whisper of thy human speech,
But in celestial silence let us tell
Of the great waves of God that through us swell,
Revealing what no tongue could ever teach;
Break not the omnipotent calm, even by a prayer,
Filled with Infinite, seek no lesser boon:

But with these pines, and with the all-loving moon,
Asking naught, yield thee to the Only Fair;
So shall these moments so divine and rare,
These passing moments of the soul's high noon,
Be of thy day the first pale blush of morn;
Clad in white raiment of God's newly born,
Thyself shalt see when the great world is made
That flows forever from a Love unstayed.

Josiah Gilbert Holland (b. 1819)

Intimations

What glory then! What darkness now!
　　A glimpse, a thrill, and it is flown!
　　I reach, I grasp, but stand alone,
With empty arms and upward brow!

Ye may not see, O weary eyes!
　　The band of angels, swift and bright,
　　That pass, but cannot wake your sight,
Down trooping from the crowded skies.

O heavy ears! Ye may not hear
　　The strains that pass my conscious soul,
　　And seek, but find no earthly goal,
Far falling from another sphere.

Ah! soul of mine! Ah! soul of mine!
　　Thy sluggish senses are but bars
　　That stand between thee and the stars,
And shut thee from the world divine.

For something sweeter far than sound,
　　And something finer than the light
　　Comes through the discord and the night
And penetrates, or wraps thee round.

Nay, God is here, couldst thou but see;
    All things of beauty are of Him;
    And heaven, that holds the cherubim,
As lovingly embraces thee!

If thou has apprehended well
    The tender glory of a flower,
    Which moved thee, by some subtle power
Whose source and sway thou couldst not tell;

If thou hast kindled to the sweep
    Of stormy clouds across the sky,
    Or gazed with tranced and tearful eye,
And swelling breast, upon the deep;

If thou hast felt the throb and thrill
    Of early day and happy birds,
    While peace, that drowned thy chosen words
Has flowed from thee in glad good-will,

Then hast thou drunk the heavenly dew;
    Then have thy feet in rapture trod
    The pathway of a thought of God;
And death can show thee nothing new.

For heaven and beauty are the same, –
    Of God the all-informing thought,
    To sweet, supreme expression wrought,
And syllabled by sound and flame.

The light that beams from childhood's eyes,
    The charm that dwells in summer woods,
    The holy influence that broods
O'er all things under twilight skies, –

The music of the simple notes
    That rise from happy human homes,
    The joy in life of all that roams
Upon the earth, and all that floats,

Proclaim that heaven's sweet providence
    Enwraps the homely earth in whole,
    And finds the secret of the soul
Through channels subtler than the sense.

O soul of mine! Throw wide thy door,
    And cleanse thy paths from doubt and sin;
    And the bright flood shall enter in
And give thee heaven evermore!

Julia Ward Howe (b. 1819)

Battle Hymn of the Republic

Glory! Glory! Hallelujah!
Glory! Glory! Hallelujah!
Glory! Glory! Hallelujah!
His truth is marching on.

Mine eyes have seen the glory of the coming of the Lord:
He is trampling out the vintage where the grapes of wrath are stored;
He has loosed the fateful lightning of His terrible swift sword:
His truth is marching on.

I have seen Him in the watch-fires of a hundred circling camps;
They have builded Him an altar in the evening dews and damps;
I can read His righteous sentence by the dim and flaring lamps.
His day is marching on.

I have read a fiery gospel writ in burnish'd rows of steel:
"As ye deal with my contemners, So with you my grace shall deal;
Let the Hero, born of woman, crush the serpent with his heel,
Since God is marching on."

He has sounded forth the trumpet that shall never call retreat;
He is sifting out the hearts of men before His judgment-seat:
Oh, be swift, my soul, to answer Him! be jubilant, my feet!
Our God is marching on.

In the beauty of the lilies Christ was born across the sea,
With a glory in His bosom that transfigures you and me:
As He died to make men holy, let us die to make men free,
While God is marching on.

Stanzas

Of the heaven is generation:
Fruition in the deep earth lies:
And where the twain have broadest blending,
The stateliest growths of life arise.

Set, then, thy root in earth more firmly:
Raise thy head erect and free:
And spread thy loving arms so widely,
That heaven and earth shall meet in thee.

Samuel Longfellow (b. 1819)

The Church Universal

One holy church of God appears
Through every age and race,
Unwasted by the lapse of years,
Unchanged by changing place.

From oldest time, on farthest shores,
Beneath the pine or palm,
One Unseen Presence she adores
With silence or with psalm.

Her priests are all God's faithful sons,
To serve the world raised up;
The pure in heart her baptized ones,
Love her communion-cup.

The truth is her prophetic gift,
The soul her sacred page;
And feet on mercy's errands swift
Do make her pilgrimage.

O living Church! thine errand speed,
Fulfill thy work sublime;
With bread of life earth's hunger feed,
Redeem the evil time!

James Russell Lowell (b. 1819)

Wisdom of the Eternal One

Therefore think not the Past is wise alone,
For Yesterday knows nothing of the Best,
And thou shalt love it only as the nest
Whence glory-wingèd things to Heaven have flown:
To the great Soul alone are all things known;
Present and future are to her as past,
While she in glorious madness doth forecast
That perfect bud, which seems a flower full-blown
To each new Prophet, and yet always opes
Fuller and fuller with each day and hour,
Heartening the soul with odor of fresh hopes,
And longings high, and gushings of wide power,
Yet never is or shall be fully blown
Save in the forethought of the Eternal One.

Herman Melville (b. 1819)

Shiloh
A Requiem (April, 1862)

Skimming lightly, wheeling still,
The swallows fly low
Over the field in clouded days,
The forest-field of Shiloh –
Over the field where April rain
Solaced the parched ones stretched in pain
Through the pause of night
That followed the Sunday fight
Around the church of Shiloh –
The church so lone, the log-built one,
That echoed to many a parting groan
And natural prayer
of dying foemen mingled there –
Foemen at morn, but friends at ever –
Fame or country least their care:
(What like a bullet can undeceive!)
But now they lie low,
While over them the swallows skim,
And all is hushed at Shiloh.

Fragments of a Lost Gnostic Poem of the Twelfth Century

Found a family, build a state,
The pledged event is still the same:
Matter in end will never abate
His ancient brutal claim.

Indolence is heaven's ally here,
And energy the child of hell:
The Good Man pouring from his pitcher clear
But brims the poisoned well.

Joseph Scriven (b. 1819)

What a Friend We Have in Jesus

What a Friend we have in Jesus,
All our sins and griefs to bear!
What a privilege to carry
Every thing to God in prayer!
O what a peace we often forfeit,
O what needless pain we bear,
All because we do not carry
Every thing to God in prayer!

Have we trials and temptations?
Is there trouble anywhere?
We should never be discouraged,
Take it to the Lord in prayer.
Can we find a friend so faithful,
Who will all our sorrows share?
Jesus knows our every weakness,
Take it to the Lord in prayer.

Are we weak and heavy laden,
Cumbered with a load of care? –
Precious Savior, still our refuge, –
Take it to the Lord in prayer.
Do thy friends despise, forsake thee?
Take it to the Lord in prayer,
In His arms He'll take and shield thee,
Thou wilt find a solace there.

Walt Whitman (b. 1819)

from *Song of Myself*

5.

I believe in you my soul, the other I am must not abase itself to you,
And you must not be abased to the other.
Loafe with me on the grass, loose the stop from your throat,
Not words, not music or rhyme I want, not custom or lecture, not even the
best,
Only the lull I like, the hum of your valvèd voice.

I mind how once we lay such a transparent summer morning,
How you settled your head athwart my hips and gently turn'd over upon me,
And parted the shirt from my bosom-bone, and plunged your tongue to my
bare-stript heart,
And reach'd till you felt my beard, and reach'd till you held my feet.

Swiftly arose and spread around me the peace and knowledge that pass all
the argument of the earth,
And I know that the hand of God is the promise of my own,
And I know that the spirit of God is the brother of my own,
And that all the men ever born are also my brothers, and the women my
sisters and lovers,
And that a kelson of the creation is love,
And limitless are leaves stiff or drooping in the fields,
And brown ants in the little wells beneath them,
And mossy scabs of the worm fence, heap'd stones, elder, mullein and
poke-weed.

A Noiseless Patient Spider

A noiseless patient spider,
I mark'd where on a little promontory it stood isolated,
Mark'd how to explore the vacant vast surrounding,
It launch'd forth filament, filament, filament, out of itself,
Ever unreeling them, ever tirelessly speeding them.

And you O my soul where you stand,
Surrounded, detached, in measureless oceans of space,
Ceaselessly musing, venturing, throwing, seeking the spheres to connect them,
Till the bridge you will need be form'd, till the ductile anchor hold,
Till the gossamer thread you fling catch somewhere, O my soul.

Vigil Strange I Kept on the Field One Night

Vigil strange I kept on the field one night;
When you my son and my comrade dropt at my side that day,
One look I but gave which your dear eyes return'd with a look I shall never
forget,
One touch of your hand to mine O boy, reach'd up as you lay on the ground,
Then onward I sped in the battle, the even-contested battle,
Till late in the night reliev'd to the place at last again I made my way,
Found you in death so cold dear comrade, found your body son of responding
kisses, (never again on earth responding,)
Bared your face in the starlight, curious the scene, cool blew the moderate
night-wind,
Long there and then in vigil I stood, dimly around me the battle-field spreading,
Vigil wondrous and vigil sweet there in the fragrant silent night,
But not a tear fell, not even a long-drawn sigh, long, long I gazed,
Then on the earth partially reclining sat by your side leaning my chin in my
hands,
Passing sweet hours, immortal and mystic hours with you dearest comrade –
not a tear, not a word,
Vigil of silence, love and death, vigil for you my son and my soldier,
As onward silently stars aloft, eastward new ones upward stole,
Vigil final for you brave boy, (I could not save you, swift was your death,
I faithfully loved you and cared for you living, I think we shall surely meet
again,)
Till at latest lingering of the night, indeed just as the dawn appear'd,
My comrade I wrapt in his blanket, envelop'd well his form,
Folded the blanket well, tucking it carefully over head and carefully under feet,
And there and then and bathed by the rising sun, my son in his grave, in his
rude-dug grave I deposited,
Ending my vigil strange with that, vigil of night and battle-field dim,
Vigil for boy of responding kisses, (never again on earth responding,)

Vigil for comrade swiftly slain, vigil I never forget, how as day brighten'd,
I rose from the chill ground and folded my soldier well in his blanket,
And buried him where he fell.

As Adam Early in the Morning

As Adam early in the morning,
Walking forth from the bower refresh'd with sleep,
Behold me where I pass, hear my voice, approach,
Touch me, touch the palm of your hand to my body as I pass,
Be not afraid of my body.

George Shepard Burleigh (b. 1821)

Dare and Know

The truths we cannot win are fruit forbidden,
That knowledge only is, by proof not ours,
Which lies beyond the measure of our powers:
Not by God's grudging are our natures chidden,
His hidden things for daring search are hidden:
The cloudy darkness that around him lowers
Burns only with his glory, and the dowers
Of Hero-hearts who have gone up and ridden
The storm like eagles! If the lightning singe
The intrepid wing, 'tis but the burning kiss
Of Victory in Espousal, – the keen bliss
Whose rapturous thrill might make the coward cringe!
He who aloft on Rood-nails hung our crown
Smiles when the bleeding hands we climb and pluck it down!

The Ideal Wins

Though hunger sharpens in the dream of food,
And thirst burns fiercer for the visioned brook,
Our souls are drawn the way our longings look,
And our ideal good is actual good.
The heavens we win are more than we pursued;
For the great Dream has cheapened the small nook
That once for all the rounded world we took,
And our sect sinks in boundless Brotherhood.
By noble climbing, though the heavens recede,
Broader expands the horizon's girdling wall;
Through misty doubts we reach the sunnier creed,
And, nearer heaven, see earth a fairer ball;
And souls that soar beyond their simple need,
To grasp the highest, are made free for all!

Frederick Goddard Tuckerman (b. 1821)

Untitled Sonnets

1.8
As when down some broad river dropping, we
Day after day behold the assuming shores
Sink and grow dim, as the great watercourse
Pushes his banks apart and seeks the sea:
Benches of pines, high shelf and balcony,
To flats of willow and low sycamores
Subsiding, till where'er the wave we see,
Himself is his horizon utterly.
So fades the portion of our early world,
Still on the ambit hangs the purple air;
Yet while we lean to read the secret there,
The stream that by green shoresides plashed and purled
Expands: the mountains melt to vapors rare,
And life alone circles out flat and bare.

1.9

Yet wear we on, the deep light disallowed
That lit our youth; in years no longer young
We wander silently, and brood among
Dead graves, and tease the sunbreak and the cloud
For import: were it not better yet to fly,
To follow those that go before the throng,
Reasoning from stone to star, and easily
Exampling this existence? Or shall I –
Who yield slow reverence where I cannot see
And gather gleams where'er by chance or choice
My footsteps draw, though brokenly dispensed –
Come into light at last? or suddenly
Struck to the knees like Saul, one arm against
The overbearing brightness, hear a voice?

1.28

Not the round natural world, not the deep mind,
The reconcilement holds: the blue abyss
Collects it not; our arrows sink amiss
And but in Him may we our import find.
The agony to know, the grief, the bliss
Of toil, is vain and vain: clots of the sod
Gathered in heat and haste and flung behind
To blind ourselves and others, what but this
Still grasping dust and sowing toward the wind?
No more thy meaning seek, thine anguish plead,
But leaving straining thought and stammered word,
Across the barren azure pass to God:
Shooting the void in silence like a bird,
A bird that shuts his wings for better speed.

2.33

One still dark night I sat alone and wrote:
So still it was that distant Chanticleer
Seemed to cry out his warning at my ear,
Save for the brooding echo in his throat.
Sullen I sat, when like the nightwind's note
A voice said, "Wherefore doth he weep and fear?

Doth he not know no cry to God is dumb?"
Another spoke: "His heart is dimmed and drowned
With grief." I knew the shape that bended then
To kiss me, when suddenly I once again
Across the watches of the starless gloom
Heard the cock scream and pause: the morning bell
Into the gulfs of night dropped One! The vision fell
And left me listening to the sinking sound.

Frances Ellen Watkins Harper (b. 1825)

Bible Defense of Slavery

Take sackcloth of the darkest dye,
  And shroud the pulpits round!
Servants of Him that cannot lie,
  Sit mourning on the ground.

Let holy horror blanch each cheek,
  Pale every brow with fears;
And rocks and stones, if ye could speak,
  Ye well might melt to tears!

Let sorrow breathe in every tone,
  In every strain ye raise;
Insult not God's majestic throne
  With th' mockery of praise.

A "reverend" man, whose light should be
  The guide of age and youth,
Brings to the shrine of Slavery
  The sacrifice of truth!

For the direst wrong by man imposed,
  Since Sodom's fearful cry,
The word of life has been unclos'd,
  To give your God the lie.

Oh! when ye pray for heathen lands,
  And plead for their dark shores,
Remember Slavery's cruel hands
  Make heathens at your doors!

Paul Hamilton Hayne (b. 1830)

Death's Self

The thought of death walks ever by my side,
    It walks in sunshine, and it walks in shade,
    A thing protean, by strange fancies made
Lovely or loathsome, dark or glorified.
But past such fantasies Death's self must hide,
    While his dread hour to smite is still delayed,
    Like a masked Presence in a cypress glade,
By all save heaven's keen vision undescried.
For me what final aspect shalt thou take,
    O Death? Or shalt thou take no shape at all,
    But viewless, soundless, on my spirit fall,
    Soft as the sleep-balm of a summer's night,
From which the flower-like soul, new-born, shall wake
    In God's fair gardens on the hills of light?

Emily Dickinson (b. 1830)

A Word Made Flesh Is Seldom

A word made Flesh is seldom
And tremblingly partook
Nor then perhaps reported
But have I not mistook

Each one of us has tasted
With ecstasies of stealth
The very food debated
To our specific strength –

A word that breathes distinctly
Has not the power to die
Cohesive as the Spirit
It may expire if He –

"Made Flesh and dwelt among us"
Could condescension be
Like this consent of Language
This loved Philology

It Was Not Saint – It Was Too Large

It was not Saint – it was too large –
Nor Snow – it was too small –
It only held itself aloof
Like something spiritual –

Helen Hunt Jackson (b. 1831)

Spinning

Like a blind spinner in the sun,
        I tread my days;
I know that all the threads will run
        Appointed ways;
I know each day will bring its task,
        And, being blind, no more I ask.

I do not know the use or name
      Of that I spin:
I only know that some one came
      And laid within
My hand the thread, and said, "Since you
Are blind, but one thing you can do."

Sometimes the threads so rough and fast
      And tangled fly,
I know wild storms are sweeping past,
      And fear that I
Shall fall; but dare not try to find
A safer place, since I am blind.

I know not why, but I am sure
      That tint and place,
In some great fabric to endure
      Past time and race,
My threads will have; so from the first,
Though blind, I never felt accurst.

I think, perhaps, this trust has sprung
      From one short word
Said over me when I was young, –
      So young, I heard
It, knowing not that God's name signed
My brow, and sealed me His, though blind.

But whether this be seal or sign
      Within, without,
It matters not. The bond divine
      I never doubt.
I know he set me here, and still,
And glad, and blind, I wait His will;

But listen, listen, day by day,
      To hear their tread
Who bear the finished web away,
      And cut the thread,
And bring God's message in the sun,
"Thou poor blind spinner, work is done."

The Love of God

Like a cradle rocking, rocking,
Silent, peaceful, to and fro,
Like a mother's sweet looks dropping
On the little face below,
Hangs the green earth, swinging, turning,
Jarless, noiseless, safe, and slow;
Falls the light of God's face bending
Down and watching us below.

And as feeble babes that suffer,
Toss, and cry, and will not rest,
Are the ones the tender mother
Holds the closest, loves the best, –
So when we are weak and wretched,
By our sins weighed down, distressed,
Then it is that God's great patience
Holds us closest, loves us best.

Sydney Henry Morse (b. 1833)

Open Secret

Not through Nature shineth
Godhead fair and free;
'Tis the Heart divineth
What the God must be.

Nature all concealing,
Dim her outer light,
Finite forms revealing,
Not the infinite.

All the Godhead's planning
Not with striving learn –
Inner eye – Heart scanning –
Sees the God-bush burn.

The Way

They find the way who linger where
The soul finds fullest life;
The battle brave is carried on
By all who wait, and waiting, dare
Deem each day's least that's fitly done
A victory worthy to be won,
Nor seek their gain in strife.

Mark Twain (b. 1835)

from *The War Prayer*

An aged stranger entered and moved with slow and noiseless step up the main aisle, his eyes fixed upon the minister . . . The stranger touched his arm, motioned him to step aside – which the minister did – and took his place. During some moments he surveyed the spellbound audience with solemn eyes in which burned an uncanny light; then in a deep voice he said: . . .
"When you have prayed for victory you have prayed for many unmentioned results which follow victory – *must* follow it, cannot help but follow it. Upon the listening spirit of God the Father fell also the unspoken part of the prayer. He commandeth me to put into words:
LISTEN!
O Lord our Father,
our young patriots,
idols of our hearts,
go forth to battle –
be Thou near them!
With them, in spirit,
we also go forth
from the sweet peace
of our beloved firesides
to smite the foe.
O Lord our God,
help us

to tear their soldiers
to bloody shreds
with our shells;
help us
to cover their smiling fields
with the pale forms
of their patriot dead;
help us
to drown the thunder
of the guns
with the shrieks
of their wounded,
writhing in pain;
help us
to lay waste
their humble homes
with a hurricane of fire;
help us
to wring the hearts
of their unoffending widows
with unavailing grief;
help us
to turn them out roofless
with their little children
to wander unfriended
the wastes
of their desolated land
in rags and hunger
and thirst,
sports of the sun flames
of summer
and the icy winds
of winter,
broken in spirit,
worn with travail,
imploring Thee
for the refuge of the grave
and denied it –
for our sakes
who adore Thee, Lord,

blast their hopes,
blight their lives,
protract their bitter pilgrimage,
make heavy their steps,
water their way with tears,
stain the white snow
with the blood
of their wounded feet!
We ask it,
in the spirit of love,
of Him Who is the Source of Love,
and Who is the ever-faithful
refuge and friend
of all that are sore beset
and seek His aid
with humble and contrite hearts.
AMEN.

After a pause:
"Ye have prayed it; if ye still desire it, speak! The messenger of the Most High waits."
It was believed afterward that the man was a lunatic, because there was no sense in what he said.

Joaquin Miller (b. 1837)

Grant at Shiloh

The blue and the gray! Their work was well done!
They lay as to listen to the water's flow.
Some lay with their faces upturned to the sun,
As seeking to know what the gods might know.
Their work was well done, each soldier was true.
But what is the question that comes to you?

For all that men do, for all that men dare,
That river still runs with its stateliest flow.
The sun and the moon I scarcely think care
A fig for the fallen, of friend or of foe.
But the moss-mantled cypress, the old soldiers say,
Still mantles in smoke of that battle day!

These men in the dust! These pitiful dead!
The gray and the blue, the blue and the gray,
The headless trunk and the trunkless head;
The image of God in the gory clay!
And who was the bravest? Say, can you tell
If Death throws dice with a loaded shell?

Abram Joseph Ryan (b. 1838)

Song of the Mystic

I walk down the Valley of Silence –
  Down the dim, voiceless valley – alone!
And I hear not the fall of a footstep
  Around me, save God's and my own;
And the hush of my heart is as holy
  As hovers where angels have flown!

Long ago was I weary of voices
  Whose music my heart could not win;
Long ago was I weary of noises
  That fretted my soul with their din;
Long ago was I weary of places
  Where I met but the human – and sin.

I walked in the world with the worldly;
  I craved what the world never gave;
And I said: "In the world each Ideal,
  That shines like a star on life's wave,

Is wrecked on the shores of the Real,
  And sleeps like a dream in a grave."

And still did I pine for the Perfect,
  And still found the False with the True:
I sought 'mid the Human for Heaven,
  But caught a mere glimpse of its Blue:
And I wept when the clouds of the Mortal
  Veiled even that glimpse from my view.

And I toiled on, heart-tired of the Human;
  And I moaned 'mid the mazes of men;
Till I knelt, long ago, at an altar
  And I heard a voice call me: – since then
I walk down the Valley of Silence
  That lies far beyond mortal ken.

Do you ask what I found in the Valley?
  'Tis my Trysting Place with the Divine.
And I fell at the feet of the Holy,
  And above me a voice said: "Be mine."
And there arose from the depths of my spirit
  An echo – "My heart shall be thine."

Do you ask how I live in the Valley?
  I weep – and I dream – and I pray.
But my tears are as sweet as the dewdrops
  That fall on the roses in May;
And my prayer, like a perfume from Censers,
  Ascendeth to God night and day.

In the hush of the Valley of Silence
  I dream all the songs that I sing;
And the music floats down the dim Valley,
  Till each finds a word for a wing,
That to hearts, like the Dove of the Deluge,
  A message of Peace they may bring.

Bur far on the deep there are billows
  That never shall break on the beach;

And I have heard songs in the Silence,
  That never shall float into speech;
And I have had dreams in the Valley,
  Too lofty for language to reach.

And I have seen Thought in the Valley –
  Ah! me, how my spirit was stirred!
And they wear holy veils on their faces,
  Their footsteps can scarcely be heard:
They pass through the Valley like Virgins,
  Too pure for the touch of a word!

Do you ask me the place of the Valley,
  Ye hearts that are harrowed by Care?
It lieth afar between mountains,
  And God and His angels are there:
And one in the dark mount of Sorrow,
  And one the bright mountain of Prayer!

Shaker Hymns (1840s)

Walk Softly

When we assemble here to worship God,
To sing his praises and to hear his word
    We will walk softly.

With purity of heart; and with clean hands,
Our souls are free, we're free from Satan's bands
    We will walk softly.

While we are passing thro' the sacred door,
Into the fold where Christ has gone before,
    We will walk softly.

We'll worship and bow down we will rejoice
And when we hear the shepherd's gentle voice
    We will walk softly.

I Will Bow and Be Simple

I will bow and be simple
I will bow and be free
I will bow and be humble
Yea ,bow like the willow tree
I will bow, this is the token
I will wear the easy yoke
I will bow and be broken
Yea, I'll fall upon the rock.

John White Chadwick (b. 1840)

Nirvana

Along the scholar's glowing page
I read the Orient thinker's dream
Of things that are not what they seem,
Of mystic chant and Soma's rage.

The sunlight flooding all the room
To me again was Indra's smile,
And on the hearth the blazing pile
For Agni's sake did fret and fume.

Yet most I read of who aspire
To win Nirvana's deep repose, –
Of that long way the spirit goes
To reach the absence of desire.

But through the music of my book
Another music smote my ear, –
A tinkle silver-sweet and clear, –
The babble of the mountain-brook.

"Oh! leave," it said, "your ancient seers;
Come out into the woods with me;
Behold an older mystery
Than Buddhists' hope or Brahmans' fears!"

The voice so sweet I could but hear.
I sallied forth with staff in hand,
Where, mile on mile, the mountain land
Was radiant with the dying year.

I heard the startled partridge whirr,
And crinkling through the tender grass
I saw the striped adder pass,
Where dropped the chestnut's prickly burr.

I saw the miracle of life
From death upspringing evermore;
The fallen tree a forest bore
Of tiny forms with beauty rife.

I gathered mosses rare and sweet,
The acorn in its carven cup;
'Mid heaps of leaves, wind-gathered up,
I trod with half-remorseful feet.

The maple's blush I made my own,
The sumac's crimson splendor bold,
The poplar's hue of paly gold,
The faded chestnut, crisp and brown.

I climbed the mountain's shaggy crest,
Where masses huge of molten rock,
After long years of pain and shock,
Fern-covered, from their wanderings rest.

Far, far below the valley spread
Its rich, root-dotted, wide expanse;
And further still the sunlight's dance
The amorous river gayly led.

But still, with all I heard or saw
There mingled thoughts of that old time,
And that enchanted Eastern clime
Where Buddha gave his mystic law, –

Till, wearied with the lengthy way,
I found a spot were all was still,
Just as the sun behind the hill
Was making bright the parting day.

On either side the mountains stood,
Masses of color rich and warm;
And over them, in giant form,
The rosy moons serenely glowed.

My heart was full as it could hold;
The Buddha's paradise was mine;
My mountain-nook its inmost shrine,
The fretted sky its roof of gold.

Nirvana's peace my soul had found, –
Absence complete of all desire, –
While the great moon was mounting higher,
And deeper quiet breathed around.

Edward Rowland Sill (b. 1841)

Five Lives

Five mites of monads dwelt in a round drop
That twinkled on a leaf by a pool in the sun.
To the naked eye they lived invisible;
Specks, for a world of whom the empty shell
Of a mustard seed had been a hollow sky.

One was a meditative monad, called a sage;
And, shrinking all his mind within, he thought:
"Tradition, handed down for hours and hours,
Tells that our globe, this quivering crystal world,
Is slowly dying. What if, seconds hence,
When I am very old, yon shimmering dome
Come drawing down and down, till all things end?"
Then with a weazen smirk he proudly felt
No other mote of God had ever gained
Such giant grasp of universal truth.

One was a transcendental monad; thin
And long and slim in the mind; and thus he mused:
"Oh, vast, unfathomable monad-souls!
Made in the image" – a hoarse frog croaks from the pool –
"Hark! 'twas some god, voicing his glorious thought
In thunder music! Yea, we hear their voice,
And we may guess their minds from ours, their work.
Some taste they have like ours, some tendency
To wriggle about, and munch a trace of scum."
He floated up on a pin-point bubble of gas
That burst, pricked by the air, and he was gone.

One was a barren-minded monad, called
A positivist; and he knew positively:
"There is no world beyond this certain drop.
Prove me another! Let the dreamers dream
Of their faint dreams, and noises from without,
And higher and lower; life is life enough."
Then swaggering half a hair's breadth, hungrily
He seized upon an atom of bug, and fed.

One was a tattered monad, called a poet;
And with shrill voice ecstatic thus he sang:
"Oh the little female monad's lips!
Oh, the little female monad's eyes:
Ah, the little, little, female, female monad!"

That last was a strong-minded monadess,
Who dashed amid the infusoria,
Danced high and low, and wildly spun and dove
Till the dizzy others held their breath to see.

But while they led their wondrous little lives
Aeonian moments had gone wheeling by.
The burning drop had shrunk with fearful speed;
A glistening film – 'twas gone; the leaf was dry.
The little ghost of an inaudible squeak
Was lost to the frog that goggled from his stone;
Who, at the huge, slow tread of a thoughtful ox
Coming to drink, stirred sideways fatly, plunged,
Launched backward twice, and all the pool was still.

Life

Forenoon and afternoon and night, – Forenoon,
And afternoon, and night, – Forenoon, and –
 what!
The empty song repeats itself. No more?
Yes, that is Life: make this forenoon sublime,
This afternoon a psalm, this night a prayer,
And Time is conquered, and thy crown is won.

Sidney Lanier (b. 1842)

from *The Marshes of Glynn*

O braided dusks of the oak and woven shades of the vine,
While the riotous noon-day sun of the June-day long did shine,
Ye held me fast in your heart and I held you fast in mine;
 But now when the noon is no more, and riot is rest,
 and the sun is a-wait at the ponderous gate of the West,
 And the slant yellow beam down the wood-aisle doth seem
 Like a lane into heaven that leads from a dream, –
Ay, now, when my soul all day hath drunken the soul of the oak,
And my heart is at ease from men, and the wearisome sound of the stroke

Of the scythe of time and the trowel of trade is low,
And belief overmasters doubt, and I know that I know
And my spirit is grown to a lordly great compass within,
That the length and the breadth and the sweep of the marshes of Glynn
Will work no fear like the fear they have wrought me of yore
When length was fatigue, and when breadth was but bitterness sore,
And when terror and shrinking and dreary unnamable pain
Drew over me out of the merciless miles of the plain, –
Oh, now, unafraid, I am fain to face
The vast visage of space.
To the edge of the wood I am drawn, I am drawn,
Where the gray beach glimmering runs, as a belt of the dawn,
For a mete and a mark
To the forest-dark: –
So:
Affable live-oak, leaning low, –
Thus – with your favor – soft, with a reverent hand,
(Not lightly touching your person, Lord of the land!)
Bending your beauty aside, with a step I stand
On the firm-packed sand,
Free
By a world of marsh that borders a world of sea.
.....
And the sea lends large, as the marsh: lo, out of his plenty the sea
Pours fast: full soon the time of the flood-tide must be:
Look how the grace of the sea doth go
About and about through the intricate channels that flow
Here and there,
Everywhere,
Till his waters have flooded the uttermost creeks and the low-lying lanes,
And the marsh is meshed with a million veins,
That like as with rosy and silvery essences flow
In the rose-and-silver evening glow.
Farewell, my lord Sun!
The creeks overflow, a thousand rivulets run
'Twixt the roots of the sod; the blades of the marsh-grass stir;
Passeth a hurrying sound of wings that westward whirr;
Passeth, and all is still; and the currents cease to run;
And the sea and the marsh are one.

How still the plains of the waters be!
The tide is in his ecstasy.
The tide is at his highest height:
And it is night.
And now from the Vast of the Lord will the waters of sleep
Roll in on the souls of men.
But who will reveal to our waking ken
The forms that swim and the shapes that creep
Under the waters of sleep?
And I would I could know what swimmeth below when the tide comes in
On the length and the breadth of the marvelous marshes of Glynn.

A Ballad of Trees and the Master

Into the woods my Master went,
Clean forspent, forspent.
Into the woods my Master came,
Forspent with love and shame.
But the olives they were not blind to Him,
The little gray leaves were kind to Him:
The thorn-tree had a mind to Him
When into the woods He came.

Out of the woods my Master went,
And He was well content,
Out of the woods my Master came,
Content with death and shame.
When Death and Shame would woo Him last,
From under the trees they drew Him last:
'Twas on a tree they slew Him – last
When out of the woods He came.

John Banister Tabb (b. 1845)

Poetry

A gleam of heaven; the passion of a star
Held captive in the clasp of harmony;
A silence, shell-like breathing from afar
The rapture of the deep – eternity.

Evolution

Out of the dusk a shadow,
Then a spark;
Out of the cloud a silence,
Then a lark;
Out of the heart a rapture,
Then a pain;
Out of the dead, cold ashes,
Life again.

Emma Lazarus (b. 1849)

In the Jewish Synagogue at Newport

Here, where the noises of the busy town,
The ocean's plunge and roar can enter not,
We stand and gaze around with tearful awe,
And muse upon the consecrated spot.

No signs of life are here: the very prayers
Inscribed around are in a language dead;
The light of the "perpetual lamp" is spent
That an undying radiance was to shed.

What prayers were in this temple offered up,
Wrung from sad hearts that knew no joy on earth,
By these lone exiles of a thousand years,
From the fair sunrise land that gave them birth!

Now as we gaze, in this new world of light,
Upon this relic of the days of old,
The present vanishes, and tropic bloom
And Eastern towns and temples we behold.

Again we see the patriarch with his flocks,
The purple seas, the hot blue sky o'erhead,
The slaves of Egypt, – omens, mysteries, –
Dark fleeing hosts by flaming angels led.

A wondrous light upon a sky-kissed mount,
A man who reads Jehovah's written law,
'Midst blinding glory and effulgence rare,
Unto a people prone with reverent awe.

The pride of luxury's barbaric pomp,
In the rich court of royal Solomon –
Alas! we wake: one scene alone remains, –
The exiles by the streams of Babylon.

Our softened voices send us back again
But mournful echoes through the empty hall;
Our footsteps have a strange unnatural sound,
And with unwonted gentleness they fall.

The weary ones, the sad, the suffering,
All found their comfort in the holy place,
And children's gladness and men's gratitude
Took voice and mingled in the chant of praise.

The funeral and the marriage, now, alas!
We know not which is sadder to recall;
For youth and happiness have followed age,
And green grass lieth gently over all.

Nathless the sacred shrine is holy yet,
With this lone floors where reverent feet once trod.
Take off your shoes as by the burning bush,
Before the mystery of death and God.

The Crowing of the Red Cock

Across the Eastern sky has glowed
The flicker of a blood-red dawn,
Once more the clarion cock has crowed,
Once more the sword of Christ is drawn.
A million burning rooftrees light
The world-wide path of Israel's flight.

Where is the Hebrew's fatherland?
The folk of Christ is sore bestead;
The Son of man is bruised and banned,
Nor finds whereon to lay his head.
His cup is gall, his meat is tears,
His passion lasts a thousand years.

Each crime that wakes in man the beast,
Is visited upon his kind.
The lust of mobs, the greed of priest,
The tyranny of kings, combined
To root his seed from earth again,
His record is one cry of pain.

When the long roll of Christian guilt
Against his sires and kin is known,
The flood of tears, the life-blood spilt,
The agony of ages shown,
What oceans can the stain remove,
From Christian law and Christian love?

Nay, close the book; not now, not here,
The hideous tale of sin narrate,
Reechoing in the martyr's ear,
Even he might nurse revengeful hate,
Even he might turn in wrath sublime,
With blood for blood and crime for crime.

Coward? Not he, who faces death,
Who singly against the worlds has fought,
For what? A name he may not breathe,
For liberty of prayer and thought.
The angry sword he will not whet,
His nobler task is – to forget.

Nineteenth-Century Poems from Native American Song

Ojibwa

Song for the Metai or for Medicine Hunting

Now I hear it, my friends, of the Metai, who are sitting about me.
Who makes this river flow?
The Spirit, he makes this river flow.
Look at me well, my friends; examine me, and let us understand that we are all companions.
Who maketh to walk about, the social people?
A bird maketh to walk about the social people.
I fly about, and if anywhere I see an animal, I can shoot him.
I shoot your heart; I hit your heart, oh animal, your heart, I hit your heart.
I make myself look like fire.
I am able to call water from above, from beneath, and from around.
I cause to look like the dead, a man I did.
I cause to look like the dead, a woman I did.
I cause to look like the dead, a child I did.
I am such, I am such, my friends; any animal, any animal, my friends, I hit him right, my friends.

Song for Medicine Hunting

I wished to be born, I was born, and after I was born I made all spirits.
I created the spirits.
He sat down Na-na-bush; his fire burns forever.
Notwithstanding you speak evil of me, from above are my friends, my friends.
I can use many kinds of wood to make a bear unable to walk.
Of you I think, that you use the We-nis-ze-bug-gone, I think this of you.
That which I take is blood, that which I take.
Now I have something to eat.
I cover my head, sitting down to sleep, ye spirits.
I fill my kettle for the spirit.
Long ago, in the old time, since I laid myself down, ye are spirits.
I open you for a bear, I open you.
That is a Spirit which comes both from above and below.
I am he that giveth success, because all spirits help me.
The feather, the feather; it is the thing, the feather.
Who is a spirit? He that walketh with the serpent, walking on the ground; he is a spirit.
Now they will eat something, my women; now I tell them they will eat.
This yellow ochre, I will try it.
Now I wish to try my bird; sometimes I used to try, and sometimes it used to be something.
I can kill any animal, because the loud-speaking thunder helps me; I can kill any animal.
I take a bear, a heart I take.
A rattle snake makes a noise on the pole of my lodge; he makes a noise.
To a Shawnee, the four sticks used in this song belonged.
When struck together they were heard all over the country.
I come up from below; I came down from above; I see the spirit; I see beavers.
I can make an east wind come and pass over the ground.
Thus have I sat down, and the earth above and below has listened to me sitting here.
I make to crawl, a bear, I make to crawl.

Medicine Song of an Indian Lover

Who, maiden, makes this river flow?
The Spirit – he makes its ripples glow –
But I have a charm that can make thee, dear,
Steal o'er the wave to thy lover here.

Who, maiden, makes this river flow?
The Spirit – he makes its ripples glow –
Yet every blush that my lover would hide,
Is mirror'd for me in the tell-tale tide.

And though thou shouldst sleep on the farthest isle,
Round which these dimpling waters smile –
Yet I have a charm that can make thee, dear,
Steal over the wave to thy lover here.

Death Song

Under the center of the sky,
I utter my baim wa wa.

Every day, thou star!
I abide – gazing
Ye warlike birds.

They fly round the circuit of the sky.
The birds – circling
Round half the circuit of the sky.

They cross the enemy's line
The birds.

The high gods
My praise
They sound.

Full happy – I
To lie on the battle-field
Over the enemy's line.

Chants to the Deity

I am the living body of the Great Spirit above,
(The Great Spirit, the Ever-living Spirit above,)
The living body of the Great Spirit,
(Whom all must heed.)
 Heh! heh! heh! heh!

I am the Great Spirit of the sky,
The overshadowing power.
I illuminate earth,
I illuminate heaven.
 Way, ho! ho! ho!

Ah say! what Spirit, or Body, is this Body?
(That fills the world around,
Speak man!) ah say!
What Spirit, or Body, is this Body?
 Way, ho! ho! ho!

Prophetic Powers

At the place of light –
At the end of the sky –
I (the Great Spirit)
Come and hang
 Bright sign.

Lo! with the sound of my voice,
(The prophet's voice)
I make my sacred lodge to shake –
(By unseen hands my lodge to shake,)
 My sacred lodge.

Haih! the white bird of omen,
He flies around the clouds and skies –
(He sees, – unuttered sight!)
Around the clouds and skies –
By his bright eyes I see – I see – I know.

Imploration for Clear Weather

I swing the spirit like a child.
The sky is what I am telling you about.
We have lost the sky.
I am helping you.
I have made an error.
I am using my heart.
What are you saying to me, and I am "in my senses"?
The spirit wolf.
I do not know where I am going.
I depend on the clear sky.
I give you the other village, spirit that you are.
The thunder is heavy.
We are talking to another.

Sia

A Rain Song

White floating clouds. Clouds like the plains come and water the earth. Sun embrace the earth that she may be fruitful. Moon, lion of the north, bear of the west, badger of the south, wolf of the east, eagle of the heavens, shrew of the earth, elder war hero, younger war hero, warriors of the six mountains of the world, intercede with the cloud people for us, that they may water the earth. Medicine bowl, cloud bowl, and water vase give us your hearts, that the earth may be watered. I make the ancient road of meal, that my song may pass straight over it – the ancient road. White shell bead woman who lives where the sun goes down, mother whirlwind, father Sus'sistinnako, mother Ya'ya, creator of good thoughts, yellow woman of the north, blue woman of the west, red woman of the south, white woman of the east, slightly yellow woman of the zenith, and dark woman of the nadir, I ask your intercession with the cloud people.

Zuni

The Origin of Corn

Lo! ye children of men and the Mother,
Ye Brothers of Seed,
Elder, younger,
Behold the seed plants of all seeds!
The grass-seeds ye planted, in secret,
Were seen of the stars and the regions,
Are shown in the forms of these tassels!
The plumes that ye planted beside them
Were felt in the far away spaces,
Are shown in the forms of their leaf-blades!
But the seed that ye see growing from them,
Is the gift of my seven bright maidens,
The stars of the house of my children!
Look well, that ye cherish their persons,
Nor change ye the gift of their being –
As fertile of flesh for all men
To the bearing of children for men –
Lest ye lose them, to seek them in vain!
Be ye brothers ye people, and people;
Be ye happy ye Priests of the Corn!
Lo! the seed of all seed-plants is born!

Konkau

Red Cloud's Song

I am the Red Cloud.
My father formed me out of the sky.
I sing among the mountain flowers.
I sing among the flowering chamize of the mountains.
I sing in the mountains like the wek-wek.
I sing among the rocks like the wek-wek.
In the morning I cry to the mountains.
In the morning I walk the path.
I cry to the morning stars.

Navajo

from *The Night Chant*

In the House of the Red Rock,
There I enter;
Half way in, I am come.
The corn-plants shake.

In the House of Blue Water,
There I enter;
Half way in, I am come.
The plants shake.
.....
In the house made of dawn,
In the house made of the evening twilight,
In the house made of the dark cloud,
In the house made of the he-rain,
In the house made of the dark mist,
In the house made of the she-rain,
In the house made of pollen,
In the house made of grasshoppers,
Where the dark mist curtains the doorway,
The path to which is on the rainbow,
Where the zigzag lightning stands high on top,
Where the he-rain stands high on top,
Oh, male divinity!
With your moccasins of dark cloud come to us.
With your mind enveloped in dark cloud, come to us.
.....
With the darkness on the earth, come to us.
With these I wish the foam floating on the flowing water over the roots of
the great corn.
I have made your sacrifice.
I have prepared a smoke for you.
My feet restore for me.
My limbs restore for me.
My body restore for me.
My mind restore for me.
My voice restore for me.

Today, take out your spell for me.
Today, take away your spell for me.
Away from me it is taken.
Far off you have done it.
Happily I recover.
Happily my interior becomes cool.
Happily my eyes regain their power.
.....
Happily the children will regard you.
Happily the chiefs will regard you.
Happily, as they scatter in different directions, they will regard you.
Happily, as they approach their homes, they will regard you.
Happily, may their roads home be on the trail of pollen.
Happily may they all get back.
In beauty I walk.
With beauty before me, I walk.
With beauty behind me, I walk.
With beauty below me, I walk.
With beauty above me, I walk.
With beauty all around me, I walk.
It is finished again in beauty,
It is finished in beauty,
It is finished in beauty,
It is finished in beauty.

Iroquois

The Thanksgivings

We who are here present thank the Great Spirit that we are here to praise Him.
We thank Him that He has created men and women, and ordered that these beings shall always be living to multiply the earth.
We thank Him for making the earth and giving these beings its products to live on.
We thank Him for the water that comes out of the earth and runs for our lands.
We thank Him for all the animals on the earth.
We thank Him for certain timbers that grow and have fluids coming from them for us all.
We thank Him for the branches of the trees that grow shadows for our shelter.

We thank Him for the beings that come from the west, the thunder and lightning that water the earth.

We thank Him for the light which we call our oldest brother, the sun that works for our good.

We thank Him for all the fruits that grow on the trees and vines.

We thank Him for his goodness in making the forests, and thank all its trees.

We thank Him for the darkness that gives us rest, and for the kind Being of the darkness that gives us light, the moon.

We thank Him for the bright spots in the skies that give us signs, the stars.

We give Him thanks for our supporters, who have charge of our harvests.

We give thanks that the voice of the Great Spirit can still be heard through the words of Ga-ne-o-di-o.

We thank the Great Spirit that we have the privilege of this pleasant occasion.

We give thanks for the persons who can sing the Great Spirit's music, and hope they will be privileged to continue in his faith.

We thank the Great Spirit for all the persons who perform the ceremonies on this occasion.

Kiowa

Ghost Dance Songs

The father will descend,
The father will descend.
The earth will tremble,
The earth will tremble.
Everybody will rise,
Everybody will rise.
Stretch out your hands,
Stretch out your hands.

•

The spirit army is approaching,
The spirit army is approaching.
The whole world is moving onward,
The whole world is moving onward.
See! Everybody is standing watching,
See! Everybody is standing watching.
Let us all pray,
Let us all pray.

•

God has had pity on us,
God has had pity on us.
Jesus has taken pity on us,
Jesus has taken pity on us.
He teaches me a song,
He teaches me a song.
My song is a good one,
My song is a good one.

Phillips Brooks (b. 1850)

O Little Town of Bethlehem

O little town of Bethlehem,
How still we see thee lie!
Above thy deep and dreamless sleep
The silent stars go by:
Yet in thy dark streets shineth
The everlasting light;
The hopes and fears of all the years
Are met in thee tonight.

For Christ is born of Mary,
And gathered all above,
While mortals sleep, the angels keep
Their watch of wond'ring love.
O morning stars, together
Proclaim thy holy birth!
And praises sing to God the King,
And peace to men on earth!

How silently, how silently,
The wondrous gift is given!
So God imparts to human hearts
The blessings of this heaven.

No ear may hear his coming,
But in this world of sin,
Where meek souls will receive him, still
The dear Christ enters in.

O holy Child of Bethlehem,
Descend to us, we pray,
Cast out our sin, and enter in,
Be born in us today!
We hear the Christmas angels
The great glad tidings tell;
O come to us, abide with us,
Our Lord Emmanuel!

Edmund Hamilton Sears (b. 1850)

It Came upon a Midnight Clear

It came upon the midnight clear,
That glorious song of old,
From angels bending near the earth,
To touch their harps of gold:
'Peace on the earth, good-will to men,
From heav'n's all gracious King.'
The world in solemn stillness lay
To hear the angels sing.

Still through the cloven skies they come,
With peaceful wings unfurled;
And still their heavenly music floats
O'er all the weary world:
Above its sad and lowly plains
They bend on hovering wing,
And ever o'er its Babel sounds
The blesséd angels sing.

But with the woes of sin and strife
    The world has suffered long;
Beneath the angel-strain have rolled
    Two thousand years of wrong;
And man, at war with man, hears not
    The love song which they bring:
O hush the noise, ye men of strife,
    And hear the angels sing!

And ye, beneath life's crushing load
    Whose forms are bending low,
Who toil along the climbing way,
    With painful steps and slow, –
Look now; for glad and golden hours
    Come swiftly on the wing:
O rest beside the weary road,
    And hear the angels sing!

For, lo! the days are hastening on
    By prophet bards foretold,
When with the ever-circling years
    Comes round the age of gold:
When peace shall over all the earth
    Its ancient splendors fling,
And the whole world give back the song
    Which now the angels sing.

Edwin Markham (b. 1852)

Song Made Flesh

I have no glory in these songs of mine:
  If one of them can make a brother strong,
It came down from the peaks of the divine –
  I heard it in the Heaven of Lyric Song.

The one who builds the poem into fact,
He is the rightful owner of it all:
The pale words are with God's own power packed
When brave souls answer to the bugle-call.

And so I ask no man to praise my song,
But I would have him build it in his soul;
For that great praise would make me glad and strong,
And build the poem to a perfect whole.

Lizette Woodworth Reese (b. 1856)

Doubt

Creeds go thick along the way,
Their boughs hide God; I cannot pray.

Spring Ecstasy

Oh, let me run and hide,
Let me run straight to God;
The weather is so mad and white
From sky down to the clod!

If but one thing were so,
Lilac, or thorn out there,
It would not be, indeed,
So hard to bear.

The weather has gone mad with white;
The cloud, the highway touch;
White lilac is enough;
White thorn too much!

Benjamin Franklin King (b. 1857)

Nobody Knows

Nobody knows when de col' winds am blowin',
Whar all de po' little chillun am a-goin'.
Nobody knows when de night time's hoverin'
How many little ones am des'tute ob coverin'.
Nobody sees, but de Lo'd done see 'em,
An' bime-by de Lo'd 'll tell humanity ter free 'em.

Nobody knows jes' how many am in rags,
A-sleepin' in de hot blocks an' 'roun' on de flags,
Nobody sees all dis poverty an' woe,
An' bime-by de Lo'd 'll tell humanity ter free 'em.

Nobody nows whar dis poverty all comes –
How many po' folks am sleepin' in de slums.
Nobody knows jes' how few am befriendin',
But de good Lo'd knows dar mus' soon be an endin'.
Nobody sees, but de Lo'd done see 'em,
An' bime-by de Lo'd 'll tell humanity ter free 'em.

Horace Logo Traubel (b. 1858)

Cosmos

Hosts of evil beset me,
The darkness falls and doubt unwraps its cabal scroll,
While I, peaked nearest heaven, seek heaven's escape.

Outspread broad wings, O soul!
Defiantly pierce the spaces upward,
Carol for lower ears the victory and the hope,
And melt in skies eternal!

Flooded in light, outleaping ties sordid and black,
Mixing shadows to suns, ascending still and still,
Upborne in arms nerved to the ceaseless flight,
I, joyant, full circling day and night,
Sing all love's songs and live all thought and deed!

Louise Imogen Guiney (b. 1861)

Summum Bonum

Waiting on Him who knows us and our need,
Most need have we to dare not, nor desire,
But as He giveth, softly to suspire
Against His gift, with no inglorious greed,
For this is joy, tho' still our joys recede;
And, as in octaves of a noble lyre,
To move our minds with His, and clearer, higher,
Sound forth our fate; for this is strength indeed.

Thanks to His love let earth and man dispense
In smoke of worship when the heart is stillest,
A praying more than prayer: "Great good have I,
Till it be greater good to lay it by;
Nor can I lose peace, power, permanence,
For these smile on me from the thing Thou willest!"

Emily Pauline Johnson (Tekahionwake) (b. 1861)

Fire Flowers

And only where the forest fires have sped,
Scorching relentlessly the cool north lands,
A sweet wild flower lifts its purple head,
And, like some gentle spirit sorrow-fed,
It hides the scars with almost human hands.

And only to the heart that knows of grief,
Of desolating fire, of human pain,
There comes some purifying sweet belief,
Some fellow-feeling beautiful, if brief.
And life revives, and blossoms once again.

The Happy Hunting Grounds

Into the rose gold westland, its yellow prairies roll,
World of the bison's freedom, home of the Indian's soul.
Roll out, O seas! in sunlight bathed,
your plains wind-tossed, and grass enswathed.

Farther than vision ranges, farther than eagles fly,
Stretches the land of beauty, arches the perfect sky,
Hemm'd through the purple-mists afar
By peaks that gleam like star on star.

Fringing the prairie billows, fretting horizon's line,
Darkly green are slumb'ring wildernesses of pine,
Sleeping until the zephyrs throng
To kiss their silence into song.

Whispers freighted with odour swinging into the air,
Russet needles as censers swing to an altar, where
The angels' songs are less divine
Than duo sung twixt breeze and pine.

Laughing into the forest, dimples a mountain stream,
Pure as the airs above it, soft as a summer dream,
O! Lethean spring thou'rt only found
Within this ideal hunting ground.

Surely the great Hereafter cannot be more than this,
Surely we'll see that country after Time's farewell kiss.
Who would his lovely faith condole?
Who envies not the Red-skin's soul?

Sailing into the cloud land, sailing into the sun,
Into the crimson portals ajar when life is done?
O! dear dead race, my spirit too
Would fain sail westward unto you.

Edith Wharton (b. 1862)

Survival

When you and I, like all things kind or cruel,
The garnered days and light evasive hours,
Are gone again to be a part of flowers
And tears and tides, in life's divine renewal,

If some grey eve to certain eyes should wear
A deeper radiance than mere light can give,
Some silent page abruptly flash and live,
May it not be that you and I are there?

Chartres

I.

Immense, august, like some Titanic bloom,
  The mighty choir unfolds its lithic core,
Petalled with panes of azure, gules and or,
  Splendidly lambent in the Gothic gloom,
And stamened with keen flamelets that illume
  The pale high-altar. On the prayer-worn floor,
By worshippers innumerous thronged of yore,
  A few brown crones, familiars of the tomb,
The stranded driftwood of Faith's ebbing sea –
  For these alone the finials fret the skies,
The topmost bosses shake their blossoms free,
  While from the triple portals, with grave eyes,
Tranquil, and fixed upon eternity,
  The cloud of witnesses still testifies.

II.

The crimson panes like blood-drops stigmatise
  The western floor. The aisles are mute and cold.
A rigid fetich in her robe of gold,
  The Virgin of the Pillar, with blank eyes,
Enthroned beneath her votive canopies,
  Gathers a meagre remnant to her fold.
The rest is solitude; the church, grown old,
  Stands stark and grey beneath the burning skies.
Well-nigh again its mighty framework grows
  To be a part of nature's self, withdrawn
From hot humanity's impatient woes;
  The floor is rigid like some rude mountain lawn,
And in the east one giant window shows
  The roseate coldness of an Alp dawn.

George Santayana (b. 1863)

O World

O World, thou choosest not the better part!
It is not wisdom to be only wise,
And on the inward vision close the eyes,
But it is wisdom to believe the heart.
Columbus found a world, and had no chart.
Save one that faith deciphered in the skies;
To trust the soul's invincible surmise
Was all his science and his only art.
Our knowledge is a torch of smoky pine
That lights the pathway but one step ahead
Across a void of mystery and dread.
Bid, then, the tender light of faith to shine
By which alone the mortal heart is led
Unto the thinking of the thought divine.

Richard Hovey (b. 1864)

When the Priest Left

What did he say?
To seek love otherwhere
Nor bind the soul to clay?
It may be so – I cannot tell –
But I know that life is fair,
And love's bold clarion in the air
Outdins his little vesper-bell.

Love God? Can I touch God with both my hands?
Can I breathe in his hair and brush his cheek?

He is too far to seek.
This love is but a name that wise men speak.
God hath no lips to kiss.

Let God be; surely, surely if he will,
At the end of days,
He can win love as well as praise.
Why must we spill
The human love out at his feet?
Let be this talk of good and ill!
Though God be God, art thou not fair and sweet?

Open the window; let the air
Blow in on us.
It is enough to find you fair,
To touch with fingers timorous
Your sunlit hair, –
To turn my body to a prayer,
And kiss you – thus.

Madison Cawein (b. 1865)

Penetralia

I am a part of all you see
In Nature; part of all you feel:
I am the impact of the bee
Upon the blossom; in the tree
I am the sap, – that shall reveal
The leaf, the bloom, – that flows and flutes
Up from the darkness through its roots.

I am the vermeil of the rose,
The perfume breathing in its veins;
The gold within the mist that glows
Along the west and overflows

The heaven with light; the dew that rains
Its freshness down and strings with spheres
Of wet the webs and oaten ears.

I am the egg that folds the bird,
The song that breaks and breaks its shell;
The laughter and the wandering word
The water says; and, dimly heard,
The music of the blossom's bell
When soft winds swing it; and the sound
Of grass slow-creeping o'er the ground.

I am the warmth, the honey-scent
That throats with spice each lily-bud
That opens, white with wonderment,
Beneath the moon; or, downward bent,
Sleeps with a moth beneath its hood:
I am the dream that haunts it too,
That crystallizes into dew.

I am the seed within its pod;
The worm within its closed cocoon:
The wings within the circling clod,
The germ that gropes through soil and sod
To beauty, radiant in the noon:
I am all these, behold! and more –
I am the love at the world-heart's core.

C. D. Martin (b. 1866)

His Eye Is on the Sparrow

Why should I feel discouraged,
Why should the shadows come,
Why should my heart be lonely
And long for Heav'n and home,

When Jesus is my portion?
My constant Friend is He:
His eye is on the sparrow,
And I know He watches me;
His eye is on the sparrow,
And I know He watches me.

"Let not your heart be troubled,"
His tender word I hear,
And resting on His goodness,
I lose my doubts and fears:
Tho' by the path He leadeth
But one step I may see:
His eye is on the sparrow,
And I know He watches me;
His eye is on the sparrow,
And I know He watches me.

Whenever I am tempted,
Whenever clouds arise,
When songs give place to sighing,
When hope within me dies,
I draw the closer to Him,
From care He sets me free;
His eye is on the sparrow,
And I know He watches me;
His eye is on the sparrow,
And I know He watches me.

W. E. B. Du Bois (b. 1868)

A Litany at Atlanta
Done at Atlanta in the Day of Death, 1906

O Silent God, Thou whose voice afar in mist and mystery hath left our ears a-hungered in these fearful days –

Hear us, good Lord!

Listen to us, Thy children: our faces dark with doubt are made a mockery in Thy sanctuary. With uplifted hands we front Thy heaven, O God, crying:

We beseech Thee to hear us, good Lord!

We are not better than our fellows, Lord, we are but weak and human men. When our devils do deviltry, curse Thou the doer and the deed: curse them as we curse them, do to them all and more than ever they have done to innocence and weakness, to womanhood and home.

Have mercy upon us, miserable sinners!

And yet whose is the deeper guilt? Who made these devils? Who nursed them in crime and fed them on injustice? Who ravished and debauched their mothers and their grandmothers? Who bought and sold their crime, and waxed fat and rich on public iniquity?

Thou knowest, good God!

Is this Thy Justice, O Father, that guile be easier than innocence, and the innocent crucified for the guilt of the untouched guilty?

Justice, O judge of men!

Wherefore do we pray? Is not the God of the fathers dead? Have not seers seen in Heaven's halls Thine hearsed and lifeless form stark amidst the black and rolling smoke of sin, where all along bow bitter forms of endless dead?

Awake, Thou that sleepest!

Thou are not dead, but flown afar, up hills of endless light through blazing corridors of suns, where worlds do swing of good and gentle men, of women strong and free – far from the cozenage, black hypocrisy and chaste prostitution of this shameful speck of dust!

Turn again, O Lord, leave us not to perish in our sin!

From lust of body and lust of blood,
Great God, deliver us!

From lust of power and lust of gold,
Great God, deliver us!

From the leagued lying of despot and brute,
Great God, deliver us!

A city in travail, God our Lord, and from her loins sprang twin Murder and Black Hate. Red was the midnight; clang, crack and cry of death and fury filled the air and trembled underneath the stars when church spires pointed silently to Thee. And all this was to sate the greed of greedy men who hide behind the veil of vengeance!

Bend us Thine ear, O Lord!

In the pale, still morning we looked upon the deed. We stopped our ears and held our leaping hands, but they – did they not wag their heads and leer and cry with bloody jaws: *Cease from Crime!* The word was mockery, for thus they train a hundred crimes while we do cure one.

Turn again our captivity, O Lord!

Behold this maimed and broken thing, dear God; it was an humble black man, who toiled and sweat to save a bit from the pittance paid him. They told him: Work and Rise! He worked. Did this man sin? Nay, but someone told how someone said another did – one whom he had never seen nor known.

Yet for that man's crime this man lieth maimed and murdered, his wife naked to shame, his children to poverty and evil.

Hear us, O heavenly Father!

Doth not this justice of hell stink in Thy nostrils, O God? How long shall the mounting flood of innocent blood roar in Thine ears and pound in our hearts for vengeance? Pile the pale frenzy of blood-crazed brutes, who do such deeds, high on Thine Altar, Jehovah Jireh, and burn it in hell forever and forever!

Forgive us, good Lord; we know not what we say!

Bewildered we are and passion-tossed, mad with the madness of a mobbed and mocked and murdered people; straining at the armposts of Thy throne, we raise our shackled hands and charge Thee, God, by the bones of our stolen fathers, by the tears of our dead mothers, by the very blood of Thy crucified Christ: What meaneth this? Tell us the plan; give us the sign!

Keep not Thou silent, O God!

Sit no longer blind, Lord God, deaf to our prayer and dumb to our dumb suffering. Surely Thou, too, art not white, O Lord, a pale, bloodless, heartless thing!

Ah! Christ of all the Pities!

Forgive the thought! Forgive these wild, blasphemous words! Thou art still the God of our black fathers and in Thy Soul's Soul sit some soft darkenings of the evening, some shadowings of the velvet night.

But whisper – speak – call, great God, for Thy silence is white terror to our hearts! The way, O God, show us the way and point us the path!

Whither? North is greed and South is blood; within, the coward, and without, the liar. Whither? To death?

Amen! Welcome, dark sleep!

Whither? To life? But not this life, dear God, not this. Let the cup pass from us, tempt us not beyond our strength, for there is that clamoring and clawing within, to whose voice we would not listen, yet shudder lest we must, – and it is red. Ah! God! It is a red and awful shape.

Selah!

In yonder East trembles a star.

Vengeance is Mine; I will repay, saith the Lord!

Thy Will, O Lord, be done!

Kyrie Eleison!

Lord, we have done these pleading, wavering words.

We beseech Thee to hear us, good Lord!

We bow our heads and hearken soft to the sobbing of women and little children.

We beseech Thee to hear us, good Lord!

Our voices sink in silence and in night.

Hear us, good Lord!

In night, O God of a godless land!

Amen!

In silence, O Silent God.

Selah!

William Vaughn Moody (b. 1869)

from *Jetsam*

I wonder can this be the world it was
At sunset? I remember the sky fell
Green as pale meadows, at the long street-ends,
But overheard the smoke-wrack hugged the roofs
As if to shut the city from God's eyes
Till dawn should quench the laughter and the lights.
Beneath the gas flare stolid faces passed,
Too dull for sin; old loosened lips set hard
To drain the stale lees from the cup of sense:
Or if a young face yearned from out the mist
Made by its own bright hair, the eyes were wan
With desolate fore-knowledge of the end.
My life lay waste about me; as I walked,
From the gross dark of unfrequented streets
The face of my own youth peered forth at me,
Struck white with pity at the thing I was;
And globed in ghostly fire, thrice-virginal,
With lifted face star-strong, went one who sang
Lost verses from my youth's gold canticle.
Out of the void dark came my face and hers
One vivid moment – then the street was there;
Bloat shapes and mean eyes blotted the sear dusk;
And in the curtained window of a house
Whence sin reeked on the night, a shameful head
Was silhouetted black as Satan's face
Against eternal fires. I stumbled on
Down the dark slope that reaches riverward,
Stretching blind hands to find the throat of God
And crush Him in his lies. The river lay
Coiled in its factory filth and few lean trees.
All was too hateful – I could not die there!
I whom the Spring had strained unto her breast,
Whose lips had felt the wet vague lips of dawn.
So under the thin willows' leprous shade
And through the tangled ranks of riverweed
I pushed – till lo, God heard me! I came forth

Where, 'neath the shoreless hush of region light,
Through a new world, undreamed of, undesired,
Beyond imagining of man's weary heart,
Far to the white marge of the wondering sea
This still plain widens, and this moon rains down
Insufferable ecstasy of peace.

James Weldon Johnson (b. 1871)

The Creation

And God stepped out on space,
And he looked around and said:
I'm lonely –
I'll make me a world.

And far as the eye of God could see
Darkness covered everything,
Blacker than a hundred midnights
Down in a cypress swamp.

Then God smiled,
And the light broke,
And the darkness rolled up on one side,
And the light stood shining on the other,
And God said: That's good!

Then God reached out and took the light in his hands,
And God rolled the light around in his hands
Until he made the sun;
And he set that sun a-blazing in the heavens.
And the light that was left from making the sun
God gathered it up in a shining ball
And flung it against the darkness,
Spangling the night with the moon and stars.
Then down between
The darkness and the light

He hurled the world;
And God said: That's good!

Then God himself stepped down—
And the sun was on his right hand,
And the moon was on his left;
The stars were clustered about his head,
And the earth was under his feet.
And God walked, and where he trod
His footsteps hollowed the valleys out
And bulged the mountains up.

Then he stopped and looked and saw
That the earth was hot and barren.
So God stepped over the edge of the world
And he spat out the seven seas –
He batted his eyes, and the lightnings flashed –
He clapped his hands, and the thunders rolled –
And the waters above the earth came down,
The cooling waters came down.

Then the green grass sprouted,
And the little red flowers blossomed,
The pine tree pointed his fingers to the sky,
And the oak spread out his arms,
The lakes cuddled down in the hollows of the ground,
And the rivers ran down to the sea;
And God smiled again,
And the rainbow appeared,
And curled itself around his shoulders.

Then God raised his arm and he waved his hand
Over the sea and over the land,
And he said: Bring forth! Bring forth!
And quicker than God could drop his hand,
Fishes and fowls
And beasts and birds
Swam the rivers and the seas,
Roamed the forests and the woods,
And split the air with their wings.
And God said: That's good!

Then God walked around,
And God looked around
On all that he had made.
He looked at his sun,
And he looked at his moon,
And he looked at his little stars;
He looked on his world
With all its living things,
And God said: I'm lonely still.

Then God sat down –
On the side of a hill where he could think;
By a deep, wide river he sat down;
With his head in his hands,
God thought and thought,
Till he thought: I'll make me a man!

Up from the bed of the river
God scooped the clay;
And by the bank of the river
He kneeled him down;
And there great God Almighty
Who lit the sun and fixed it in the sky,
Who flung the stars to the most far corner of the night,
Who rounded the earth in the middle of his hand;
This Great God,
Like a mammy bending over her baby,
Kneeled down in the dust
Toiling over a lump of clay
Till he shaped it in his own image;

Then into it he blew the breath of life,
And man became a living soul.
Amen. Amen.

Paul Laurence Dunbar (b.1872)

The Light

Once when my soul was newly shriven,
When perfect peace to me was given,
Pervading all in all with currents bright,
I saw shine forth a mighty Light;
And myriad lesser lights to this were joined,
Each light with every other light entwined;
And as they shone a sound assailed my ears,
Alike the mighty music of the spheres.
The greater light was Love and Peace and Law,
And it had power toward it the rest to draw;
It was the Soul of souls, the greatest One,
The Life of lives, of suns the sun.
And floating through it all, my soul could see
The Christ-light, shining for humanity;
And silently I heard soft murmurs fall,
"Look up, earth child; the light is all."

An Ante-Bellum Sermon

We is gathahed hyeah, my brothahs,
  In dis howlin' widaness,
Fu' to speak some words of comfo't
  To each othah in distress.
An' we chooses fu' ouah subjic'
  Dis – we'll 'splain it by an' by;
  "An' de Lawd said, 'Moses, Moses,'
  An' de man said, 'Hyeah am I.'"

Now ole Pher'oh, down in Egypt,
  Was de wuss man evah bo'n,
An' he had de Hebrew chillun
  Down dah wukin' in hi co'n;
'Twell de Lawd got tiahed o' his foolin',
  An' sez he: "I'll let him know –
Look heyah, Moses, go tell Pher'oh
  Fu' to let dem chillun go."

"An' ef he refuse to do it,
  I will make him rue de houah,
Fu' I'll empty down on Egypt
  All de vials of my powah."
Yes, he did – an' Pher'oh's ahmy
  Wasn't wuth a ha'f a dime;
Fu' de Lawd will he'p his chillun,
  You kin trust him evah time.

An' yo' enemies may 'sail you
  In de back an in de front;
But de Lawd is all aroun' you,
  Fu' to ba' de battle's brunt.
Dey kin fo'ge yo' chains an' shackles
  F'om de mountains to de sea;
But de Lawd will sen' some Moses
  Fu' to set his chillun free.

An' de lan' shall hyeah his thundah,
  Lak a blas' f'om Gab'el's ho'n,
Fu' de Lawd of hosts is mighty
  When he girds hi ahmor on.
But fu' feah some one mistakes me,
  I will pause right hyeah to say,
Dat I'm still a-preachin' ancient,
  I ain't talkin' 'bout to-day.

But I tell you, fellah christuns,
  Things'll happen mighty strange;
Now, de Lawd done dis fu' Isrul,
  An' his ways don't nevah change,
An' de love he showed to Isrul
  Wasn't all on Isrul spent;
Now don't run an' tell yo' mastahs
  Dat I's preachin' discontent.

'Cause I isn't; I'se a-judgin'
  Bible people by deir ac's;
I'se a-givin you de Scriptuah,
  I'se a-handin' you de fac's.

Cose ole Pher'oh b'lieved in slav'ry,
  But de Lawd he let him see,
Dat de people he put bref in – ,
  Evah mothah's son was free.

An' dah's othahs thinks lak Pher'oh,
  But dey calls de Scriptuah liar,
Fu' de Bible says "a servant
  Is a-worthy of his hire."
An' you cain't git roun' nor thoo dat,
  An you cain't git ovah it,
Fu'whatevah place you git in,
  Dis hyeah Bible too'll fit.

So you see de Lawd's intention,
  Evah sence de worl' began,
Was dat His almighty freedom
  Should belong to evah man,
But I think it would be bettah,
  Ef I'd pause agin to say,
Dat I'm talkin' 'bout ouah freedom
  In a Bibleistic way.

But de Moses is a-comin',
  An' he's comin', suah an' fas'
We kin hyeah his feet a trompin',
  We kin hyeah his trumpit blas'.
But I want to wa'n you people,
  Don't you git too brigity
An' don't you git to braggin'
  'Bout dese things, you wait an' see.

But when Moses wif his powah
  Comes an' sets us chillun free,
We will praise de gracious Mastah
  Dat has gin us liberty;
An' we'll shout ouah halleluyahs,
  On dat mighty reck'nin' day,
When we'se reco'nised ez citiz' –
  Hu huh! Chillun, let us pray!

Sympathy

I know what the caged bird feels, alas!
  When the sun is bright on the upland slopes;
When the wind stirs soft through the springing grass,
And the river flows like a stream of glass;
  When the first bird sings and the first bud opes,
And the faint perfume from its chalice steals –
I know what the caged bird feels!

I know why the caged bird beats his wing
  Till its blood is red on the cruel bars;
For he must fly back to his perch and cling
When he fain would be on the bough a-swing;
  And a pain still throbs in the old, old scars
And they pulse again with a keener sting –
I know why he beats his wing!

I know why the caged bird sings, ah me,
  When his wing is bruised and his bosom sore, –
When he beats his bars and he would be free;
It is not a carol of joy or glee,
  But a prayer that he sends from his heart's deep core,
But a plea, that upward to Heaven he flings –
I know why the caged bird sings!

The Mystery

I was not; now I am – a few days hence,
I shall not be; I fain would look before
And after, but can neither do; some Pow'r
Or lack of pow'r says "no" to all I would.
I stand upon a wide and sunless plain,
Nor chart nor steel to guide my steps aright.
Whene'er, o'ercoming fear, I dare to move,
I grope without direction and by chance.
Some feign to hear a voice and feel a hand
That draws them ever upward thro' the gloom.
But I – I hear no voice and touch no hand,
Tho' oft thro' silence infinite, I list,

And strain my hearing to supernal sounds;
Tho' oft thro' fateful darkness do I reach,
And stretch my hand to find that other hand.
I question of th' eternal bending skies
That seem to neighbor with the novice earth;
But they roll on and daily shut their eyes
On me, as I one day shall do on them,
And tell me not the secret that I ask.

Resignation

Long had I grieved at what I deemed abuse;
  But now I am as grain within the mill.
If so be thou must crush me for thy use,
  Grind on, O potent God, and do thy will!

George Bennard (b. 1873)

The Old Rugged Cross

So I'll cherish the old rugged cross,
Till my trophies at last I lay down.
I will cling to the old rugged cross,
And exchange it some day for a crown.

On a hill far away, stood an old rugged cross,
The emblem of suff'ring and shame;
And I love that old cross where the dearest and best
For a world of lost sinners was slain.

Oh, that old rugged cross so despised by the world
Has a wondrous attraction for me;
For the dear Lamb of God left his glory above,
To bear it to dark Calvary.

In the old rugged cross, stained with blood so divine,
A wondrous beauty I see;
For 'twas on that old cross Jesus suffered and died,
To pardon and sanctify me.

To the old rugged cross I will ever be true,
Its shame and reproach gladly bear;
Then he'll call me some day to my home far away,
Where his glory forever I'll share.

Robert Frost (b. 1874)

Rose Pogonias

A saturated meadow,
  Sun-shaped and jewel-small
A circle scarcely wider
  Than the trees around were tall;
Where winds were quite excluded,
  And the air was stifling sweet
With the breath of many flowers, –
  A temple of the heat.

There we bowed us in the burning,
  As the sun's right worship is,
To pick where none could miss them
  A thousand orchises;
For though the grass was scattered,
  Yet every second spear
Seemed tipped with wings of color,
  That tinged the atmosphere.

We raised a simple prayer
  Before we left the spot,
That in the general mowing
  That place might be forgot;

Or if not all so favoured,
  Obtain such grace of hours,
That none should mow the grass there
  Whilse so confused with flowers.

A Prayer in Spring

Oh, give us pleasure in the flowers today;
And give us not to think so far away
As the uncertain harvest; keep us here
All simply in the springing of the year.

Oh, give us pleasure in the orchard white,
Like nothing else by day, like ghosts by night;
And make us happy in the happy bees,
The swarm dilating round the perfect trees.

And make us happy in the darting bird
That suddenly above the bees is heard,
The meteor that thrusts in with needle bill,
And off a blossom in mid air stands still.

For this is love and nothing else is love,
The which it is reserved for God above
To sanctify to what far ends He will,
But which it only needs that we fulfill.

The Trial by Existence

Even the bravest that are slain
  Shall not dissemble their surprise
On waking to find valor reign,
  Even as on earth, in paradise;
And where they sought without the sword
  Wide fields of asphodel fore'er,
To find that the utmost reward
  Of daring should be still to dare.

The light of heaven falls whole and white
  And is not shattered into dyes,

The light for ever is morning light;
  The hills for verdured pasture-wise;
The angel hosts with freshness go,
  And seek with laughter what to brave; –
And binding all is the hushed snow
  Of the far-distant breaking wave.

And from a cliff-top is proclaimed
  The gathering of the souls for birth,
The trial by existence named,
  The obscuration upon earth.
And the slant spirits trooping by
  In streams and cross- and counter-streams
Can but give ear to that sweet cry
  For its suggestion of what dreams!

And the more loitering are turned
  To view once more the sacrifice
Of those who for some good discerned
  Will gladly give up paradise.
And a white shimmering concourse rolls
  Toward the throne to witness there
The speeding of devoted souls
  Which God makes his especial care.

And none are taken but who will,
  Having first heard the life read out
That opens earthward, good and ill,
  Beyond the shadow of a doubt;
And very beautifully God limns,
  And tenderly, life's little dream,
But naught extenuates or dims,
  Setting the thing that is supreme.

Nor is there wanting in the press
  Some spirit to stand simply forth,
Heroic in its nakedness,
  Against the uttermost of earth.
The tale of earth's unhonored things
  Sounds nobler there than 'neath the sun;
And the mind whirls and the heart sings,
  And a shout greets the daring one.

But always God speaks at the end:
  'One thought in agony of strife
The bravest would have by for friend,
  The memory that he chose the life;
But the pure fate to which you go
  Admits no memory of choice,
Or the woe were not earthly woe
  To which you give the assenting voice.'

And so the choice must be again,
  But the last choice is still the same;
And the awe passes wonder then,
  And a hush falls for all acclaim.
And God has taken a flower of gold
  And broken it, and used therefrom
The mystic link to bind and hold
  Spirit to matter till death come.

'Tis of the essence of life here,
  Though we choose greatly, still to lack
The lasting memory at all clear,
  That life has for us on the wrack
Nothing but what we somehow chose;
  Thus are we wholly stripped of pride
In the pain that has but one close,
  Bearing it crushed and mystified.

Fragmentary Blue

Why make so much of fragmentary blue
In here and there a bird, or butterfly,
Or flower, or wearing-stone, or open eye,
When heaven presents in sheets the solid hue?

Since earth is earth, perhaps, not heaven (as yet) –
Though some savants make earth include the sky;
And blue so far above us comes so high,
It only gives our wish for blue a whet.

Amy Lowell (b. 1874)

Wheat-in-the-Ear

You stand between the cedars and the green spruces,
Brilliantly naked
And I think:
What are you,
A gem under sunlight?
A poised spear?
A jade cup?
You flash in front of the cedars and the tall spruces,
And I see that you are fire –
Sacrificial fire on a jade altar,
Spear-tongue of white, ceremonial fire.
My eyes burn,
My hands are flames seeking you,
But you are as remote from me as a bright pointed planet
Set in the distance of an evening sky.

A Decade

When you came, you were like red wine and honey,
And the taste of you burnt my mouth with its sweetness.
Now you are like morning bread,
Smooth and pleasant.
I hardly taste you at all for I know your savour,
But I am completely nourished.

Gertrude Stein (b. 1874)

from *Tender Buttons*

Dirt and Not Copper.

Dirt and not copper makes a color darker. It makes the shape so heavy and makes no melody harder.

It makes mercy and relaxation and even a strength to spread a table fuller. There are more places not empty. They see cover.

A Red Stamp.

If lilies are lily white if they exhaust noise and distance and even dust, if they dusty will dirt a surface that has no extreme grace, if they do this and it is not necessary it is not at all necessary if they do this they need a catalogue.

More.

An elegant use of foliage and grace and a little piece of white cloth and oil.

Wondering so winningly in several kinds of oceans is the reason that makes red so regular and enthusiastic. The reason that there is more snips are the same shining very colored rid of no round color.

A Waist.

A star glide, a single frantic sullenness, a single financial grass greediness.

Object that is in wood. Hold the pine, hold the dark, hold in the rush, make the bottom.

A piece of crystal. A change, in a change that is remarkable there is no reason to say that there was a time.

A woolen object gilded. A country climb is the best disgrace, a couple of practices any of them in order is so left.

In Between.

In between a place and candy is a narrow foot-path that shows more mounting than anything, so much really that a calling meaning a bolster measured a whole thing with that. A virgin a whole virgin is judged made and so between curves and outlines and real seasons and more out glasses and a perfectly unprecedented arrangement between old ladies and mild colds there is no satin wood shining.

from *A Plate.*

Plates and a dinner set of colored china. Pack together a string and enough with it to protect the centre, cause a considerable haste and gather more as it is cooling, collect more trembling and not any even trembling, cause a whole thing to be a church.

from *Rooms.*

A religion, almost a religion, any religion, a quintal in religion, a relying and a surface and a service in indecision and a creature and a question and a syllable in answer and more counting and no quarrel and a single scientific statement and no darkness and no question and an earned administration and a single set of sisters and an outline and no blisters and the section seeing yellow and the centre having spelling and no solitude and no quaintness and yet solid quite so solid and the single surface centred and the question in the placard and the singularity, is there a singularity, and the singularity, why is there a question and the singularity why is the surface outrageous, why is it beautiful why is it not when there is no doubt, why is anything vacant, why is not disturbing a centre no virtue, why is it when it is and why is it when it is and there is no doubt, there is no doubt that the singularity shows.

.....

A light in the moon the only light is on Sunday. What was the sensible decision.

The sensible decision was that notwithstanding many declarations and more music, not even notwithstanding the choice and a torch and a collection, notwithstanding the celebrating hat and a vacation and even more noise than cutting, notwithstanding Europe and Asia and being overbearing, not even notwithstanding an elephant and a strict occasion, not even withstanding more cultivation and some seasoning, not even with drowning and with the ocean being encircling, not even with more likeness and any cloud, not even with terrific sacrifice of pedestrianism and a special resolution, not even more likely to be pleasing. The care with which the rain is wrong and the green is wrong and the white is wrong, the care with which there is a chair and plenty of breathing. The care with which there is incredible justice and likeness, all this makes a magnificent asparagus, and also a fountain.

Trumbull Stickney (b. 1874)

Live Blindly

Live blindly and upon the hour. The Lord,
Who was the Future, died full long ago.
Knowledge which is the Past is folly. Go,
Poor child, and be not to thyself abhorred.
Around thine earth sun-winged winds do blow
And planets roll; a meteor draws his sword;
The rainbow breaks his seven-coloured chord
And the long strips of river-silver flow:
Awake! Give thyself to the lovely hours.
Drinking their lips, catch thou the dream in flight
About their fragile hairs' aerial gold.
Thou art divine, thou livest, – as of old
Apollo springing naked to the light,
And all his island shivered into flowers.

Carl Sandburg (b. 1878)

Grass

Pile the bodies high at Austerlitz and Waterloo,
Shovel them under and let me work –
    I am the grass; I cover all.

And pile them high at Gettysburg
And pile them high at Ypres and Verdun.
Shovel them under and let me work.
Two years, ten years, and passengers ask the conductor:
What is this place?
Where are we now?

I am the grass.
Let me work.

Wallace Stevens (b. 1879)

Sunday Morning [1917]

I

Complacencies of the peignoir, and late
Coffee and oranges in a sunny chair,
And the green freedom of a cockatoo
Upon a rug, mingle to dissipate
The holy hush of ancient sacrifice.
She dreams a little, and she feels the dark
Encroachment of that old catastrophe,
As a calm darkens among water-lights.
The pungent oranges and bright, green wings
Seem things in some procession of the dead,
Winding across wide water, without sound.
The day is like wide water, without sound,
Stilled for the passing of her dreaming feet
Over the seas, to silent Palestine,
Dominion of the blood and sepulchre.

II

She hears, upon that water without sound,
A voice that cries: "The tomb in Palestine
Is not the porch of spirits lingering;
It is the grave of Jesus, where he lay."

We live in an old chaos of the sun,
Or old dependency of day and night,
Or Island solitude, unsponsored, free,
Of that wide water, inescapable.
Deer walk upon our mountains, and the quail
Whistle about us their spontaneous cries;
Sweet berries ripen in the wilderness;
And, in the isolation of the sky,
At evening, casual flocks of pigeons make
Ambiguous undulations as they sink,
Downward to darkness, on extended wings.

III

She says: "I am content when wakened birds,
Before they fly, test the reality
Of misty fields, by their sweet questionings;
But when the birds are gone, and their warm fields
Return no more, where, then, is paradise?"
There is not any haunt of prophecy,
Nor any old chimera of the grave,
Neither the golden underground, nor isle
Melodious, where spirits gat them home,
Nor visionary South, nor cloudy palm
Remote on heaven's hill, that has endured
As April's green endures; or will endure
Like her remembrance of awakened birds,
Or her desire for June and evening, tipped
By the consummation of the swallow's wings.

IV

She says, "But in contentment I still feel
The need of some imperishable bliss."
Death is the mother of beauty; hence from her,
Alone, shall come fulfilment to our dreams
And our desires. Although she strews the leaves
Of sure obliteration on our paths –
The path sick sorrow took, the many paths
Where triumph rang its brassy phrase, or love
Whispered a little out of tenderness –
She makes the willow shiver in the sun
For maidens who were wont to sit and gaze

Upon the grass, relinquished to their feet.
She causes boys to bring sweet-smelling pears
And plums in ponderous piles. The maidens taste
And stray impassioned in the littering leaves.

V

Supple and turbulent, a ring of men
Shall chant in orgy on a summer morn
Their boisterous devotion to the sun –
Not as a god, but as a god might be,
Naked among them, like a savage source.
Their chant shall be a chant of paradise,
Out of their blood, returning to the sky;
And in their chant shall enter, voice by voice,
The windy lake wherein their lord delights,
The trees, like seraphim, and echoing hills,
That choir among themselves long afterward.
They shall know well the heavenly fellowship
Of men that perish and of summer morn –
And whence they came and whither they shall go,
The dew upon their feet shall manifest.

Witter Bynner (b. 1881)

God's Acres

Because we felt there could not be
A mowing in reality
So white and feathery-blown and gay
With blossoms of wild caraway,
I said to Celia, "Let us trace
The secret of this pleasant place!"

We knew some deeper beauty lay
Below the bloom of caraway,
And when we bent the white aside

We came to paupers who had died:
Rough wooden shingles row on row,
And God's name written there – *John Doe.*

William Carlos Williams (b. 1883)

Metric Figure

There is a bird in the poplars –
It is the sun!
The leaves are little yellow fish
Swimming in the river;
The bird skims above them –
Day is on his wings.
Phoenix!
It is he that is making
The great gleam among the poplars.
It is his singing
Outshines the noise
Of leaves clashing in the wind.

Sara Teasdale (b. 1884)

On the Dunes

If there is any life when death is over,
    These tawny beaches will know much of me,
I shall come back, as constant and as changeful
    As the unchanging, many-colored sea.

If life was small, if it has made me scornful,
    Forgive me; I shall straighten like a flame
In the great calm of death, and if you want me
    Stand on the sea-ward dunes and call my name.

Ezra Pound (b. 1885)

Ballad for Gloom

For God, our God is a gallant foe
That playeth behind the veil.

I have loved my God as a child at heart
That seeketh deep bosoms for rest,
I have loved my God as a maid to man –
But lo, this thing is best:

To love your God as a gallant foe that plays behind the veil;
To meet your God as the night winds meet beyond Arcturus' pale.

I have played with God for a woman,
I have staked with my God for truth,
I have lost to my God as a man, clear-eyed –
His dice be not of truth.

For I am made as a naked blade,
But hear ye this thing in sooth:

Who loseth to God as man to man
Shall win at the turn of the game.
I have drawn my blade where the lightnings meet
But the ending is the same:
Who loseth to God as the sword blades lose
Shall win at the end of the game.

For God, our God is a gallant foe that playeth behind the veil.
Whom God deigns not to overthrow hath need of triple mail.

H. D. (b. 1886)

Orchard

I saw the first pear
as it fell –
the honey-seeking, golden-banded,
the yellow swarm
was not more fleet than I,
(spare us from loveliness)
and I fell prostrate
crying:
you have flayed us
with your blossoms,
spare us the beauty
of fruit-trees.

The honey-seeking
paused not,
the air thundered their song,
and I alone was prostrate.
O rough-hewn
god of the orchard,
I bring you an offering –
do you, alone unbeautiful,
son of the god,
spare us from loveliness:

these fallen hazel-nuts,
stripped late of their green sheaths,
grapes, red-purple,
their berries
dripping with wine,
pomegranates already broken,
and shrunken figs
and quinces untouched,
I bring you as offering.

The Cliff Temple

I

Great, bright portal,
shelf of rock,
rocks fitted in long ledges,
rocks fitted to dark, to silver granite,
to lighter rock –
clean cut, white against white.

High – high – and no hill-goat
tramples – no mountain-sheep
has set foot on your fine grass;
you lift, you are the-world-edge,
pillar for the sky-arch.

The world heaved –
we are next to the sky:
over us, sea-hawks shout,
gulls sweep past –
the terrible breakers are silent
from this place.

Below us, on the rock-edge,
where earth is caught in the fissures
of the jagged cliff,
a small tree stiffens in the gale,
it bends – but its white flowers
are fragrant at this height.

And under and under,
the wind booms:
it whistles, it thunders,
it growls – it presses the grass
beneath its great feet.

II

I said:
for ever and for ever, must I follow you
through the stones?
I catch at you – you lurch:
you are quicker than my hand-grasp.

I wondered at you.
I shouted – dear – mysterious – beautiful –
white myrtle-flesh.

I was splintered and torn:
the hill-path mounted
swifter than my feet.

Could a daemon avenge this hurt,
I would cry to him – could a ghost,
I would shout – O evil,
follow this god,
taunt him with his evil and his vice.

III

Shall I hurl myself from here,
shall I leap and be nearer you?
Shall I drop, beloved, beloved,
ankle against ankle?
Would you pity me, O white breast?

If I woke, would you pity me,
would our eyes meet?

Have you heard,
do you know how I climbed this rock?
My breath caught, I lurched forward –
I stumbled in the ground-myrtle.

Have you heard, O god seated on the cliff,
how far toward the ledges of your house,
how far I had to walk?

IV

Over me the wind swirls.
I have stood on your portal
and I know –
you are further than this,
still further on another cliff.

Joyce Kilmer (b. 1886)

Trees

I think that I shall never see
A poem lovely as a tree.

A tree whose hungry mouth is prest
Against the earth's sweet flowing breast;

A tree that looks at God all day,
And lifts her leafy arms to pray;

A tree that may in Summer wear
A nest of robins in her hair;

Upon whose bosom snow has lain;
Who intimately lives with rain.

Poems are made by fools like me,
But only God can make a tree.

T. S. Eliot (b. 1888)

The Hippopotamus

Similiter et omnes revereantur Diaconos, ut mandatum Jesu Christi; et Episcopum, ut Jesum Christum, existentem filium Patris; Presbyteros autem, ut concilium Dei et conjunctionem Apostolorum. Sine his Ecclesia non vocatur; de quibus suadeo vos sic habeo.
S. Ignatii Ad Trallianos.

And when this epistle is read among you, cause that it be read also in the church of the Laodiceans.

The broad-backed hippopotamus
Rests on his belly in the mud;
Although he seems so firm to us
He is merely flesh and blood.

Flesh and blood is weak and frail,
Susceptible to nervous shock;
While the True Church can never fail
For it is based upon a rock.

The hippo's feeble steps may err
In compassing material ends,
While the True Church need never stir
To gather in its dividends.

The 'potamus can never reach
The mango on the mango-tree;
But fruits of pomegranate and peach
Refresh the Church from over sea.

At mating time the hippo's voice
Betrays inflexions hoarse and odd,
But every week we hear rejoice
The Church, at being one with God.

The hippopotamus's day
Is passed in sleep; at night he hunts;
God works in a mysterious way –
The Church can sleep and feed at once.

I saw the 'potamus take wing
Ascending from the damp savannas,
And quiring angels round him sing
The praise of God, in loud hosannas.

Blood of the Lamb shall wash him clean
And him shall heavenly arms enfold,
Among the saints he shall be seen
Performing on a harp of gold.

He shall be washed as white as snow,
By all the martyr'd virgins kist,
While the True Church remains below
Wrapt in the old miasmal mist.

Preludes

I

The winter evening settles down
With smell of steaks in passageways.
Six o'clock.
The burnt-out ends of smoky days.
And now a gusty shower wraps
The grimy scraps
Of withered leaves about your feet
And newspapers from vacant lots;
The showers beat
On broken blinds and chimneypots,
And at the corner of the street
A lonely cab-horse steams and stamps.
And then the lighting of the lamps.

II

The morning comes to consciousness
Of faint stale smells of beer
From the sawdust-trampled street
With all its muddy feet that press
To early coffee-stands.
With the other masquerades
That time resumes,
One thinks of all the hands
That are raising dingy shades
In a thousand furnished rooms.

III

You tossed a blanket from the bed
You lay upon your back, and waited;
You dozed, and watched the night revealing
The thousand sordid images
Of which your soul was constituted;
They flickered against the ceiling.
And when all the world came back
And the light crept up between the shutters
And you heard the sparrows in the gutters,

You had such a vision of the street
As the street hardly understands;
Sitting along the bed's edge, where
You curled the papers from your hair,
Or clasped the yellow soles of feet
In the palms of both soiled hands.

IV

His soul stretched tight across the skies
That fade behind a city block,
Or trampled by insistent feet
At four and five and six o'clock;
And short square fingers stuffing pipes,
And evening newspapers, and eyes
Assured of certain certainties,
The conscience of a blackened street
Impatient to assume the world.

I am moved by fancies that are curled
Around these images, and cling:
The notion of some infinitely gentle
Infinitely suffering thing.

Wipe your hand across your mouth, and laugh;
The worlds revolve like ancient women
Gathering fuel in vacant lots.

Fenton Johnson (b. 1888)

Tired

I am tired of work; I am tired of building up somebody
else's civilization.
Let us take a rest, M'lissy Jane.
I will go down to the Last Chance Saloon, drink a gallon
or two of gin, shoot a game or two of dice and
sleep the rest of the night on one of Mike's barrels.

You will let the old shanty go to rot, the white people's
clothes turn to dust, and the Calvary Baptist Church
sing to the bottomless pit.
You will spend your days forgetting you married me and
your nights hunting the warm gin Mike serves the
ladies in the rear of the Last Chance Saloon.
Throw the children into the river; civilization has given
us too many. It is better to die than it is to grow
up and find out that you are colored.
Pluck the stars out of the heavens. The stars mark out
destiny. The stars marked my destiny.
I am tired of civilization.

Conrad Aiken (b. 1889)

Miracles

Twilight is spacious, near things in it seem far,
And distant things seem near.
Now in the green west hangs a yellow star.
And now across old waters you may hear
The profound gloom of bells among still trees,
Like a rolling of huge boulders beneath seas.

Silent as though in evening contemplation
Weaves the bat under the gathering stars.
Silent as dew, we seek new incarnation,
Meditate new avatars.
In a clear dusk like this
Mary climbed up the hill to seek her son,
To lower him down from the cross, and kiss
The mauve wounds, every one.

Men with wings
In the dusk walked softly after her.
She did not see them, but may have felt
The winnowed air around her stir;

She did not see them, but may have known
Why her son's body was light as a little stone.
She may have guessed that other hands were there
Moving the watchful air.

Now, unless persuaded by searching music
Which suddenly opens the portals of the mind,
We guess no angels,
And are contented to be blind.
Let us blow silver horns in the twilight,
And lift our hearts to the yellow star in the green,
To find perhaps, if, while the dew is rising,
Clear things may not be seen.

Edna St. Vincent Millay (b. 1892)

God's World

O world, I cannot hold thee close enough!
 Thy winds, thy wide grey skies!
 Thy mists, that roll and rise!
Thy woods, this autumn day, that ache and sag
And all but cry with colour! That gaunt crag
To crush! To lift the lean of that black bluff!
World, World, I cannot get thee close enough!

Long have I known a glory in it all,
  But never knew I this;
  Here such a passion is
As stretcheth me apart, – Lord, I do fear
Thou'st made the world too beautiful this year;
My soul is all but out of me, – let fall
No burning leaf; prithee, let no bird call.

B. G. De Sylva (b. 1895)

Stairway to Paradise

All you preachers
Who delight in panning the dancing teachers,
Let me tell you there are a lot of features
Of the dance that carry you through
The Gates of Heaven.

It's madness
To be always sitting around in sadness,
When you could be learning the Steps of Gladness.
(You'll be happy when you can do
Just six or seven.)

Begin today. You'll find it nice:
The quickest way to Paradise.
When you practice,
Here's the thing to do –
Simply say as you go:

I'll build a Stairway to Paradise,
With a new Step ev'ry day.
I'm going to get there at any price;
Stand aside, I'm on my way!
I got the blues,
and up above it's so fair;
Shoes,
Go on and carry me there!
I'll build a Stairway to Paradise
With a new Step ev'ry day.

Stephen Vincent Benét (b. 1898)

from *John Brown's Body*

[The Captive Sings Below Deck:]
Oh Lordy Je-sus
Won't you come and find me?
They put me in jail, Lord,
Way down in the jail.
Won't you send me a pro-phet
Just one of your prophets
Like Moses and Aaron
To get me some bail?

I'm feeling poorly
Yes, mighty poorly,
I aint got no strength, Lord,
I'm all trampled down.
So send me an angel
Just any old angel
To give me a robe, Lord,
And give me a crown.

Oh Lordy Je-sus
It's a long time comin'
It's a long time co-o-min'
That Jubilee time.
We'll wait and we'll pray, Lord,
We'll wait and we'll pray, Lord,
But it's a long time, Lord,
Yes, it's a long time.

The dark sobbing ebbed away.
The captain was still talking. "Yes," he said,
"And yet we treat 'em well enough. There's no one
From Salem to the Guinea Coast can say
They lose as few as I do."

.....

John Brown's Prayer

Omnipotent and steadfast God,
Who, in Thy mercy, hath
Upheaved in me Jehovah's rod
And his chastising wrath,
For fifty-nine unsparing years
Thy Grace hath worked apart
To mould a man of iron tears
With a bullet for a heart.

Yet, since this body may be weak
With all it has to bear,
Once more, before Thy thunders speak,
Almighty, hear my prayer.

I saw Thee when Thou did display
The black man and his lord
To bid me free the one, and slay
The other with the sword.

I heard Thee when Thou bade me spurn
Destruction from my hand
And, though all Kansas bleed and burn,
It was at Thy command.

I hear the rolling of the wheels,
The chariots of war!
I hear the breaking of the seals
And the opening of the door!

The glorious beasts with many eyes
Exult before the Crowned.
The buried saints arise, arise
Like incense from the ground!

Before them march the martyr-kings,
In bloody sunsets drest,
O, Kansas, bleeding Kansas,
You will not let me rest!

I hear your sighing corn again,
I smell your prairie-sky,
And I remember five dead men
By Pottawattomie.

Lord God it was a work of Thine,
And how might I refrain?
But Kansas, bleeding Kansas,
I hear her in her pain.

Her corn is rustling in the ground,
An arrow in my flesh.
And all night long I staunch a wound
That ever bleeds afresh.

Get up, get up, my hardy sons,
From this time forth we are
No longer men, but pikes and guns
In God's advancing war.

And if we live, we free the slave,
And if we die, we die.
But God has digged His saints a grave
Beyond the western sky.

Oh, fairer than the bugle-call
Its walls of jasper shine!
And Joshua's sword is on the wall
With space beside for mine.

And should the Philistine defend
His strength against our blows,
The God who doth not spare His friend,
Will not forget His foes.

Traditional Spirituals and Hymns of the Nineteenth Century

Deep River

Deep river,
My home is over Jordan,
Deep river,
Lord, I want to cross over into camp ground,

Oh, don't you want to go to that Gospel feast,
That promis'd land where all is peace?

I'll go into heaven, and take my seat,
Cast my crown at Jesus' feet.

Oh, when I get to heav'n, I'll walk all about,
There's nobody there for to turn me out.

Free at Last

Free at last, free at last;
I thank God I'm free at last;
Free at last, free at last,
I thank God I'm free at last,
O free at last.

'Way down in the grave-yard walk,
I thank God I'm free at last,
Me and my Jesus goin' to meet and talk,
I thank God I'm free at last,
O free at last.

On-a my knees when the light pass'd by,
I thank God I'm free at last,
Thought my soul would rise and fly,
I thank God I'm free at last,
O free at last.

Some of these mornings, bright and fair,
I thank God I'm free at last,
Goin' meet King Jesus in the air,
I thank God I'm free at last,
O free at last.

Wayfaring Stranger

I'm just a poor wayfaring stranger,
A-trav'lin through this world of woe,
But there's no sickness, toil, or danger
In that bright land to which I go.
    I'm going there to see my father,
    I'm going there no more to roam,
    I'm just a-going over Jordan,
    I'm just a-going over home.

John Brown's Body

John Brown's body lies a-mould'ring in the grave,
John Brown's body lies a-mould'ring in the grave,
John Brown's body lies a-mould'ring in the grave,
    His soul is marching on.

Glory, glory, hallelujah!
Glory, glory, hallelujah!
Glory, glory, hallelujah!
His soul is marching on!

The stars of heaven are looking kindly down,
    On the grave of old John Brown.

He's gone to be a soldier in the army of the Lord,
    His soul is marching on.

John Brown died that the slave might be free,
    But his soul goes marching on.

He captured Harper's Ferry with his nineteen men so true,
And he frightened old Virginia till she trembled through and through;

They hung him for a traitor, themselves the traitor crew,
    But his soul goes marching on.

John Brown's knapsack is strapped to his back,
    His soul is marching on.

His pet lambs will meet on the way,
    And they'll go marching on.

They will hang Jeff Davis on a sour apple tree,
    As they go marching on.

Now has come the glorious jubilee,
    When all mankind are free.

Nobody Knows the Trouble I've Seen

Nobody knows de trouble I've seen,
Nobody knows but Jesus,
Nobody knows de trouble I've seen,
Glory Hallelu!

One morning I was a-walking down,
O yes, Lord!
I saw some berries a-hanging down,
O yes, Lord!

I pick de berry and I suck de juice,
O yes, Lord!
Just as sweet as the honey in de comb,
O yes, Lord!

Sometimes I'm up, sometimes I'm down,
O yes, Lord!
Sometimes I'm almost on de groun',
O yes, Lord!

What make ole Satan hate me so?
O yes, Lord!
Because he got me once and he let me go,
O yes, Lord!

Steal Away

Steal away, steal away, steal away to Jesus!
Steal away, steal away home,
I hain't got long to stay here.

My Lord calls me,
  He calls me by the thunder;
The trumpet sounds it in my soul:
  I hain't got long to stay here.

Green trees are bending,
  Poor sinners stand trembling;
The trumpet sounds it in my soul:
  I hain't got long to stay here.

My Lord calls me,
  He calls me by the lightning;
The trumpet sounds it in my soul:
  I hain't got long to stay here.

Tombstones are bursting,
  Poor sinners stand trembling;
The trumpet sounds it in my soul:
  I hain't got long to stay here.

Langston Hughes (b. 1902)

The Negro Speaks of Rivers

I've known rivers:
I've known rivers ancient as the world and older than the flow
  of human blood in human veins.

My soul has grown deep like the rivers.

I bathed in the Euphrates when dawns were young.
I built my hut near the Congo and it lulled me to sleep.

I looked upon the Nile and raised the pyramids above it.
I heard the singing of the Mississippi when Abe Lincoln went
  down to New Orleans, and I've seen its muddy bosom turn
  all golden in the sunset.

I've known rivers:
Ancient, dusky rivers.

My soul has grown deep like the rivers.

Various Anonymous Chinese Immigrants (1910s) (translated by Marlon K. Hom)

[Untitled]

Life is like a vast, long dream.
Why grieve over poverty?
A contented life soothes ten thousand matters.
Value the help from other people.
In all earnest, just endure:
You can forget about cold and hunger, as you
  see them often.
After lasting through winter's chill and snow's
  embrace,
You will find joy in life when happiness comes
  and sorrow fades.

[Untitled]

A brave man meeting an untimely adversity,
All day long, unable to eat or sleep.
Rushing about over ten thousand miles,
  deep in sorrow,
Every hour, every minute, mind and body
  toil in pain.

Heaven's will is extreme!
This big roc wants to spread its wings.
Yet scores are not evened up; the mind is not
at ease.
Alas, I can't rest in peace, I just can't rest
in peace.

[Untitled]

A cool breeze, a warm day,
A leisurely walk around the New Garden.
Willows green, peaches red, all are marvelous
sights;
I don't mind the fragrant paths leading a
distance away.
All the more delighted,
I wander along, to the east, to the west.
Each blade of grass and every blooming flower
can cheer a troubled mind.
O, why not take it easy and enjoy everything all
over again?

[Untitled]

I have finished my needlework for the night.
My mood is as chaotic as hemp fibers.
My blossoming years have been wrongly wasted
And I cannot even share with you the parting
sorrow, a sorrow so immense in my mind.
A heart left dangling.
One day is three autumns.
Privately I pray Heaven to grant me this wish:
Let my husband come home early and in triumph.

[Untitled]

Life is a dream, an illusion:
A twenty-year span of fun and games.
Hugging the one in red, leaning on the one in green,
O, what joy and gaiety!

Treasure the youthful years: once gone, they never
return.
Before that time comes –
What man won't hanker after pretty faces
Like a butterfly lingering around lustrous flowers?
A death from passion is really nothing.

William Everson (b. 1912)

The Song the Body Dreamed in the Spirit's Mad Behest

I am black but beautiful, O ye daughters of Jerusalem. Look not upon me because I am black, because the Sun has looked upon me.
– The Song of Songs

Call Him the Lover and call me the Bride.
Lapsing upon the couch of His repose
I heard the elemental waters rise,
Divide, and close.

I heard Him tremble and I turned my head.
Behold, the pitiless fondness of His eyes;
Dark, the rapacious terror of the heart
In orgy cries.

His eyes upon me wanton into life
What has slept long and never known the surge;
Bequeath an excess spilt of the blood's delight,
And the heart's purge.

His lips have garnished fruits out of my breast
That maddens Him to forage on my throat,
Moan against my dread the finite pang
Of the soul's gloat.

He is the Spirit but I am the Flesh.
Out of my body must He be reborn,
Soul from the sundered soul, Creation's gout
In the world's bourn.

Mounted between the thermals of my thighs
Hawklike He hovers surging at the sun,
And feathers me a frenzy ringed around
That deep drunk tongue.

The Seal is broken and the Blood is gushed.
He does not check but boldens in His pace.
The fierce mouth has beaked out both my eyes,
And signed my face.

His tidal strength within me shores and brunts,
The ooze of oil, the slaver of the bitch,
The bull's gore, the stallion's famished gnash,
And the snake's itch.

Grit of great rivers boasting to the sea,
Geysers in spume, islands that leveled lie,
One snow-peak agonized against the bleak
Inviolate sky.

Folding Him in the chaos of my loins
I pierce through armies tossed upon my breast,
Envelop in love's tidal dredge of faith
His huge unrest.

But drifting into depth that what might cease
May be prolonged until a night is lost,
We starve the splendor lapsing in the loins,
Curb its great cost.

Mouthless we grope for meaning in that void
That melds between us from our listening blood,
While passion throbs the chopped cacophony
Of our strange good.

Proving what instinct sobs of total quest
When shapeless thunder stretches into life,
And the Spirit, bleeding, rears to overreach
The buttock's strife.

That will be how we lose what we have gained,
The incremental rapture at the core,
Spleened of the belly's thick placental wrath,
And the seed's roar.

Born and reborn we will be groped, be clenched
On ecstasies that shudder toward crude birth,
When His great Godhead peels its stripping strength
In my red earth.

God Germed in Raw Granite

God germed in raw granite, source-glimpsed in stone?
Or imaged out in the black-flamed
Onyx-open line, smoldered in the tortured
Free-flow of lava, the igneous
Instant of conception? As maiden-form
Swells in the heaviness of wold, sleeps
Rumped and wanton-bulged in the boulder's
Bulk, is shaped in tree-forms everywhere
As any may see: dropped logs, say, or those crotched
Trunks pronged like a reckless nymph
Head-plunged into the earth – so Godhood
Wakes under water, shape-lurked, or grave and somber,
Where sea falls, mocks through flung foam . . .

Ghost!

Can this be? Breather of elemental truths,
She stirs, she coaxes! Out of my heart's howk,
Out of my soul's wild wrath
I make oath! I my emptiness
These arms gall for her, bride's mouth,
Spent-breathed in laughter, or that night's
First unblushing revealment, the flexed
Probity of the flesh, the hymen-hilted troth,
We closed, we clung on it, the stroked
And clangorous rapture!

I am dazed.

Is this she? Woman within!

Can this be? Do we, His images, float
Time-spun on that vaster drag
His timelessness evokes?
In the blind heart's core, when we
Well-wedded merge, by Him
Twained into one and solved there,
Are these still three? Are three
So oned, in the full-forthing
(Heart's reft, the spirit's great
Unreckonable grope, and God's
Devouring splendor in the stroke) are we –
This all, this utterness, this terrible
Total truth – indubitably He?

The Word

One deepness,
That mammoth inchoation,
Nothingness freighted on its term of void,
Oblivion abandoned to its selflessness,
Aching for a clue.

What clue?

Syllabled,
Shaken in its fixèd trance,
A far shuddering.

Who?

Blooms,
Subsumed in its sheer
Quality of inflection.

Endowed, the syllable
Focusing,
Determination conceives.

The concept
Borns of its pure consistency.

Not willed but perceived,
Not declared but acknowledged,
Yielded into the dimensional,
A salutation from the without.

Bearing within its strange liberties,
Consanguinations,
Dissolutions of oldness.

Rarer than the splendor it invokes,
More of wonder than its focal
Justness of perfection.

You, God

A land of darkness, and of the shadow of death, without any order, where the light is as darkness.
– The Book of Job

Nor any day gone,
Nor any night,
Measureless over the rimrock.

Nor those black imaginary suns
Roaring under the earth,
Roasting the roots of trees.

If I beg death, God, it is of you.

If I seize life, it is out of you.
If I lose, if I lose,
It is into you.

God of death,
Great God of no-life,
Existence is mine,
But you
Broach a nothingness
Breached out of nowhere.

Always you are not yet.

Deep in my guts,
Choked on oblivion,
Split, hearted on annihilation,
Caught through,
Smothered out,
A terror of emptiness,
Spat.

Immutable silence
Enormous over the snow mesa,
Enormous over the lava crag,
The wind-worked cloud.

My brain
Burns on your pierce.
My blood spits.
I shriek each nerve.

God!

Suck me in!

Alan Dugan (b. 1923)

Letter to Eve

The lion and lioness are intractable,
the leaves are covered with dust,
and even the peacocks will not
preen. You should come back,
burnish us with your former look,
and let the search for truth
go. After a loud sleep last night
I got up late and saw a new
expression on the faces of the deer;

the shrews and wolves are gaunt
and out of sorts: they nosed
their usual fruits and do not know
what they intend to do. The dogs
got tangled up in an unusual way:
one put its urinary tube
into the other's urinary tract
and could not get it out.
Standing tail to tail for hours,
they looked at me with wise,
supplicatory eyes. I named
two new sounds: snarl and shriek,
and hitherto unnoticed bells,
which used to perform the air,
exploded!, making a difference.
Come back before the garden does
what I'll call "die," not that it
matters. Rib, Rib, I have a new
opinion of your Eve, called "lust"
or Love, I don't know which,
and want to know how I will choose.

Argument to Love as a Person

The cut rhododendron branches
flowered in our sunless flat.
Don't complain to me, dear,
that I waste your life in poverty:
you and the cuttings prove: Those
that have it in them to be beautiful
flower wherever they are!, although
they are, like everything else, ephemeral.
Freedom is as mortal as tyranny.

On Gaining a Soul

As I explained the rules,
quarters, and conveniences,
the bloodless animal
I'll call "my soul"
tongued at my blackest tooth
in absent-minded joy
and asked about the truth
of feeling: it has a short
vacation in the flesh
and everything to do,
so I should take great pains
to satisfy the guest
so that it does not leave
before I make it pay.

Religious Question

When my wife said, "Oh angel, angel, angel, you'll save me"
in her sleep
I wondered who in hell this angel was and why
the Judeo-Christian-Islamic tradition is such a god-damned
chronic, infectious, unbeatable brain disease
that even my own true wife, my passionate atheist,
my politically anticlerical lover must dream
of an angelic love and savior to devil her sleep
and I must be jealous of her devilishly heavenly incubus.

On Inter-Relatedness in the Universe

I want to tear you apart.
I said to the butterfly,
in a sexy way,
and did, and it did
not matter: the tear
did not tear up the air
and rip the sky apart
the way it should
in a moral universe

because, you know,
morality is only human,
the universe and bugs
are not. I only made
a butterfly into a worm
like me. But oh
the wings, the wings:

Do not say these wings
are little frittilary fripperies.
They are great works of art
though small, say, compared
to the Milky Way, or you,
love in your various scales.
The great question is
why are they so beautiful
as the flying stained glass
flimsy windows of the worm's
evanescent flying cathedral.

Julie Suk (b. 1924)

The Architecture of Ruin

At a distance:
seemingly intact piers,
dark recesses, blind arcades.

Nearer, the sky
pours through arches,
a drizzle of rain inside the nave,
the passage crumbling,
open to grass and grazing sheep.

On good days
strokes of sun the trespasser,
devastation given a kind of splendor,

the strobe lights of memory
playing out impressions of a tower
you know is not there,

nor are the bells,
nor the stalls, nor choir,
not one finger tapping time
on the carved arms of chairs
or intertwined

here the church,
here the steeple,
open the door

no vaulting hosannnas, the chalice
and wine of remembrance
long removed,

as were the tapestries,
as was the incense of flesh
not yet carrion, not yet stringing off
into sorrow, base silence.

Maxine Kumin (b. 1925)

Where Any of Us

Where any of us is
going in tomorrow's reckless Lexus is
the elemental mystery: despite

instructions he left behind, Houdin-
i, who could outwit
ropes and chains, padlocks and steam-

er trunks, could extricate
himself from underwater metal crates,
could send forth, he was certain,

a message from the other side,
never cracked the curtain
and Mary Baker Eddy's telephone

said to be hooked up in her crypt –
would it have been
innocence or arrogance,

such trust in the beyond? –
has, mythic, failed to ring. If
they knew the script

these two (God may be love
or not) they left, tightlipped
and unfulfilled.

As we will.

Gerald Stern (b. 1925)

American Heaven

A salt water pond in the Hamptons near David
Ignatow's house, the water up to my chest,
an American Heaven, a dog on the shore, this time
his mouth closed, his body alert, his ears
up, a dog *belongs* in heaven, at least our
kind. An egret skidding to a stop, I'm sure
water snakes and turtles, grasses and weeds,
and close to the water sycamores and locusts,
and pitch pine on the hill and sand in the distance,
and girls could suckle their babies standing in water,
so that was our place of origin, that was
the theory in 1982 – David
had his own larder, Rose had hers, he brought
tuna fish into her kitchen, it was a triptych,
the centerpiece was the pond, the left panel
was his, his study, and he was stepping naked

across the frame into the pond holding an
open can and hers was the right, her arms had
entered the pond, holding a bowl, it was her
studio, we ate on a dry stone
and talked about James Wright and Stanley Kunitz,
and there was a star of the fourth magnitude
surrounded by planets, shining on all of us.

Allen Ginsberg (b. 1926)

Psalm IV

Now I'll record my secret vision, impossible sight of the face of God:
It was no dream, I lay broad waking on a fabulous couch in Harlem
having masturbated for no love, and read half naked an open book of Blake
on my lap
Lo & behold! I was thoughtless and turned a page and gazed on the living
Sun-flower
and heard a voice, it was Blake's, reciting in earthen measure:
the voice rose out of the page to my secret ear never heard before –
I lifted my eyes to the window, red walls of buildings flashed outside, endless
sky sad in Eternity
sunlight gazing on the world, apartments of Harlem standing in the universe –
each brick and cornice stained with intelligence like a vast living face –
the great brain unfolding and brooding in wilderness! – Now speaking
aloud with Blake's voice –
Love! thou patient presence & bone of the body! Father! thy careful
watching and waiting over my soul!
My son! My son! the endless ages have remembered me! My son! My son!
Time howled in anguish in my ear!
My son! My son! my father wept and held me in his dead arms.

Magic Psalm

Because this world is on the wing and what cometh no man can know
O phantom that my mind pursues from year to year descend from heaven
to this shaking flesh
catch up my fleeting eye in the vast Ray that knows no bounds –
Inseparable – Master –
Giant outside Time with all its falling leaves – Genius of the Universe –
Magician in Nothingness where appear red clouds –
Unspeakable King of the roads that are gone – Unintelligible horse riding
out of the graveyard – Sunset spread over Cordillera and insect –
Gnarl Moth –
Griever – Laugh with no mouth, heart that never had flesh to die –
Promise that was not made – Reliever, whose blood burns in a million
animals wounded –
O mercy, Destroyer of the World, O mercy, Creator of Breasted Illusions,
O Mercy, cacophonous warmouthed doveling, Come,
invade my body with the sex of God, choke up my nostrils with corruption's
infinite caress,
transfigure me to slimy worms of pure sensate transcendency I'm still alive,
croak my voice with uglier than reality, psychic tomato speaking Thy
million mouths,
Myriad-tongued my Soul, Monster or Angel, Lover that comes to fuck me
forever – white gown on the Eyeless Squid –
Asshole of the Universe into which I disappear – Elastic Hand that spoke
to Crane – Music that passes into the phonograph of years from
another Millennium – Ear of the buildings of NY –
That which I believe – have seen – seek endlessly in leaf dog eye – fault
always, lack – which makes me think –
Desire that created me, Desire I hide in my body, Desire all Man know
Death, Desire surpassing the Babylonian possible world
that makes my flesh shake orgasm of Thy Name which I don't know never
will never speak –
Speak to Mankind to say the great bell tolls a golden tone on iron balconies
in every million universe,
I am Thy prophet come home this world to scream an unbearable name
thru my 5 senses hideous sixth
that knows Thy Hand on its invisible phallus, covered with electric bulbs
of death –
Peace, Resolver where I mess up illusion, Softmouth Vagina that enters my
brain from above, Ark-Dove with a bough of Death.

Drive me crazy, God I'm ready for disintegration of my mind,
disgrace me in the eye of the earth,
attack my hairy heart with terror eat my cock Invisible croak of deathfrog
leap on me pack of heavy dogs salivating light,
devour my brain One flow of endless consciousness, I'm scared of your
promise must make scream my prayer in fear –
Descend O light Creator & Eater of Mankind, disrupt the world in its
madness of bombs and murder,
Volcanos of flesh over London, on Paris a rain of eyes – truckloads of
angel-hearts besmearing Kremlin walls – the skullcup of light to
New York –
myriad jeweled feet on the terraces of Pekin – veils of electrical gas de-
scending over India – cities of Bacteria invading the brain – the
Soul escaping in the rubber waving mouths of Paradise –
This is the Great Call, this is the Toscin of the Eternal War, this is the cry
of Mind slain in Nebulae,
this is the Golden Bell of the Church that has never existed, this is the
Boom in the heart of the sunbeam, this is the trumpet of the Worm
at Death,
Appeal of the handless castrate grab Alm golden seed of Futurity thru the
quake & volcan of the world –
Shovel my feet under the Andes, splatter my brains on the Sphinx, drape
my beard and hair over Empire State Building,
cover my belly with hands of moss, fill up my ears with your lightning,
blind me with prophetic rainbows
That I taste the shit of Being at last, that I touch Thy genitals in the
palmtree,
that the vast Ray of Futurity enter my mouth to sound Thy Creation
Forever Unborn, O Beauty invisible to my Century!
that my prayer surpass my understanding, that I lay my vanity at Thy foot,
that I no longer fear Judgement over Allen of this world
born in Newark come into Eternity in New York crying again in Peru for
human Tongue to psalm the Unspeakable,
that I surpass desire for transcendency and enter the calm water of the
universe
that I ride out this wave, not drown forever in the flood of my imagination
that I not be slain thru my own insane magic, this crime be punished in
merciful jails of Death,
men understand my speech out of their own Turkish heart, the prophets
aid me with Proclamation,
the Seraphim acclaim Thy Name, Thyself at once in one huge Mouth of
Universe make meat reply.

Frank O'Hara (b. 1926)

Poem

God! love! sun! all dear and singular things!
I am not bad although I am wicked,
perhaps, and not too rare. Beat, yes, liquored
to exhaustion, dead tired in sheets, still sings

to me the thunderous redwood's laughings
at my ears, a lover patient and picked,
and the crooning violet's not panicked
by my bloodshot foreskin, swollen lips, wings,

her tongue stays in my ear and sings. Purple
clouds, doubting, say hello across the lawn
and linen, wondering if I'm too gay

with exits, too abrupt with doors. Away,
far! the scratchy tune "L'amant du peuple":
I see a girl tap-dancing on the dawn.

Samuel Hazo (b. 1928)

The Art Professor Discussed Bernini's Teresa in Ecstasy

Depicting her, Bernini did not sculpt
  the woman who would counsel popes
  or dance flamenco in the convent
  when the nuns were bored.
                                        Instead,
  he focused solely on her face
  contorted in an agony of pleasure,
  her eyes half-lidded

and her parted lips unwilling
to return the oval of her mouth
to silence.
A bride outspread
and straddling her lover's loins
would look like this, her body
primed for what she hopes will happen
and desires more than breath
itself.
It's possible Bernini
could have posed or fantasized
a woman locked in such a tussle.
Why not transfer this image
to a sainted nun?
With consummation
as his parable, Bernini carved Teresa
swooning in God's orgy
as any woman might when yielding
to a love both wanton and permissible.

Jane Augustine (b. 1931)

Endgame

(Purkhang: temporarily constructed ceremonial oven for cremation of Tibetan lamas)

Hiked that last retreat day
the rutted road under evergreens
whose black branches kept
massive snowmounds frozen,
slick, blocking the log-roads,
feet slipping till I slowed
and held each step with care
not to break a leg crossing
till ice became mud and the way

widened out of deep gloom
into meadow where the *purkhang* stands,
isolated, white-plastered, square
on a lonely rise, bare bone against green,
its four oven mouths shut tight
facing the four directions,
its chimney-tower pointing
into directionless gray space
whose cold winds whirl
a torment of wet flakes
out of the bowed fir-tree tops
tangled and overgrown at the
shaggy meadow's edge that backs off
from the cremation place.

Here the remains of a body
that had once held a mind
and had decomposed to water
packed in salt had gone to fire
and then to air (but not this air
of now) and in that air set
an arc of gold, two arcs, green-tinged,
the hoped-for rainbows in the smoke
created by the logs of *arborvitae*,
juniper, sacred fuel of enlightenment.

The fire has long been out.
White paint peels from the ledge
where a few dry flowers lie
and coins, a velvet hairpin
disintegrating in the weather.
They offered what little they had
thought up on the spur of the moment
at this temporary furnace, reminder
of a transient life declaring transience
the rule, as everyone knew and knows
and won't admit, so to gaze fixed
on this crumbling structure is deluded
and generally useless –

A sudden furious flurry of snow
whips its wild white scarves
around the white pinnacle:
    such a thunderstorm will not
    come again soon.

Of you, my world, I got an eyeful. Your turbulence
isn't internal. You cry aloud: get up,
go, why are you waiting around
    as if your heartbeat were not sufficient?

Jack Collom (b. 1931)

Save

Save the moment
green, through porch window
(sunblaze highlights dust),
imported trees, hiding most
of the next-door brick, blue sky with
extravagant August clouds;
moment saves itself,

slow, folding semblance...
pearl in the looseness of memory, metal leaves
leopardy green-black in the sumac!
A little red garage on the alley
across 19th. There's the assortment of words
as if into crazy mail-slots.
An insect white in motion
zigzagging against the wafers.
Bicyclist flashing south.

Green
blue air and water dust
fire sand, sun

bits of car book reflection call
it the intricacies
of light at
present

Linda Pastan (b. 1932)

Soul Song

The snake slips from its skins,
leaving ghosts of itself
to haunt rocks
and the furrows
of fields. Still it remains
solid and supple as ever,
no closer to the marrow
of snake.

And the onion whose simple secret
I think to uncover layer
by transparent layer
leaves nothing, finally,
for the hand to close on
but pungency.

Yet there is something
hard as a peach pit to which
the flesh clings stubbornly.
I feel it move in the lonely cavity
of the chest, or high up in the skull
like a queen bee that must
be evicted in the end
from the hive.

Jo McDougall (b. 1935)

Mercy

The night after his two children burned
in a frame house in a searing drought,
the man, the neighbors said,
wandered through his yard
murmuring "Lord have mercy."
And the Lord sent rain.

Rennie McQuilkin (b. 1936)

Ascension

Left behind, I've followed her
to this windy height in the hills of West Virginia.
Under a rattling canopy
I shiver, listen to the Word, hear praises sung.
Her cherry box is poised on slings above a gape
too like her open mouth those days she lay there
waiting, dark gargle rising in her throat.
I look away.
Overhead, a Red Shoulder riding the wind
is not, of course, what I wish it to be.
A hawk's a hawk, focused
on matters of moment – milk snake, rabbit, vole.
The box sways on its slings, the winch grinding
out of sync with the Twenty-third Psalm, and there
she goes. Dear God,
I feel my mind slipping.
Let me think – of anything – of the underground
deposit of salt that made this town –
muddy water superheated to steam, pressured
down through sixty feet of shale to melt the salt,

the brine pumped back (hue of the death collecting
in a dun deposit on her lips)
to evaporating tanks, from which the fine white
salt of West Virginia comes. How good to believe
her bones will rise like so, do their dance.
Now the box hits bottom bluntly. I'm brought up
short, in time for the dive of the hawk, the kill,
the small life rising, completely loved, reusable.

Gail Mazur (b. 1937)

Insomnia at Daybreak

So many years, so many months and seasons
re-lived in the turnings of one night:
a night of pacing, every comfortless hour
punctuated by the bells of Town Hall.
And now, why should the slow light
of morning hurt so? Like the face
of God, overwhelming, blinding –
hard, effacing face I've taken
for a mirror as the world wakes
yet again.
Give me the words I need,
the words that would calm my soul,
words that would make my life work.

—after Vittorio Sereni

Alicia Ostriker (b. 1937)

Four Psalms

I am not lyric any more
I will not play the harp
for your pleasure

I will not make a joyful
noise to you, neither
will I lament

for I know you drink
lamentation, too,
like wine

so I dully repeat
you hurt me
I hate you

I pull my eyes away from the hills
I will not kill for you
I will never love you again

unless you ask me

•••••

I endure impure periods
when I cannot touch you

or even look at you
you are a storm I would be electrocuted

by your approach then I feel some sort of angelic laughter
like children behind a curtain

come, I think
you are at my fingertips my womb

you are the wild driver of my vehicle
the argument in my poem

nothing between us
only breath

•

my head is uncovered to my naked hair
I am dressed immodestly

my old body lacks teeth, lacks a breast
still cherishes itself

I eat what I want I am
an animal of flesh

as you know for you formed me in the womb
and made my desires what they are

I am waiting for you
in a bed of pleasure

•

like a skin on milk
I write to you

I hurl the letters of your name
onto every page, one and many

I know you are reading over my shoulder
look each of us possesses a book of life

each attempts to read what the other has scripted
in these almost illegible letters tipped by crowns

what is the story
we want to know

Stephen Dunn (b. 1939)

The Soul's Agents

Every night before bed, say for a week,
we recommend admitting a lie
or a deception, sotto voce, a rogue's prayer
to the soul you know you have,
no matter how tattered or dormant.
Trust us, your secrets differentiate you
from no one, but the soul awakens
a little when it hears them.
We have its interests at heart,
which means your interests as well.

Try to practice unsettling
what remains settled in you –
those ideas, for example,
inherited, still untested.
And if only you could raise
your hypocrisy to the level of art,
like forgery, there might be
real hope for you.

Some people of course expect
to be rewarded for stumbling
and rising from the floor
and stumbling again, but we give
no credit for living. We favor vitality
over goodness, even over effort;
we love a great belly laugh
more than anything.

In your case we do worry
there may not be enough
quarrel in you, or enough courage
to acknowledge your worst inclinations.
Know that the soul converts them
into tenderness. Nothing pleases it more.

So next week why not admit
that what Raskolnikov did
has always made you dream?
The more you expose yourself
the more you become unrecognizable.
Remember, we are here to help.
What you decide to keep
from the world, tell us. We understand
everything. We pass it on.

Norah Pollard (b. 1940)

Introduction to the Spiritual Life

St. Leo's basement,
down there in the serious dark,
bumping, fumbling,
the air raid siren wailing,
we knelt bent over,
our hands on our heads,
crouched in the dust like
so many turnips waiting to be
harvested. The nuns
in their black robes
swished up and down the rows,
our own scarecrows,
rosaries rattling like bones,
black straps slapping,
hissing "Silence!" at the small
nervous giggle.

And down there in that heavy dark,
each Lent we witnessed
(for a dime) sweet-faced Jesus
murdered on the tattered screen.
The projector would break down

somewhere near Gethsemane,
exposing our stunned dread,
snapping us to reality.
But reality was up there on the screen
and when those spikes tore flesh,
the bitter sponge sent up
to that poor downturned mouth,
sorrow dense as drowning
filled our lungs;
we were sodden with it for days,
remembering the agonized eye,
the cry for "Father! Father!"
going unanswered, as usual.

Down there in the basement
where we were sent when we had disobeyed,
blinded and buried, both,
we could only hear, far and faint,
the trucks rumbling in the street,
the bell of the changing class,
the scraping overhead
of a hundred wooden chairs.
We shivered in the darkness
waiting for the hoof-footed devil
and his slavering rats
until, over time,
that dark became a place
to suffer freely in,
to luxuriate in alienation,
to watch the dust motes drift,
to feel the rapture of
the placelessness of the blackness,
to imagine,
with all the power of darkness,
new, brave sins.

Billy Collins (b. 1941)

The Night House

Every day the body works in the fields of the world
mending a stone wall
or swinging a sickle through the tall grass –
the grass of civics, the grass of money –
and every night the body curls around itself
and listens for the soft bells of sleep.

But the heart is restless and rises
from the body in the middle of the night,
leaves the trapezoidal bedroom
with its thick, pictureless walls
to sit by herself at the kitchen table
and heat some milk in a pan.

And the mind gets up too, puts on a robe
and goes downstairs, lights a cigarette,
and opens a book on engineering.
Even the conscience awakens
and roams from room to room in the dark,
darting away from every mirror like a strange fish.

And the soul is up on the roof
in her nightdress, straddling the ridge,
singing a song about the wildness of the sea
until the first rip of pink appears in the sky.
Then, they all will return to the sleeping body
the way a flock of birds settles back into a tree,

resuming their daily colloquy,
talking to each other or themselves
even through the heat of the long afternoons.

Toi Derricotte (b. 1941)

Boy at the Paterson Falls

I am thinking of that boy who bragged about the day he threw
a dog over and watched it struggle to stay upright all
the way down.
I am thinking of that rotting carcass on the rocks,
and the child with such power he could call to a helpless
thing as if he were its friend, capture it, and think of
the cruelest punishment.
It must have answered some need, some silent screaming in a
closet, a motherless call when night came crashing;
it must have satisfied, for he seemed joyful, proud, as if he
had once made a great creation out of murder.
That body on the rocks, its sharp angles, slowly took the shape of
what was underneath, bones pounded, until it lay on the bottom
like a scraggly rug.
Nothing remains but memory – and the suffering of those who
would walk into the soft hands of a killer for a crumb of bread.

Jack Myers (b. 1941)

The Flicker

This is in honor of the flicker
that sings its heart out on my roof everyday
though no other flicker comes.

If I can't be sure of the language of joy
can I at least know something that is?

There is a flicker flapping its wings and playing
with the name of whatever it's doing.

The tiny bit of him that weighs something
is holding down the house

while the larger part of him that weighs nothing
lifts it up.

Albert Glover (b. 1942)

Further

Thinking of "breath" as "spirit"
as in Hatch's hymn
"Breathe on Me, Breath of God"

heard after Olson's "Projective Verse Essay"
and yet later Coltrane's 1957 statement
concerning his "spiritual awakening"

more than twenty years after
Bill W's: "I felt lifted up, as though
the great clean wind of a mountain top

blew through and through" which itself
echoes DHL's "Not I, not I, but the wind
that blows through me!"

provides plenty of precedent
for anyone, as I was that Spring,
alone, down, and out

on the front lawn of my
No. Count. home waiting for
something to blow me away

like the breeze which did come
to release me from
much of what I owned

and then all through the 90s
after that initiation into what
I'd only read about or

"understood" in some mental manner,
the *idea* of it became embodied
and "natural" (unthought) as a wing.

The Source was outside of me
until recently, on the golf course
in retirement sitting on a bench

under red pine boughs and allowing
that familiar air to reach me, I
noticed also the warmth

of sun as "equivalent" in primacy,
– touched the lower Dan Tien coincident
with Taoist breathing out –

instantly the Source was inside also,
the same Source which I'd known
out there was equally

in here   without any loss
of boundary   no merge
awoke

B.H. Fairchild (b. 1942)

The Deposition

And one without a name
Lay clean and naked there, and gave commandments.
Rilke, "Washing the Corpse" (trans. Jarrell)

Dust storm, we thought, a brown swarm
plugging the lungs, or a locust-cloud,
but this was a collapse, a slow sinking
to deeper brown, and deeper still, like the sky
seen from inside a well as we are lowered down,
and the air twisting and tearing at itself.

But it was done. And the body hung there
like a butchered thing, naked and alone
in a sudden hush among the ravaged air.
The ankles first – slender, blood-caked,
pale in the sullen dark, legs broken
below the knees, blue bruises smoldering
to black. And the spikes. We tugged iron
from human flesh that dangled like limbs
not fully hacked from trees, nudged
the cross beam from side to side until
the sign that mocked him broke loose.
It took all three of us. We shouldered the body
to the ground, yanked nails from wrists
more delicate, it seemed, than a young girl's
but now swollen, gnarled, black as burnt twigs.
The body, so heavy for such a small man,
was a knot of muscle, a batch of cuts
and scratches from the scourging, and down
the right side a clotted line of blood,
the sour posca clogging his ragged beard,
the eyes exploded to a stare that shot
through all of us and still speaks in my dreams:
I know who you are.
So, we began to wash
the body, wrenching the arms, now stiff

and twisted, to his sides, unbending
the ruined legs and sponging off the dirt
of the city, sweat, urine, shit – all the body
gives – from the body, laying it out straight
on a sheet of linen rank with perfumes
so that we could cradle it, haul it
to the tomb. The wind shouted.
The foul air thickened. I reached over
to close the eyes. *I know who you are.*

Sydney Lea (b. 1942)

Recovery

So here are the Andes, and here the fabled chollos,
ponies strong enough to bear his flesh
and weight accrued
  – failed suicide, guilt and tears –
ten thousand feet to this world-commanding mesa.
The guide reports that one may with luck behold
a condor. Two have nested here for years.

The horse surefoots a shale that would daunt a man
on foot, the clouds hang planet-vast, he hopes
the rain will wait:
  he imagines on his own
that his self, which counts so little among these grand
immensities, or anywhere, will wash
downhill to the crashing rio, on which his bones

will ride to the cold Atlantic, dissolve within it,
as he once believed they were meant long since to do.
Yet here he sits
  a noble horse. He's well.
Sweet wind conspires with scent of lather, leather.

Years back, rock-bottomed, he'd have never dreamed a condor,
and still he all but fears a welcoming world.

The guide calls out, *Serà allà*! The bird
will be up there. He's pointing at a crag
as bleak and boding
  as childhood terror. Gray.
The bird is not *allà*, will not be found
today, and it comes clear again that wonder
lies in the thought of God, which makes him say,

O I have seen that soaring after all,
because he's known what it can be to be
poised at an edge
  more deadly than any he's climbed
just now. He feels as if he's turned much lighter
than a lump of man like him has a right to turn.
Into his mind – or out of some greater mind –

the wide-flung wings come gliding, gold as sun.

Maxwell King (b. 1944)

Crossing Laurel Run

Climbing the arc
of the high-pasture hill
in six inches of new wet snow,
we track through a stubble
of the season's last cut of hay,
our boot prints puddling
with dark water.
Two old oaks are down
with ice in the branches;
as we cross Laurel Run

we hear a cracking and turn back
to see a towering poplar
fall dead with the weight.

In the evening,
together by the wood stove,
we sit in silence.
I stare at the page number
in my book; your needles
tick for a moment, then fall still.
I watch your face:
eyes closing, high cheeks
darkening with some thought
not shared with me.
I could tell you what I've lost;
that it is the same
as what you've lost.
And then we would fight again –
our struggle to move past
the truth, to find a way
to lend the greater weight to hope.

I put a hand on your arm;
you put a hand on my hand.
Isn't there something we might understand,
something we could know
in order to know what to say to each other?
You would say there is nothing to say.
For me, there is this,
perhaps only this:
the ice will come soon enough,
and we must try, until then,
to hold each other
in the incandescence of our own arc.

Elton Glaser (b. 1945)

Church of the Downtown Redeemer and Twiceborn Saints

Sunday, and the air's gone slack and thick,
Peeled back from the tight night before, until the reverend
Straps it on and knobs it loud, hitting his quick licks
About the Lord, about the going down and the getting up again,
About the slickery pitfalls of body and bottle, and then
He's strangling the live mic like a serpent's head,
Long cord whipping from side to side in the death throes of sin,

Sermon with a backbeat, gutbucket gospel in a neon suit,
And thunder among the pews, lightning in the aisles, a great
Ricochet of amens as he preaches the lid up from darkness
And lets the low souls loose, jitter of black electrics
Through the jacked-up strings and the brazen tambourine,
Crackle of salvation racing down the stormfront, making
The pulpit jump and the benches tremble, putting
Mama on the good foot, daddy off the dime,

And the reverend's still kicking it, Fender in full thrash and twang,
Choir behind him at wide-open throttle, angels in fat satin,
So heavy they can lift themselves only by the voice, blessing
The sweat and the spasm and the steam of jubilee,
Reverb pulsing from the amp like waves washing the stain away,
Pools and pools of it, in the rinse of rhythm, the sluice of blues,
A baptism that takes so hard it lasts until the fires of hell
Hiss out and the cinders sizzle and the skin of the damned
Gives off a glow like sweet Easter shining high on
The churchhouse windows, glass in a rapture of risen light.

Gary Margolis (b. 1945)

First Spring

"About Ten A Clocke we came into a deepe Valley full of Brush, Wood-gaile and Long Grass, Through which we found little paths or tracks and there we saw a deere and found springs of fresh water of which we were heartily glad and sat us downe and drunke our first new england water with as much delight as ever we drunke drinks in all our lives—"
(November 16, 1620, Truro, Massachusetts)

They must have heard surf breaking the sand
into coast, and dry from drinking the left-over
dust of the ship's kegs, they went searching
for new water, tramping through the Cape's woods
toward the salty sound that carried them here.
Everywhere the blood-seeking mosquito bore
its small transfusion and the green-headed deerfly
branded the backs of their necks and arms.
How could they stay, not being blood-drinkers,
not having found yet and aged a fermentable fruit
into a fruit wine that could help them forget

and remember the beauty and loneliness of crossing,
of being here beautiful and alone? Thinking of freedom,
or rather a different pain, they risked going thirsty,
living on what they could find to take the place
of water. Rightfully, they thought of deer bending
to drink, trout that could not live in the sea.
And themselves, one dry day, stepping where they had
never been, not born here, but bound now to this
salt-free spring which could take their knees and hands
and lips, turning each of them into a body of water
through which the tearless Truro fish could swim.

Michael Poage (b. 1945)

Night Jasmine

That was your
big mistake. You realized
then it's better
to be a little lost
than entirely
found. Resurrection
just means things
are not as they seem.
I keep having
to learn that. Can you
smell the fragrance
from the open window? You think
of a place where the jasmine
would be at home
with you. Watch the live,
tilting-to-one-side
man. He is actually
an angel spinning
on the head
of God. Then you remember
the hawks
are really vultures.

Anne Waldman (b. 1945)

Mantra

...was...
In the mouth all sound
Denied in night & then
Hell, no! out out

A breeze towards lines of philology
Lines of philosophy towards cohesiveness
Towards traces of pilgrimage
Air gets in being humble
The word gets in the marrow
Being mantra
OM AH HUM
And a place to visit gets in
Being humble, also holy
You might propose
An offer of poetry
Recited as jewels in a lotus
As you turn (body) turn (speech) turn (mind)
OM MANI PADME HUM

Might be a sound easy to offer
Linguistics: state of grace
OM TARE TAM SOHA
Easy to consider goddess Tara
born of Avalokitesvara's tear
Wheel: perpetual riddle
Myth of the weapon is
objectifying it as a turn
around the block for a
gorgeous pointed thing
It must be used!
So said the jaguar
in another religion
in the great debate
that signaled "war"
A heart sighs "bodhicitta"
"bodhicitta
& signals "come back"
to haunt you – back to compassion,
to the negotiating table

NOTE:
Religion exists on earth as the fuller
form of the eternal art of poetry...
It works like poetry which bonds
to the Infinite putting off the Indefinite
into most holy forms of thought...
—paraphrase of John Milton

Frank X. Gaspar (b. 1946)

Bodhidharma Preaches the Wake-Up Sermon

There's no language that isn't the Dharma. Language is essentially free. It has nothing to do with attachment. And attachment has nothing to do with language.
– Bodhidharma

Somehow or another, something is missing in me. I should
be satisfied with the household gods. I should learn my place
and understand that they are enough for any one man or woman.
Of course we are at their mercy. They suffer us every small thing.
And we thank you, god of the kitchen drainboard and goddess of
the gas-log hearth. We thank you for your benevolence and kindness,
and god of the grocery sacks for your capacious heart, and goddess
of linoleum and green lawns, and winged goddess of the laughter
of neighborhood children, but always we are wandering from
your groves and bowers, your gardens, your abundant pantries.
For instance, what does anyone's life mean, now, in this third
millennium, so-called? I am talking about what you can and can't
live without, which is a way of talking about attachment. Is there
a language that isn't the Dharma? *To seek nothing is bliss,* said
the saint Bodhidharma, but isn't he the one who cut off his eyelids
in the search for a more perfect meditation? No, no, this is not
the way, in the heat of night, in the heat of fevers, the blue gas jets
wavering in the hot breeze on the kitchen range (the goddess of the
four burners, the goddess of the coffee pot, our acknowledgment,
our gratitude), not the way when we open the door to the small
empty street and look down its length, first one way and then the other.
It's what you can or can't live without. It's all streetlight and crickets
on this particular night. It's all language and breath in this particular
trial. It's all delicacy and power lines. It's all asphalt and glass. That's
why I am up night after night. That's why I walk so softly on the floors
and rugs. I am bowing and kneeling in every little corner, at every little
helpful shrine, but I couldn't say if I am praying or if I am simply
looking for some small button or short piece of string that I've lost.
Most nights I really couldn't tell you what on earth I'm doing.

Andrea Hollander Budy (b. 1947)

A Way of Speaking

of saying hello
to everything that deserves
notice, even while it

hides: ice patterns
scarcely seen behind
the shower curtain

on the inside
of the bathroom window,
or wild

grass pushed up
along that unseeable line it finds
between the parking lot

and Sears, the way
the mouth stays open
while the sleeper sleeps, and moves

sometimes and makes
undecipherable sounds,
the way hands

close tight around
a blanket fold,
steering you

through the world you're
in now, the one where
you speak

invisibly, as a poem
tries to do, travelling
to a lost place,

and everyone who hears it
finally home.

Bin Ramke (b. 1947)

All Saints

Ariadne
If the stained things of the earth lie, as in
lie, and a thread on the floor is remarked,
there's a story to tell but not the one
that leads out, only, for instance, beginning,
or to begin again leads in, torn from
elsewhere, now here, nowhere you know
but still the face rises as in dream and speaks
as in dream but that's a real child in the corner
small and weak and beginning
its own sort of threaded passage.

Now it makes you want to touch only
surface, a blind tongueless traveler
when the word alone is witness to all,
the word which comes out of lung from
an act of breath and constriction of
the various parts of the throat – the breath

a thread dissolving on its way out –
a child out of the warmth into the world
ready to be fed, ready to listen: Listen,

Rusalka
Dvorak told this story: another creature of water
wants to be mortal (to have sex with a human), needs

permission from her father to die; there she sits
beneath the inconstant moon she sings
an aria for him which asks the moon to say
Mine are the arms that shall hold him, That between
waking and sleeping he may Think of the love that enfolds him.

This mortality allows us to touch one another and thread our way out into bluish air and tinted anemones persistent in our paths, temptation and a kind of hunger

Saint Alphais

which only some can resist – hunger's catastrophe of touch – remember Alphais' inedia, her gift of subsistence on only the host, the wafer of bread received daily. To waste to essentials is one form of grace. Having lost her arms and legs, living in a lean-to next to the church – these legends grow beautiful in their cruelty, a thread thrown to the drowning, a sound which enlightens, even hunger quivers bird-like within the mouth

imitating with the mouth the birds'
liquid sounds came before men could delight
their own ears by singing sweet songs (De Rerum Natura)

Sacrificial Sanctity

The habit of hope saints evade, and the pettiness of life viewed from a certain angle. Avoid the certain angle. If the air were flavored lemon, say, or any accidental floral that lines the walk, the habitual path from home compounding the inarticulate with despair, the last remaining virtue one learns with age to trust, to greet with a nod in the morning, ever waiting in the bathroom mirror, ready to carry on, to care. Among the things a long life teaches, none matter beyond a mirrored silvery way among the plants thick with insects eating each other into other forms, larva to pupa to the serial splendor of wings and delicate dining on nectar; such liquefaction of appetite can be learned in such a world can be learned by the singularly attentive, that the best birds are pigeons, next are sparrows; the full avian hierarchy founded on commonness – crows, boat-tailed grackles, etc. Nothing rare counts to the saint who has seen all things familiar and contained, who has seen and is content to see, and sigh.
I can do all that angels can Wallace Stevens

Baron Wormser (b. 1948)

Christmas

Celebration becomes stupefaction
And when we sit in church our minds wander
To the little tree and our transferred bounty.
"Miracle" feels like the farthest of words:

You couldn't drive there in the fastest car.
It's numberless. Standing in a line
Or coming out of a store, a tincture of joy
Arises from what seems like nowhere:

Something that happened so long ago,
Something that has always been a good rumor,
Something that didn't use the front door
Is central and in its raw beauty unbearable.
I forget my business. When I look up at
The winter stars, I could begin to repent.

Agha Shahid Ali (b. 1949)

God

"In the Name of the Merciful" let night begin.
I must light lamps without her – at every shrine?
God then is only the final assassin.

The prayers end. Emptiness waits to take her in.
With laments found lost on my lips, I resign
myself to His every Name. Let night begin

without any light, for as they carry the coffin
from the mosque to the earth, no stars shine
to reveal Him as only the final assassin.

The mourners, at the dug earth's every margin,
fill emptiness with their hands. Their eyes meet mine
when with no Name of His I let my night begin.

In the dark the marble of each tomb grows skin.
I tear it off. I make a holocaust. I underline
God is the only, the only assassin

as flames put themselves out, at once, on her shrine
(they have arrived like moths from temples and mosques).
In no one's name but hers I let night begin.

Prayer Rug

Those intervals
between the day's
five calls to prayer

the women of the house
pulling thick threads
through vegetables

rosaries of ginger
of rustling peppers
in autumn drying for winter

in those intervals this rug
part of Grandma's dowry
folded

so the Devil's shadow
would not desecrate
Mecca scarlet-woven

with minarets of gold
but then the sunset
call to prayer

the servants
their straw mats unrolled
praying or in the garden

in summer on grass
the children wanting
the prayers to end

the women's foreheads
touching Abraham's
silk stone of sacrifice

black stone descended
from Heaven
the pilgrims in white circling it

this year my grandmother
also a pilgrim
in Mecca she weeps

as the stone is unveiled
she weeps holding on
to the pillars

(for Begum Zafar Ali)

Robert Cording (b. 1949)

Parable of the Moth

Consider this: a moth flies into a man's ear
One ordinary evening of unnoticed pleasures.

When the moth beats its wings, all the winds
Of the earth gather in his ear, roar like nothing
He has ever heard. He shakes and shakes

His head, has his wife dig deep into his ear
With a Q-tip, but the roar will not cease.
It seems as if all the doors and windows
Of his house have blown away at once –
The strange play of circumstances over which
He never had control, but which he could ignore
Until the evening disappeared as if he had
Never lived it. His body no longer
Seems his own; he screams in pain to drown
Out the wind inside his ear, and curses God,
Who, hours ago, was a benign generalization
In a world going along well enough.

On the way to the hospital, his wife stops
The car, tells her husband to get out,
To sit in the grass. There are no car lights,
No streetlights, no moon. She takes
A flashlight from the glove compartment
And holds it beside his ear and, unbelievably,
The moth flies towards the light. His eyes
Are wet. He feels as if he's suddenly a pilgrim
On the shore of an unexpected world.
When he lies back in the grass, he is a boy
Again. His wife is shining the flashlight
Into the sky and there is only the silence
He has never heard, and the small road
Of light going somewhere he has never been.

Leonard Gontarek (b. 1949)

prayer.net

Do I want the night   The one who made it   Extraordinary demon

I do not knock   I made the night   Do I

Believe that? I remember
Standing in the moonlight

Stealing tulips

The world carries the scent of water   Like a child a handful of fireflies

The head makes wings
From axioms and gray aura
The everyday eats

The man who dreams of flying wants nothing

Would trade those dreams for nothing   Not even flight

I want the tree   The peach

& pear   Arranged in heirloom bowl

Wet & shining, the objects   Curse

& arise from the lake of It

The self follows on its throne

The court littered with failed abductions & adorations

Prayer,

Balled-up & crushed paper   Peonies

Such a sad & lovely king

The crown, memories, Beauty, Lies, the weight of water, fragments of each song of the field

Arthur Sze (b. 1950)

Earthstar

Opening the screen door, you find a fat spider
poised at the threshold. When I swat it,

hundreds of tiny crawling spiders burst out.
What space in the mind bursts into waves

of wriggling light? As we round a bend,
a gibbous moon burnishes lava rocks and waves.

A wild boar steps into the road, and, around
another bend, a mongoose darts across our headlights.

As spokes to a hub, the very far converges
to the very near. A row of Siberian irises

buds and blooms in the yard behind our bedroom.
A moth flutters against a screen and sets

off a light. I had no idea carded wool spun
into yarn could be dipped and oxidized into bliss.

Once, hunting for chanterelles in a meadow,
I flushed quail out of the brush. Now

you step on an unexpected earthstar, and it
bursts in a cloud of brown spores into June light.

Peter Blair (b. 1951)

Mantra

Francis knelt by the bed,
weeping after his host
had fallen asleep,
prayed, *My God and my all,*
his mantra, the whole night.
He threw his spirit into the words
as the ghostly seeds
of a dandelion leap into the wind
that bends its stalk
in hard prayer. His host,
pretending to sleep, listened
in shocked rapture all night.

In Saint Francis psych ward,
Mr. Heally lies half off a bed
bolted to the floor. Tangled
in straps, he moans to curtainless,
screened windows: *My God,*
I'm all done. Yesterday, he searched
the phone book for a new doctor,
muttering, *Fucking shock treatments.*
The pages fluttered, rasped.
Thorazine cures dualism.

Now the drugs, the doctors,
splinter like broken glass.
I gaze at him through wire mesh
at 3 a.m. Walter, the other aide, dozes
in the lounge, but like Francis' host,
I can't sleep. I listen to the voice,
the weeping whisper that echoes
in the darkness, the mind
on the other side of dualism.

Brenda Hillman (b. 1951)

; ; ; ; ; ; ; ; ; ; ; ; ;   ; ; ; ; ; ; ; ; ; ; ; ; ;

Patterns of Paint in Certain Small Missions

, When next I saw the bright light /
, There were several /
, /
, Day had followed itself, for a second half /
, /
, A pattern crawled with experience /
, Entwined /
, /
, A movement less fickle than the grievous /
, Gold wings /
, /
, It looked as if a piece of breath had been dragged /
Through two thoroughly types of dull red dirt

Till dread   learned a brushstroke

, History had put it there   to cure it /
, /
, Vibrations from fruit trucks   Earth acting /
, /
, Beyond horror   with the joy ideas have /
, /
, A pattern so skinny considering what went on /
, /
, Scooping out half-wings that had been /
, Helping a little bit /
, /

, Artist stay general /

Mother of god be specific

? ?

San Rafael 1817

Brigit Pegeen Kelly (b. 1951)

The Foreskin

I planted the little curl of skin under the magnolia. For a long time I could not remember the name for it, because though I had heard the word and its definition many times, when confronted with the tiny curl of flesh, the word did not seem to resemble the thing I held in hand, as words so often do not resemble the things they represent, or what we imagine them to represent; words can even destroy in their saying the very thing for which they stand. The little curl was pinkish, like an overbred white rabbit's eyes, and yellowing white, like the petals of the magnolia blooms, and a soft blue; and it had a crust of red, for no one had washed it, those who might have done so unprepared for the request for it, so they handed it over in its sullied form, which made it, I thought, more beautiful. And then I did not know what to do with it, for it seemed that the pain, too, the boy had felt when the knife peeled the portion away, and the pain of the one watching, who was afraid to follow the ancient covenants and afraid not to, were folded into this piece of flesh. So I planted it in the black dirt at the crest of the field, and then I planted the magnolia over it. That was the order, first the little petal, now dried, and then the new bush, and in one year or two the bush made blossoms that began as furred buds, like the budding horns of young deer, and turned into large flowers that seemed to have been pieced together with curls of flesh, but magnified, as if under glass, magnified and made dazzling by the sun.

Sidney Wade (b. 1951)

Grace

Thank you for the buzzing body,
    high blood singing in the ears,
        for the strong and ever-willing appetites

thank you for black violets in the grass
    for timothy, fescue, foxtail, cheat
        for zinnias in their starched and brilliant colors

thank you for the sudden gifts of time and money
    and for articles of chocolate from carry-out heaven
        and for all those other bright addictions

thank you for The Love Supreme, O sauvage,
    and the infinite CD, for grandiloquent fire and hardbed frost
        thank you for major weather in all its ardent forms

thank you for moth-eaten, feather-bedded, meat-balled things
    for the last nibble in the mess hall
        for the pied and pickled fall into failure

thank you for The Patron Saint of a Happy Death
    and for miracles that come disguised as children
        thank you for achromatic interfero coronography

and for hormonal drift, the utterly groundless fall of spirit
    thank you for flathead noodlers and feral poetry
        for the large and resilient misery of our hopeless culture

thank you for this tatterdemalion and passionate scenery
    which is what keeps the blood in a boil, the tongue in flux
        and for all our prodigious mowing, bringing in the sheaves

Mark Jarman (b. 1952)

On the Street

He jogs in, a v of sweat on his t-shirt. He strides in, pushing a baby carriage. Wearing a Walkman, he saunters in. He barrels in in his truck, and stops, and gets out. He tells the taxi driver to let him off here. He thanks the person who gave him a lift, opens the car door, and invites her to stay. Brakes his bicycle at the brush heap in the cul de sac, dismounts, and starts calling our names. Our first names. Appears one day, like the blossoms on the redbud, and captures our attention. We know it's spring, and we know him.

What's the word on the street? The word is made flesh on the street. The word is made person, place, and thing. The word is steel, concrete, fibre-optic cable, ceramic and saliva, aluminum and blood, axle grease and fingernails, hair and glass. It is the leaf of the sidewalk weed and the soft desiring soul inside the truck cab. It is the footprint tracked a little ways beyond the puddle and the foot still thinking of where it stepped. Anonymous and public, the word is that if you're good, you'll be happy, if you're happy, you'll be good. Suffer and remain private. Receive aid, and see your savior on the news. Out the door, into the blaring, shining welcome, from which there is no escape, the word on the street is lord. Tang of diesel fumes, fellow fragrance of men and women, music of the spheres of influence burning to illuminate the word, the word in every molecule that starts a sense, these – and that face that passes and travels with you a little way beyond the sight of it. They are the word on the street. And the word is knowledge like a cellphone ringing with all the others.

Inside, behind the showroom window, two men in shirtsleeves and ties and a woman in her power suit watched. One held a telephone. Outside we passed the group beginning to assemble around the lady who lay on her right cheek. She wore a felt hat and a cloth coat, both a grayer version of her blue eye, her left eye which stared at our feet. The right side of her face – cheek, eye, half her mouth – was pressed hard against the sidewalk. The half of her mouth we could see showed, in its grin, an effort to do or say – no one knew. Her eye, watching our feet, was painted marble, showing outer and inner knowledge, straining to know more. As if she were studying the street itself – the pavement where we were passing and our feet – studying for a clue to why she had fallen there, why she walked there, lived there, put on her old lady's attire on an early spring day, and went out, to do errands, and found her way to this vigil, this post.

What was she looking at? At the grain of the cement she felt under her cheek and its color. At the rims of shoe soles that stopped and those that pivoted and moved on. The soles made a grainy scraping that her hidden ear caught and she was looking at the source of that sound. There is too much on the street. All you can do is know the smallest portion. May it save her.

Dorianne Laux (b. 1952)

Sunday

We sit on the lawn, an igloo
cooler between us. So hot, the sky
is white. Above gravel rooftops
a spire, a shimmering cross.

You pick up the swollen hose, press
your thick thumb into the silver nozzle.
A fan of water sprays rainbows
over the dying lawn. Hummingbirds

sparkle green. Bellies powdered
with pollen from the bottle-brush tree.
The bells of twelve o'clock.
Our neighbors return from church.

I bow my head as they ease
clean cars into neat garages, file
through screen doors in lace gloves,
white hats, Bible-black suits.

The smell of barbeque rises, hellish
thick and sweet. I envy their weekly
peace of mind. They know
where they're going when they die.

Charcoal fluid cans contract in the sun.
I want to be Catholic. A Jew. Maybe
a Methodist. I want to kneel
for days on rough wood.

Their kids appear in bright shorts,
bathing suits, their rubber thongs
flapping down the hot cement.
They could be anyone's children;

they have God inside their tiny bodies.
My god, look how they float, like birds
through the *scissor-scissor-scissor*
of lawn sprinklers.

Down the street, a tinny radio bleats.
The sun bulges above our house
like an eye. I don't want to die.
I never want to leave this block.

I envy everything, all of it. I know
it's a sin. I love how you can shift
in your chair, take a deep drink
of gold beer, curl your toes under, and hum.

Alberto Ríos (b. 1952)

A Physics of Sudden Light

This is just about light, how suddenly
One comes upon it sometimes and is surprised.

In light, something is lifted.
That is the property of light,

And in it one weighs less.
A broad and wide leap of light

Encountered suddenly, for a moment –
You are not where you were

But you have not moved. It's the moment
That startles you up out of dream

But the other way around: it's the moment
That startles you up out of dream,

But the other way around: It's the moment, instead,
That startles you into dream, makes you

Close your eyes – that kind of light, the moment
For which, in our language, we have only

The word *surprise*, maybe a few others,
But not enough. The moment is regular

As with all the things regular
At the closing of the twentieth century:

A knowledge that electricity exists
Somewhere inside the walls;

That tonight the moon in some fashion will come out;
That cold water is good to drink.

The way taste slows a thing
On its way into the body.

Light, widened and slowed, so much of it: It
Cannot be swallowed into the mouth of the eye,

Into the throat of the pupil, there is
So much of it. But we let it in anyway,

Something in us knowing
The appropriate mechanism, the moment's lever.

Light, the slow moment of everything fast.
Like hills, those slowest waves, light,

That slowest fire, all
Confusion, confusion here

One more part of clarity: In this light
You are not where you were but you have not moved.

Steven Cramer (b. 1953)

God's at the Top of the Stairs

It can't feel like homework.
If it requires penmanship,

Don't do it. If there's no red
Magic marker, no edible

Paste, no aroma of mimeo blue
To push a face into, forget it.

Who wants to sidle up close
To the moment inside the moment

Inside the moment, if it's not
An apple skin peppered with cloves?

Stop listening for the wind
Somewhere hushing the sweet William;

Don't demand enlightenment
From the bindweed between railroad ties

In Dover, New Hampshire –
Where once, on mushrooms, you swore

"The Brown's" brown mailbox
Shouted *brown* so loud

World married Word and moved in;
And stop waiting for your ship

While the dock rots. *God's*
At the top of the stairs. You'll see

If you sit on the edge of the bed
And stare at your feet and say

Here I am for damn good reason.

Mark Doty (b. 1953)

Theory of Multiplicity

I dislike the laundromat on Sixteenth Street in the winter,
since the single aisle between the rows of washers and dryers is too narrow to allow one to sit down,
and the women who work there
doing the laundry of others seem generally to resent one's in-the-wayness, and why aren't you paying
them to do your laundry anyway?

But in summer it's fine, you can read on the street, in white plastic chairs
set out for this purpose, or watch people go by, or, as I used to like to do
one summer, look into the garden someone had made next door,
right on the edge of the sidewalk, spilling onto the pavement,
surprisingly wild, with prairie grasses, a shrubby purple coneflower,
a strapping and frowsy black-eyed susan, even a few bees drowsing

through it (how do they live, in Manhattan?) and once
when I had been leaning back on the legs of the white chair
and staring into the garden I thought of myself as one its many viewers.
What I knew was this singular aspect, what I could see
from this vantage, in this light, but its actuality consisted

in its being seen multiply, color and dimension attracting the gaze of many,
those who did not ignore it in their hurry took it in
from the particular height or angle afforded them.
What was the garden but the sum of all those instances of looking,
however hurried or casual? Perception carried, loved, considered, dis-
 or regarded.
Though it was late in the season, the frost probably not far off, it didn't seem

to matter, the fullness of the garden, the late afternoon slanting down
from the London plane trees with their already yellowing
and thinning leaves, sunlight humming into the stalks and the flowers,
the garden I saw one occasion of many, and this was in some way
an accomplishment, a contribution to the work of the whole,

ensuring that the garden was seen, being one who helped to make
the garden known, It took all of us to see it. No one could assemble that vantage
we made together, if anyone could it would be the vision of God –
which is not God, exactly, that theoretical viewpoint, but a satisfying gesture
in that direction, a participation. I felt in that moment entirely complete.
The next summer the garden was sparse, not well tended, and offered no
 consolation.

Jane Hirshfield (b. 1953)

The Monk Stood Beside a Wheelbarrow

The monk stood beside a wheelbarrow, weeping.

God or Buddha nowhere to be seen –
these tears were fully human,
bitter, broken,
falling onto the wheelbarrow's rusty side.

They gathered at its bottom,
where the metal drank them in to make more rust.

You cannot know what you do in this life, what you have done.

The monk stood weeping.
I knew I also had a place on this hard earth.

Dale Hobson (b. 1953)

Sesshins

Sesshin is an extended Buddhist meditation retreat, often held on a seasonal basis.

Spring
First day – dime-sized leaves,
second day – quarter-sized leaves,
third day – full-blown leaves.

Summer
Who catches fireflies
just to let them go again?
Which summer is this?

Fall
Begins out of sight
becomes a leaf on the wind
falls on the far shore.

Winter
The garden Jizo
shoulders a frozen white robe.
His tuque too is snow.

Greg Rappleye (b. 1953)

In the Great Field at Mount Holyoke, Under a Dome of Stars

I said, Lord, let me speak.
I am wearied by their honeysuckle words,
their kamikaze advice.

To the south are the lights of Springfield.
North stands the house of Emily,
your difficult servant.

Save me as I travel north.

Let me stand watch
under Dead Tom's plum-colored sky
and disappear again as I vanished tonight,
into Eamon's gather-dark.

And the Lord said *Keep silent.*

And the Lord said *Dance as a child dances,*
so I dizzied myself in the field.

And the Lord said *On this star-hammered night*
slap neither the mosquito nor the gnat,
for it is me, come at last
to whisper in your ear.

Deborah Slicer (b. 1953)

This Is Why

God's prayers for us are root vegetables
that struggle to breath and stretch
in clay.

Some grow into angels
with stolid bodies of
fennel and carrots, celery,

with lazy brains that fluster
in wind, get beaten down by rain,
matted in autumn muck.

These are not the angels with wings
the size of sequoia canopies
or robes soft as bumble bee fur, though some

are messengers,
onions, we unwrap silk by
sweating

silk, until
we find the little mooncalf we buried
that fall, for good,

now hiding in its monk's cell, wailing
with its wringing
hands. This is why

we weep
so much. More
than God

himself
I love
the earth angels

who taste like cold
dew, red
mud, my
fingers.

Scott Cairns (b. 1954)

Blessèd Being

So few poor among us save the actual poor, who acquire
in due time a serene dis- interest regarding whatever
evil tomorrow may bring. So few among us quite willing
to adopt that poverty promising to adorn the heart
in efficacious tatter. And so our being yet looms large
if largely out of reach, yet retains the tremor troubling
the evening's dim diffusions enhanced just now by scotch served neat.

Where was I? And where was I prepared to go? Honest, I'd hoped
by now to have accomplished a somewhat more reliable
demeanor. I'd hoped by now to have commenced, at least, to pray.
One day, I hope to do so free of the incredulous,
glib, incessant columnist established in his box seat, beaming.
How might one dip beneath that murmur, descend into a self
unadorned, undistracted, wholly present to the Blesséd

Being in Whom another blessed being comes to be?

Donald Revell (b. 1954)

To the Lord Protector

1.

It is incredible
how cold, how far
from all feeling
the spur feels.

Me next. In the middle
way of scarecrow and
imagination, I do not
wonder. I do not open.

Against intelligible flame,
against the goad,
the craving for piety,
God established the body.

The shifting flaws of human permission made it move.

2.

Cruel to remain
in solace, such
a house whose
sound cannot consist
of humanness.

The table is
hazardous. The door
is accidental.
Loneliness never
welcomes echoes.

I taste it sharply.
As it dreams
to happen, sharp
I taste it.
I clash and conjecture.

A thing of stone is not a continuity.

3.
Many find immediate
rest and human things
exempt from harm.
Seeds and sparkles
all blaze again.

But even a famous
man may not
oblige jailers,
so wild a race
has superstition run.

If any two
tasted once
remedy for loneliness,
calamity remains.
Laws are imposed.

Cure of disease crept into the best part of human society.

4.
I trust to protect
tables, astronomy,
and the unconjugal
mind not to suffer.

Words declare
no expression.
Mind hangs off,
closing proportion.

Preposterous
to have made
provisions
while I dreamed.

Soul's lawful contentment is only the fountain.

5.
A discreet man
in wild affections
remains more alone.

More deeply rooted
in other burning
in rational burning

he honors himself
to understand himself
and be considered.

The least grain
is well enough.
Many are married.

God does not principally take care of such cattle.

6.
To end the question
men may often
borrow compulsion
from a snare.

Exhortation is angels.
Compulsion is devils.
One hides, one
bares the claw.

I saw the least sinew
of my body washed
and salted. I saw
it seeking.

The obscene evidence of the question never changed.

7. *(Dedication)*
This day will be
remarkable
or my last.
Like a beast,
I am content
and mutable,
perhaps free.

A few and easy
things, a few words
unearthed in season
revive the ruined
man on earth.
The effortless rainbow
deepens.

My author sang and was deep in her showing.

Elizabeth Kirschner (b. 1955)

Meditation

Out of myself, I was looking for God
In silken streams the moon was told
Where I bent deep in ancient night
Over my people, my death, my soul.

I think I haunt the hills around.
I think God loves the blackest sound,
The cry, the wind, the world's low whine,
God is lonely where we abound.

Though we play at war till the end
His love blazes into pain and back again
When deeply down and down we go
Embalmed in his sweet amen.

Now we are lost, we sing to thee
Joy may wander but never leave.
Now we are dead, we rise and praise,
Permit us – just once! – your glory.

Anne Marie Macari (b. 1955)

Mary's Blood

It was Mary's blood made him, her blood
sieved through meaty placenta to feed him,
grow him, though Luke wrote she was no more
than the cup he was planted in, a virgin
no man ever pressed against or urged
who could barely catch eyes with the towering
angel but felt God come to her like light
through glass, like a fingerprint left on glass;
still, it's hard to believe she never wanted
to be rid of the thing inside her, wasn't
shamed carrying him, the child's
perfect head pointing at the ground
and rubbing her cervix like the round earth
rubbing the thin wall of the sky that holds it.
All women reach the time of wanting it out
but not wanting it out, not knowing
what's coming, so she must have spread
her legs in anguish because what was inside
pressing her membranes for release
was both herself and a stranger;
and she must have cried out
as the small head crowned,
splitting her, her pelvis swung

wide to push him through the wall
of this world, till what came from her
was a child lit with her own gore,
soiled, everything open so her inside
was now outside, cracked open, it means
mother to crack open, to be rent
by what comes to replace her. Such
is love – the only way. It was Mary's
blood made him: his eyes, tongue,
his penis, her milk fattened his legs,
made hair on the crown of his head,
she grew caul to wrap him and door
to come through and nothing, not even
crying *Father, Father,* to the warped
blue sky can change it.

Cole Swensen (b. 1955)

Nocturne

and as are the nocturnes, three
in number bordered before and after by antiphon and
three lessons in   and as   darkness recited
to an end of night the many knees
kneeling and would forget
oneself and the rising voice
might have been many or any
other word for three:

thy name in the whole   mindful   hast

show forth firmament   of hands

Lift up your gates O
gates   shall enter in

shall and.

Jim Daniels (b. 1956)

Transubstantiation

School let out at noon on Good Friday.
We hurried home to pray. Thunder and wind.
Did Jesus make it dark by dying on the cross?
Hurry, the old florist said, wiping dirt
onto a shroud as I ran past.

*

Ash rained down from a lumberyard fire.
It's almost beautiful, my father said,
holding me on his shoulders.

*

An empty neighborhood lot designated
as the ass-kicking site, like the coliseum
in Rome. Chunks of cement. Glass
and trash. Blood-absorbing dust.

*

One lazy summer afternoon Darlene Pike
died in a fire down the street. *It's such*
an effort just to talk, her mother said.
Mr. Pike became a genie.

*

Ronnie cowered under his father's wild blows.
We watched from our porch. *Isn't it illegal?*
Not if it's your own kid.

*

We lied to the police about the porn
so they would not drive us home to our parents.
We watched through basement windows
as our sisters danced and stripped.

*

I joined altar boys for wine and mischief.
For tips from weddings and funerals.
I sweat sin through cassock and surplice.
In the dark church, I knelt on command.
I lit candles. When the signal came,
I rang the bells.

Stephen Murabito (b. 1956)

Benediction: How to Winter Out
(After Patricia Dobler's "Wintering Out")

Do not hide
In the cellar
Regardless of your beer supply
Value the blackbird
Without it
The robin's song falls flat
Burn the wood
And sing the blues
And let the pork roast cook
On the old iron stove
All day long
Eat garlic
And breathe poetry
Into your lover's face
And thereby open yourself
To the rare sun
Don't look when it goes down
Remember
Let all voices wait
And all flesh be silence
And all flame be a language
Perfectly understood
Yet constantly in need
Of such translation

Romella D. Kitchens (b. 1957)

Block Print of the Soul

The smell of linseed and wood. It is art and
soul carved into one glorious form.

We round-off the corner in the gallery and
find a block print.

Black and white.

It is of souls trying to make it up
a spiritual hill and some forever failing.

Their bodies tumble down, seemingly
drawn to the flesh's pull, its spine, its
sweat, fear, guilty greed
            and glorious weight.

The mountain is the consistency.
It is glorious and wide and beckoning.

It has form which perseveres
beyond bone.

Yet, it feels forgiving.
Patient with the prone, the flailing,
the frail shouldered attempts.

I look at the print for a long time.
Ponder those who fall, those nearing
the top, those rolling like fine tools
used deftly down further and further.

Black and white.

Carving.

No winged figures, no white
birds winging to heaven.

Simply people in their essence
having to strive through effort
into fruition.

Philip Terman (b. 1957)

G-d

Not even in representation, figure
or shape, nothing we can imagine
or create, no structure or sound or phrase –

not even symbols or color, formulas
or equations, nothing we can mold –
what we are incapable of calling out

or writing down. Our houses
are candles and stained glass,
in our pantries scrolls of words

we kiss and dance before.
The presence of beauty is without form,
and so the middle letter is erased,

spelling a word we can never pronounce,
our tongues stumbling for a vowel,
a syllable forbidden to be said,

for the sound itself is only a sign
of the original silence.
And what is it but silence after all,

the spaces we fill in with our prayers,
our actions with blessings? Here,
each of our images is graven

as we crave and carve your name
in our lower case, our imaginations
sealed in museums, wrung out in metal

and glass and stone, bound in ink
and cloth, where words follow
in their necessity out of that place

they fade into, as us, shaping the air
with our skins full of breath and bones
that become earth, walk, and are perfect.

Bruce Beasley (b. 1958)

Lord's Prayer

Cast thy bread upon the waters: for thou shalt find it after many days . . .
for thou knowest not what evil shall be upon the earth.
–Ecclesiastes

Old One, who art in heaven, the ground's
hacked with rain-dents in ice here,
on earth, choked as it is

through months of mud & dim, threshheld.

Old One, supraliminal,
unfathered &
extramundane:

down how many deep-settled & alien

layers will your hallowing
seep? Daily your bread's cast on the waters
& daily the sops drift in,

algae-scummed, demanna-ing. So the kingdom,

as it comes, disintegrates, grain by grain. Old One,
Tetragrammaton,
unutterable

as thy hallowed & devoweled name,

pass across us, trespass us, like that
squall of crow in the square
as it jabs its beak in the puddle's

overlapping circumferences of disturbed

surface, drop by hailed raindrop, smoothed
loose by wind
so it flashes transparent

to the underlamina's burnt-brick glaze

then deflects again, in a skim, the streetlamp's
midmorning flush. Our Father,
unfathering,

be done, be done

with thy will, with its
unbroken last testament. Giver of days
like these, trinkets & tokens, the quotidian's

temptation, all otherwhere occluded:

in the circadian, sleep's
drag & draw through daylong litanies
of sitcom & beer-guzzle &

bedlamp's spluttered *Amen*. So be it,

Old One, half-
lightstreaked & macrocosmic & half
coiled down inside the quanta, imperceptible

ground, evil-deliverable & self-clustering.

As it is
in heaven, let it seem, at least,
as if it were on earth

(the half-flayed sycamore rattling

loose its last seedballs & stalks, as the crow
flaps from the grass-sludge's
hierogram of bootmark & bird-scratch)

visible & inscrutable scrawl,

thine, let it be thine Old One, thy signatory
X: let these dimmed-
out days seem that

much *willed*, unharrowed though it is here, kingdom becoming & unbecome,
amen.

Jane Mead (b. 1958)

To the Wren, No Difference No Difference to the Jay

I came a long
way to believe
in the blue jay

and I did not cheat
anyone. I
came a long way –

through complexities
of bird-sound and calendar
to believe in nothing

before I believed
in the jay.

Lynn Stanley (b. 1958)

God Affords One Explanation

Understand, you will never be happy.
You will hang beneath time like weights
in a clock. Occasionally a girl will lift her skirts,
you'll feel you have somewhere to go.
Yes you'll have joy's aperture –
the world become spatial in its light –
but mostly a wall of bird song in the dying ivy,
the candling of a child's voice,
even the heavy roses:
beauty, in its indifference, will strip you.
Even now you are trying to cover yourselves.

Eric Pankey (b. 1959)

In Memory

If the world is created from the Word,
What can I hear amid the noise of that one
Assertion and all that rattles and diminishes

In its wake: the mockingbird's trill and grate,
The sluice and overlap where the creek narrows,
The dragonfly needling through the humid air?

And what will I hear when words are no more?
I cannot hear you now, ash-that-you-are,
My beloved, who in your passion and error,

In what was your life gave life to me,
My life from the life of your blunt body
That is no more. If I believe that Christ

Is risen, why can't I believe that we too
Will be risen, rejoined, and relieved
Of the world's tug and the body's ballast?

We are asked to testify, to bear
Witness to what we have seen and heard,
And yet our hope is in the veiled and silenced.

I take comfort in your silence,
In the absence of the voice that voiced your pain.
The body apart from the spirit is dead

But that does not mean the spirit is dead.

Catherine Barnett (b. 1960)

What the Naked Eye Looks for But Cannot Find

Why ask her to wake?
So she can look into the sky at what?
The stars keep her company but niggardly so.
She watches them as they fall, pointing out
the tiny invisibles of black
where stars have been named for her girls
who can't be seen with the naked eye
though we all pretend to follow the map she draws
into the cloak of holes.

Melanie Braverman (b. 1960)

from *Love*

It's the constant need for fixing, for repair, electric failing in the last big wind causing our clocks to blink like scared children in the dark. We set the time, we set towels against the chimney to staunch the leak there, measure the door for repair. One sets out pills in the morning and afternoon, the other knits hats against the cold. The pipes freeze. The back goes out. One mother has cancer, one has an intermittent heart that blinks like the clocks at night. One is here, one is far away. When we hit the lights at night it is a fitful sleep that greets us, dreams full of instruction as to what needs doing next, and we wake grateful for the help. We drink our coffee strong, we walk the happy dog. Some days one worries that the dog isn't happy, isn't getting out enough in the midst of all this human need, but here she comes to lay her head in your hands, tail moving at the same consistent cadence as the clock. Happiness, what is it. Six in the morning, three in the afternoon, quiet sweeps in from the corners like dust. Dusk not long after on the shortest days, evening stretching before us like a sheet, smooth after dinner and a glass of wine and television and knitting and sleep. One helps with the shower, one feeds. One makes a cashmere cap for the friend who will lose her hair to drugs. It's what happens out here where the clocks slow down, where the tides shift imperceptibly until one morning again the stairs are gone and water has overtaken the shore. Gulls like buoys mark the swells, wind shoves sand around the rocks. It's a battle out there in the wind or it's a joy ride, depending on which direction you walk. If you want to get home, you have to walk both ways: oppose and acquiesce, one way not eliminating but illuminating the other. Gratitude!

Bob Hicok (b. 1960)

A Sketch

"We know other connoisseurs of God's hunger."

You come into a place of false starts.
Into skin, into arms.

Blankets surround you.

One day you flick a switch at the same time
you say the word "mother."

Now you've tasted yourself in the world:
extension: what you'll later call honesty, cancer, soul.

It's tenth grade and you're asking so much of the sky,
the "who am I?" hours,
then there are car payments in their own little book,
a novella of debt,
then a manwoman kisses your secret folds, a womanman
bears you a son or an automobile,
a daughter and one perfect spoke to add to the wheel
of everything,
you are dead and I am sorry
say my black shoes, say the ants to the fly.

But there it was: a day of rain.
A room with you alone in a room of alone.
Light half dark half sun half night
wholly liquid.
Table, chairs, book open to a picture of a man
pointing at the unknown, the open.
Woman on the ground, her jaws so wide
it can only be anguish, loss
which frames the photo, you know this, this is why
you haven't touched your tea.
There you are, inside her dress, the mistaken folds of it,
inside his finger, the one that wants to speak,
that must have been screaming when this picture was taken,
it's early in a war, this is the clock we share.
You are the rain, the hesitant light, the number on the page,
the tendency of words to gather below pictures,
tendency of pictures to have a secret side,
you have this thought,
        I am breathing water,
and this,
        I am dreamed by the day.

When you told the manwoman, the womanman
about this moment, it didn't work, you could see by eyes, by smile,
that it was your seed alone, and you carried it
through tempests of deadlines, through blood thinners
and champagne corks dimpling ceilings.

And there it was, your dying, and it wasn't that moment again,
not that rain and not that light, that finger, that open mouth,
that feeling of inside, but when people drew near,
that's all you wanted to give them, and when you bore down,
they thought it was a grimace, and they prayed for you
using the wrong words, blessing where you'd go and not
where you'd been.

Nick Flynn (b. 1960)

Stylite (fragment # 10)

Go into the desert sometime
climb a pole & sit up there
for thirty-eight years or so

until the faithful start to call you a saint.

Spend your days waiting for pilgrims
bearing olives & bread, a jar of water
balanced on a woman's head
the dipper like the tongue of a forgotten bell.

Go to the desert for half your life
then see if God doesn't find the time.

Denise Duhamel (b. 1961)

Fall

My brother-in-law
landed with a clunk.
My sister said, "Jesus Christ!
What was that?"
Her husband
splayed
on the deck,
on top
of a pile of shingles
he was pulling off the roof.
The emergency room
doctor said, "This is your lucky day, pal,"
which wasn't exactly true

except that when
most people fall from over 18 feet
they usually break their necks
and at least my brother-in-law
didn't do that.

He's sure someone was trying
to catch him.
He felt
hands
cupping his armpits
midair,
even though that's impossible,
even though his surveillance camera
doesn't show any hands
just the slightest
pause
in which a pair of slippery wings
may have tried
to lift him back up to the roof.
"Look," he says, rewinding.
He's a gray grainy lump
coming down,
missing the grill
by just a few inches,
his impact making the flames shoot up,
his thud
almost flipping
the burgers.

Maurice Kilwein Guevara (b. 1961)

Blue Dress of Chiquinquirá

Took turns scrubbing her only dress in a metal basin
in a room lit by forearms and fists pressing

into the ribs of the washboard. Whiff of vinegar.
The hem finally stopped leaking its blood shadows.
Her hair rinsed with water from a white enamel pitcher.
Can't say where they took his tiny body with the spade,
the purpled head and torso twisted in a sheet.
Outside the day was bright and with wind.
The cordillera in the distance pine-dark,
charcoal above the medicine-bottle
blue dress wanting to fly backwards from the clothesline.

Elizabeth Robinson (b. 1961)

Speak

Address is its own metaphysics. See: the
hereafter in which I speak, now, solely
in your voice.

Certain tunes tune themselves this way.
United, but how shall I ever know, speaking
in a voice that I would adopt from you.

Here is a book in which the both of us
believe in god. One reads from the front
and the other from the back.

So states the divine voice: that there
is a middle. Where is it that we do
not meet?

I speak in your voice to say that what
I heard is also what I said, that there
is a word drawn out, something less than faith,

and where, I do not know, but that a thing I
desire could extend from me. Willful religion:
that a voice could have its impact.

I carried close my small transcendent, like
a balm, but I have your voice now. The
mutual god is all immanent, the center

that dispenses with pronouns.

Ellen McGrath Smith (b. 1962)

Halasana: The Plough

The crucifix folds.   The crucifix *can fold.*   Arms meld
    to fulcrum,   hips and legs lift
until head and toes   meet / touch   the persistent ground.

A dozen daily wars   are transformed
into ploughshares   where the chin
meets the chest   the mouth kisses
    the heart

and the crown of the head   eases out
    of its thorns.

Intestines: above.   restless organs: above.
    Vena cava,
the pelvic bone   warm   as the unlidded
    eyes of the fetus.

The spine is the furrow the plough pulls from earth.
The spine is the teeth of the plough, moving backwards
from Calvary, that whole sad progress rewound.
Different way, different truth, different life.

No one's jackknife.

Grapes before vinegar.
Dirt before dust. The torso an arbor, a blessing,
the shade of your breathing –

Live there,
if you can.

Ruth L. Schwartz (b. 1962)

Trees in Wind

How sure they are, the trees in wind,
gangly, manic, drugged, exuberant; rustling,
reckless, lost; wringing a thousand hands
over a thousand graves; placing long fingers
to long lips, saying Hush, all is not lost
that you think is lost; saying There are costs
you have not yet paid. They know more than you
want to know, you who want to know

everything. They know more than that and aim
to tell it all night long, in song you can't repeat
or translate; Don't forget, they say, and pray, equally
to the gods of wind and ground; chance and purpose;
air and failure; gods of all things fallen, their limbs
block the way, arrow toward the way.

Liz Waldner (b. 1962)

(What Virginia Woolf Means to Me, by Egress Altner)

i.
The sun comes through the leaves
and makes the air seem water
so they float and things beneath
what is seen seem possible.

I need to feel no more possible than they seem;
I need the cloud that ends the dream.

ii.
In the rain, in the bucket
where the crab walks his weakly legs around
we meet. In the things of this world
we meet. While we stream away in the meanings
we make of the things of this world.

Place is where two or more are gathered.
Meaning is the language of desire.

iii.
Please grant that I may evade the ending at the end
I will trade you my goosebumps and/or my grief
Whatever you value most, venerate least
The sound of my pen scribbling at night
The moon in my fingernails, my hair
so determinedly turning white

I chose and chose and ended here
I want to be *there* before I ever left
(and left and left and left)
I've grown but not in place
I am here
I am here
Nothing fits me and still I am here

Is that the right thought?
Is that what I stayed alive to think?
With this idea, restore me to the world
It would mean the world to me, and vice versa

Nice God, lift me to your ear for me to whisper *there*
The cares of an evening all the heres have come to bear

Olena Kalytiak Davis (b. 1963)

Six Apologies, Lord

I Have Loved My Horrible Self, Lord.
I Rose, Lord, And I Rose, Lord, And I,
Dropt. Your Requirements, Lord. 'Spite Your Requirements, Lord,
I Have Loved the Low Voltage Of the Moon, Lord,
Until There Was No Moon Intensity Left, Lord, No Moon Intensity Left
For You, Lord. I Have Loved The Frivolous, The Fleeting, The Frightful
Clouds. Lord, I Have Loved Clouds! Do Not Forgive Me, Do Not
Forgive Me LordandLover, HarborandMaster, GuardianandBread, Do Not.
HoldMe, Lord, O, Hold Me

Accountable, Lord. I am
Accountable. Lord.

Lord It Over Me,
Lord It Over Me, Lord. Feed Me

Hope, Lord. Feed Me
Hope, Lord, Or Break My Teeth.

Break My Teeth, Sir,

In This My Mouth.

Reginald Shepherd (b. 1963)

Faithless

Lily, marshwater, Saint Elmo's fire
are you there? Wishes I follow to
your name, only to fall into standing pools,
gaslights bursting like soap bubbles.
Lead me into broken glass that lines
the highway's white on asphalt, or let me take
my chances, stumbling through forests
swathed in mist that looks too much like dawn
to be so dark, combing the matted undergrowth
for tell-tale leaves. If there were stars, I'd be
that light among the trees;
and if I couldn't see inside such fog,
would you carry the torch for me?
In the darkness, in the daylight,
always your smashed lamps, but never you.

Eleni Sikelianos (b. 1965)

Untitled (The Garment of Praise)

Put on the garment of praise
    Boy and Girl of praise Joy
Move god on the lips

Joy or luck fell into a swoon
a barrel of light
sweet crude

an agent having power
to reduce, destroy, or consume
                                        (catheretic)

Oh here comes a doggess sciomancer divining love
and hate by means of shadows and clouds

a beautiful bitch communicating with
ghosts of the living and dead

Sunlight falls across the body
        The house creaks, inspiration hits

Move away

        What are we doing here? All
our movements and actions
are helping or hindering
the dead

Dana Curtis (b. 1966)

The Angel Opened

Nails through the gold shimmering
tips of the red wingspan across
the tree, stretched still,
the eyes black with color.
I stroke its body, its shudders
and twists, then split the chest,
examine the graceful ribs and veins
then pluck out the heart,
hold it, perfect, just covering my eye.
To walk these echoing chambers:
what a finely detailed joy,
what endless mirrors
and the nightmare finally opened
into a dark but open room.
I kiss the small throb
and toss it in the dirt while

the feathery eyes stare at me
and I run away singing
through all the chambers of the world,
hands glowing with tenderness,
wings, wings.

Frances Richard (b. 1967)

Regmaglypt

indentation in a meteorite, caused by ablation of minerals while passing through earth's atmosphere

i.

God put spacious hands all over it. Primordial ball
of metal or evolved rock from a differentiated world, regmaglypted
meteorite thunks down
in the cushy grass, on the hood of the car,
as a portent of big touch. Punched like Rodin with raw thumbprints
of atmospheric entry. Crystallized from solar nebulae, unchanged
for 45 billion years or burning up right now within your sudden
grasp, it is the size of a sugar-grain
aflame, a shooting star that writes *touch* *touch* for an instant
on the belly or forehead of the arcing sky
while you stand and look. While you're not looking,
a continuous gentle rain
of micrometeorites bombards the earth and God is plagioclase, iron,
nickel, silicate, pyroxene, olivine, basalt that burns
off in the transforming heat of precincts where this
world's convéx abuts the others'. Time-space
zings into your chest

Glypt: carving; *regma*: breaking; *ablation*: erosion, dissipation, excision,
amputation, carrying away (as heat or mass)

ii.

Screwform
accretions build crystals in the magma junk, the
goopy secret innards of the pulsing candy body
of the earth. Bite into it: God is all
mouth. Bore into it: screwform
self-building in the lap
of thin stratosphere, fat ionosphere, the underskirts and
upper echelons where aurora swarms. Dry cold massive vacuum-packed
lap. Core in layers, mantle in layers, crust in
layers, air in layers, atmosphere in layers, and shooting
through them. Thine eyes torn white
by something-something speed, O Skygak.

Bicarbonated. Chaos
is a nameless female space where form
is not and transformation is. Sweet teeth
in the spacious mouth. Rough tongue
and paw that finger the fireball, ablate
its substance. Cosmic magnesium
sprinkles on the ground, a ton of it
per day. Online, for sale: a meteorite shaped
modestly like an angel

iii.

God sends his golden verbal semen out
into the roiling chaos container. Water
and mud and night and milk and gunk and ick
and honey are names   for this.

The bride thumbed back to clay.
The asked-for bride dismantled in the attic.
Blind bride in a heavy headdress bowing to her
head. Her mechanism. Her doll-parts. Her malic mould and crack
and silver wire, apple-cheeked and chocolate-dipped
prosthesis. Murmuring waters, fairest

flow'r unpropp'd, I

issued from a cave; I laid mee down; thou leadeth mee;
that seem'd to mee another sky. That seem'd to mee

reduced, a billboard in a cornfield near a truck-route advertising don't be a
mannequin.com. While beside the meat-case
in the chilly-breathing aisle, the skinny, ponytailed father
converses with his diaper-wearing son. The mother standing
in the irregular space outside, at the recycling center, where oil-stains
amorphously iridesce on the asphalt, is carrying
the money in her cut-offs.

Small mass, weak
heat of money she's carrying

iv.

The aspects

come to her and bid her
be; from out the whirlwind temporary
field commanders bark on mobile staticky telephones. Invisibly, she pulls
her veil up. The fiend

coasting the outer demesne of uncreation gets a flick of it by accident
on his gold sandal, on his lapis wing. Salty
leaden cum and weeping drips of chaos
burn him, he is horny, lonesome, the bad
son. A female
touch-mark on him. Hurtles

as a piece of not-earth toward earth, from the empyrean
where chunks of iron calve from larger bodies. How they do it
is a secret, and why, and how
the envelope of flux around the planet

has been woven into a scaly basket like a rocky
seacoast to catch the drop.
She sees the drop hit. Kneels and scoops
the nectar of the reflection of her face from out the pool
in the sandstorm whose name is Eden, from the puddle in the parking-lot
post-downpour, and drinks that.

Her child, screaming
in his father's arms, has not been given what he wants. A bride –

v.

Gristle-string and muscle, the calf grazes
near the truck-route, beside the cornfield. Continuous,
gentle rain. Hang-dog expression, sickly
hope, a plastic number
grommets its left ear. It eats prefabricated bricks of superfern
and freeze-dried bone and hormone buttercup. Its failed ancestors, doelike
in their eyes, were killed off by the asteroidal impact. On one hind hoof, an
ant crawls,
and its would-be paleo-kind were glued
in amber sweating from rank trees. The fern survived.
Its thread-thin root-hairs
have mutated to accommodate a wisp of astral muck
running underground

vi.

Friability: a tendency
to break up. The parent bodies
chipping or sloughing off. Magnesium
in small type in the list of trace ingredients
on the chip-bag. Elemental
lips that double-speak hiss *touch* *touch* *Chaos*

can be structured as non-chaos.

Rebecca Wolff (b. 1967)

The Lord Is Coming: All Bets Are Off

I want to marry a toy maker
outside of my community
get so-and-so to interrupt
the motivational speaker

his eyes appear to be gray.
Hovels and shacks

in the huddle of city limits
within the constraints of my boundaries

Soon I shall be released

to the previous.

In the shadow of the street
the handsome recognize
the handsome. His eyes in the immediacy
appear to be gray. Now live together forever.

Why does it have to be so previously . . .?

Extremely clever, to make it that way,
the urge for the love of God all in the past,
loving god or man all out of proportion

to his creation: wind-up toy,
stuffed dimension. To the question,

your only possible answer:
She's *natural*
The sweater is *deep black*
The sleeves are *casually pushed up*
naturalistic

Sound of wild animal
running from spider
the tall grasses
immaculate sound

glass animals of God
hauled before the tribunal
nailed into position
freed from the freedom

in the service of which I have been.
Have you been seen by me? *In the*
shadow of the shadow
        and disappeared

into composition:
in the shade of greater longing.
what little do I want from an encounter anymore?

Set piece, a constitutional

trot in vernal time
the cankerous fear of his coming
unrealized: "People are talking about . . ."

mechanical accompaniment
precipitous mountains

the accompanying
spirits rising up the mountain
through deep infernal forest
fog-drenched but not beset

exactly: reluctant to countenance the import
fresh slick on my lips
when I go to meet you

Why do you have to be so previous?

your eyes appear to be gray
outside of your environment.
The god in you greets the god

in me summarily and we proceed:
experiment in shared reality.

Lord how I wept when I came upon it (you)
I forget when last I had it (you).
I must be in the middle now, the dead
middle. On either side, morass.
Veiled valley. Audiovisual
one word now. Hand out

for greeting, demand made upon me
I register as erotic. Experiment
in shared reality: We gather together
to ask the Lord questions.

Moments before his arrival
I was alerted to his presence
Mother let me sit and stand
stand for a moment
while I regain perspective

I went down the staircase and there was no reentry.
If I fell in love with you

hand out
on the open market

a toy offering in the shadow of
the receding backside of Yahweh

Go with me

and be absorbed.

G.C. Waldrep (b. 1968)

from *Archicembalo*

What Is a Hymn

A vault kneeling stresses rhythm from one frozen motion. This is not about time. This is not about the consideration of another's feelings. Another may come or go, may come and go, another may come or she may go and he may come again. This is not about personality. Whereas from a lectern any ice needle threads broadcloth some sure vacancy.

Another may come or go, another may come or he may go and may not come again. Purely voluntary. Or not at all voluntary else not pure. If the other is yoked, if the other is tired, if the other is frightened. If the other is very small. And so how round a vowel is it that forces static from the elms into a pale sky. We see this as candles.

The question is not which but another in his freedom, that is, in the expression of a broader interest or concern excitement or distaste. Call it nave or gable or something yet more curious eggs pelican cheese. (See *What is a viola*.)

A cantonment for one certain culture.

Threshold then is not the same as permission, i.e., may he come, may she go, may another substitute – reluctant creel – may there prick an absence, may I be alone. I am alone and want and therefore you too with me. (See *What is unison*.) Is there any strength in the mutual application of a fixed surface.

Is not then paper, is not then voice. Drawn down from scope to hand-held satisfaction the plane of a dubious embrace. I question as does each in its small way. When thrown to the harp as eggs, as pelican, as license, as cheese it makes a simple roaming, it splays tethered, it does not go far. It can be heard across the river. It is an obstruction in a winter park.

What is a hymn, a hymn is a red dress, a hymn is a red dress that keeps swinging.

What is Selah

A city inside keeps crumbling into dust.

Nothing in particular is wrong, nothing in particular is a gradual unfolding and thereby undaunted by underlying technique, this is an aesthetic reproach, a taunt, a distinction and an astonishment. Space makes weight and way for malingering artifice, for a vision touching the whole multitude thereof.

Any mock-up of the universe depends on touch for its root semblance. Is there, was there ever a demiurge. (See *What is architecture*.)

Every native with his destroying weapon looks past one wheel into another. Every David in the stateroom of his agony asks for an interpretive sign: better not to know, is this a Hebrew letter, is this an Etruscan conceit. It is. Translucent.

In which dimension hubris manifests and whereby renewed through what polarity.

A sympathy, as for cherish. A stilled dancing in the fens of the Brooklyns.

A vantage in the valley of dry bones. (Far ahead, an old woman paces the same road before you.)

Mark Wunderlich (b. 1968)

Amaryllis

after Rilke

You've seen a cat consume a hummingbird,
scoop its beating body from the pyracantha bush
and break its wings with tufted paws
before marshaling it, whole, into its bone-tough throat;
seen a boy, heart racing with cocaine, climb
from a car window to tumble on the ground,
his search for pleasure ending in skinned palms;
heard a woman's shouts as she is pushed into the police cruiser,
large hand pressing her head into the door,
red lights spinning their tornado in the street.

But all of that will fade; on the table is the amaryllis
pushing its monstrous body in the air,
requiring no soil to do so, having wound
two seasons' rot into a white and papered bulb,
exacting nutrition from the winter light,
culling from complex chemistry the tints
and fragments that tissue and pause and build
again the pigment and filament.
The flower crescendoes toward the light,
though better to say despite it,
gores through gorse and pebble

to form a throat – so breakable – open
with its tender pistils, damp with rosin,
simple in its simple sex, to burn and siphon
itself in air. Tongue of fire, tongue
of earth, the amaryllis is a rudiment
forming its meretricious petals
to trumpet and exclaim.
How you admire it. It vibrates
in the draft, a complex wheel
bitten with cogs, swelling and sexual
though nothing will touch it. You forced it
to spread itself, to cleave and grasp,
remorseless, open to your assignments –
this is availability, this is tenderness,
this red plane is given to the world.
Sometimes the heart breaks. Sometimes
it is not held hostage. The red world
where cells prepare for the unexpected
splays open at the window's ledge.
Be not human you inhuman thing.
No anxious, no foible, no hesitating hand.
Pry with fiber your course through sand.
Point your whole body toward the unknown
away from the dead.
Be water and light and land –
no contrivance, no gasp, no dream
where there is no head.

Anthony Butts (b. 1969)

Thin Places

White stick with red tip tapping the sidewalk
at casual intervals, this blind man knows his
way around: the strict passing of each stride
like a mathematics toward desire, calm world of

zeroes invisible to seemingly everyone but me –
the pace with which I lift and smoke a drag
on my cigarette just as orderly, just as rare,
as the trained smoke from my mouth seems

to others. This world is not as it
appears, our hands unimaginably linked
in their dance around the unknowingly
sighted world. It never mattered where

the buildings on campus lay, yellow bricks
like sunlight captured as solid. The world
of distances the only one worth knowing,
his sleep languishes as if the next step

would not remain alone – as if the map of the earth
could have never appeared flat. We seek the thin
places of commitment, the extraordinary vision
of a world where earth and sky meet, where

the great Sky God paces about in solace. What
connections do we have with each other,
those places where earth and sky are pressed
out of existence: into an awaiting horizon

of pink and powder blue at the steady lapping
of water on shore? She lingers there,
I believe, awaiting the "yes" that trained men
possess – a woman in periwinkle and white

as if her cloak contained the approaching dawn after
the first hues have faded from clouds. The morning
appears that bright, without sunlight, in the first moments
we believe might reveal the dawn. He walks with a

cane loosely in His hand. He walks as would
a man who knows where to go; I ask
for the same, for autumn leaves to glow
like the very sun reflecting: as if they could

grow their own light. I have walked as a blind
man in the world of light conversation, as an
angel whose wings retracted permanently
into the coffered ceiling of sky. I am not immortal;

I am the only light I know before the block and tackle
hoisting the sun, the passing of day like the building
of a community of belief – dew on lawns like songs
of lament and longing. The blind man passes

like a promise through somber morning, moisture
upon moisture until the ground seems saturated with
pleas, as if the only words I try to give resemble the ones
that would make her gown completely white.

Timothy Donnelly (b. 1969)

Chapter for Being Transformed into a Sparrow

The world tries hard to bore me to death, but not hard enough.
Today it bade me sit immobile in the bath-
water upwards of an hour, but the fact is, World –

I was totally into it. There's a canker anchored
at the root of everything. Even I know that. Now what I want
is to know it better, want to know deep down

I can return to the world what filth I receive
without compunction. I knew humility once
and she died on the floor. What power do you think

you have over me? Even fastened in your turning
tepid and beyond, what I felt was strengthened,
downright strong. *The end comes once,* I said, *then what* –

What carries me now? A sudden heartwave
moving rapidly, increasing with a pinch of recollected incense.
Steady, spirit. We will address our Dead:

– What are you now, a whisper? A vapor minnow
in the rue-blue seize that never loosens, not even

for a minute, not for a half-lived something
like a dream? I trust the eloquent have already

tried opening that grip with flattery and failed; possibly
the only currency to grease a palm that monstrous

has to be the same old prank of paper we have here –
or don't have, cheerfully (not quite cheerfully).

See what can be bartered; what sacrifice's smoke
appeases over others: there is nothing beneath me.

There is nothing beneath me: the days keep coming
as if significant: events strain the heavenly, weak-
seamed sack in which they're pent; when one slips through,

kaboom! That's history, and I'm nothing better
than a shattered passenger; I pass by. Pictures develop
more speedily than ever, in an hour if you ask.

Remember the one of us on the ocean, salt-wincing
on the red flotation device? I can't take it anymore,
photography. How it flattens memory's body down

to a roll of surfaces – insistent surfaces; persuasive, yes,
but not convincing, though they threaten everywhere
to take the place of, usurping what they save: the way

a javelin of lavender, sprung from the close of a once-
loved book, asserts a dozen verities: first that of the plant
from which it came, then of its having been removed

(and that by human hand); then of a time, however measured
(and that for waving through a field); next of the soil
from which it grew, and by extension, of the world –

inclusive of the book, and of the time, and even
of the hand – but never how it felt, what anxiety or rapture
conducted or conducts it, what faith in what ability

of anything to capture; what brought it to begin with,
what labor of the blood; what accident of lavender
dismantled now on carpet; what measure of the spirit

and of its having been removed, which is perhaps
now waving through a field, and that from which it grew:
keep waving through a field, keep *with* me, please.

After the first weeks after, I lost myself remembering
the worth of what was lost, the cost of which was nothing.
Between myself and where I stood, there fell a distance

only loss could fill, an empty world, a simpleness, its shadows
thrown across my window. Often the mind would try
to stay itself by imagining: a falling through the many

numbered levels of the air, each level its progressively
thinner shade of blue, as though the air nearest earth
was the least of its forms, or had been ruined by what happens.

And always as it fell, the mind would snag upon a saving
branch before colliding with the planet beneath it.
No small debate surrounded the origin of that branch:

had the mind itself devised it, or had you put it there?
Its significance, however, was certain: something in the mind
clearly warranted protecting, but what remained unclear.

In the shade of the need to know, to know that what was once
remains, grows the knowledge that what was

was almost certainly not that, not merely,
not once. There is a way through all of this,

a ladder, yes, but it's a ladder made of thread.
In the shade of the need, keep *with* me, please.

A day or two before they tore the pall of ivy
down from the wall that held the hill in place,

the invisible sparrows that had made of it a shelter
seemed to sing a little differently, sing a little

less, as if in apprehension, and what happened to them
keeps happening to me. My green retreat

has folded, drawn into itself without me in it,
and had I known that it would, there would be

less repeating now, or as much, but softer.
At the barren wall, where what has been

has been erased, the only phrase I stand
with loving to remember, with temper I perpetuate:

---

who had pictured the world as one of degrees,
from root to stalk, from stalk to flower, from flower to breath
has learned to suffocate at last, and will not be

found recumbent on the davenport, trawling the creases
for sweetmeats past and the fruits of human reason.
When I open the door to perceive you – you are there.

Stay, illusion. There are so many things. Be with me
on Ha'arlem Meer, where you can be alligator
grown past keeping. On with me to Gorman Park, where

stairs slant down into the dark declivity of ivy wind
and fallen brown. Late afternoon a weathered book
from which I will never leave, not breathing. Broken

vessel, broken thought: late afternoon in Gorman Park. Be with me
that in what leaves will breathe in what is broken.
You were the sparrow in the laundromat. I trapped you

in the whelm of a pillowcase, showed you to the street
with human decency, care. You looked me back into myself.
And as then, so even now: I commend you to the air.

Koshin Paley Ellison (b. 1969)

Naked

Grandma, yesterday, a giant statue of a Hindu god
toppled and killed the three people

who raised the money for
their God's construction. And I hear your voice

this morning blowing up Broadway,
over the East River,

in the park on a bench,
inside the wind on my face,

the memory of your naked
body with glassy newborn eyes –

you laying tiny in your hospice bed propped
up by a dozen pillows. Naked

with your blue gown balled up in your hands,
and you said, I'm naked.

And I smiled and began
to write this elegy for you,

and I asked, if you wanted
to stay that way.

And you looked at me,
smiled slightly and said,

That would be good,
but I'll take it off again.

I said, Take what off?
And you said, Everything.

Richard Greenfield (b. 1969)

Signs & Self-Prophecy & Such

The widow's sorrow stitched them together: the freight arrived from over long distances, undamaged. Sebastian survived the many piercings that had emptied their quivers.

I thought of the painting again, the occasion of the oculus was a fake optimism in blue, where his eyes would have sought. From a small board of cedar, his upward gaze, as obvious now as the nimbus over his head, is directed by the arrows the artist skewers him with: to Our Savior, off-screen.

Here are the millennial pines, wind-raked on a promising coast & history landed on claiming. Admit the flags had to be planted in the gentle surf of the New World & songbirds make voiceless in the tortured limbs above the scree. Revised, it remains an act of privation.

Pure water seeped through an epoch of sandstone before reaching the fissure I placed my lips to & drank from.

Sign of impending death, clung to the screen against the Pacific's offshore flow. Father said the moth must have drifted up from a South American rain forest on the winds. The curled antennas were longer than its body. It was a ghost, a quality pressed against the night.

As a child in the park's pavilion she couldn't appreciate Bernstein's *Mass*, cacophony of strings & dancers – felt excluded from the rapt crowd. What remains vivid of the summer evening is the spiral slide: the other children corkscrewing down it while her mother held her, still, on a plaid blanket beneath an overhanging tree.

Another: the psychic neighbor dropped our mother's spoons on the table & read their silver collisions as the approaching death of the matriarch a week after her death.

The thread of Sebastian's life was frayed now, & the widow, grieving, removed his bloody raiment. Cut the arrowheads & placed them into a clay bowl. She genuflected before the criminal Image, prayed for how the removals should be done.

Among ancient reefs waterless in the Mojave, the morning star sank for the seventy-millionth time. I stood where I had stood at the age of ten, a hundred years between. I saw the seams that made up the jacket. The parental knot the shoelace tied.

The idea that so costumed, one could become him: thus the child entered the contest & won with his interpretation of saint as pin-cushion.

Halfway, you turn
on a feeling.

Duriel E. Harris (b. 1969)

Meditations

for Erma Jean Weems

I.
For the beginning and the end
For promise
For moments everything seems just that
For clarity after

For stillness that approaches peace
For wind that moves me
For breath that carries the long line
the comma, the colon, the semi-colon
lull of soft sounds conducive to sleep
For light moving steadily toward us
For the cushion of the earth
For those who have come before
the dead and the living
For the now, this moment, and this one
For the tenacity of the just-past
For memory and revelation
For the path to the lake
For graciousness of trees: maple, oak, willow and evergreen
For the path to the wood that trails to . . .
the bigness and smallness of things
For the work of seasons and their willingness
For those who have come before and their legacy of strong bones and teeth
    and flesh
– all moving in unison to become what is human
For those who are still beginning: our shapes, our possibilities
For the now, this moment, and this one

II.

For eyes that reach from sleep and bring morning
        still warm glazed with strangeness
For the arc of the star and the blackening crusts of night's first offering

For dark passages of ears and their shapes and winding
For waves of sound, the major and minor chords, the trill and scat, beat and
  measure
        metronome
        the brilliance that resonates
(Epiphany, divine order echoed in carbon
the molecules rattling the body cage)
        Wound so tightly I would break
        nothing to spare, rationing breath
        all the while screaming
        take it all, take it all, and leave me
And I do break, I do, I do break

For the heaving sigh
For the diaphragm, lung, larynx, tongue and palate

For the receiving palm
For receiving until filled, receiving until unbroken
For the perpetual present – fluid existence – in infinite dimensions
        paper-thin panes (neither barrier nor shield)
        that simultaneously are
        as I am in this moment and all those before and hereafter
For the yes
For the now, this moment, and this one

Tara Moyle (b. 1969)

Amphibian Duet

The night arrives thick with frogs
                Last night I dreamt I explained
                the concept of faith to a child
their song stirring buried roots under willowed ribs.
                She contemplated my words silently, with
                reverence, like Michealangelo's cherub yet wise,
                nodding only slightly
                when I paused.
Greenless in winter I'd promised myself
such an orchestra,
                It's like a belief, I told her,
saying soon they will wake up again;
                only it comes from inside yourself
soon
                like your heart beating, or the blood
                running through your veins;
soon
                you come to know it's there
soon.

I think I hear the frogs

She took my slowly spoken words

ringing the frosty edge

like the thinnest wafer on her tongue,

of the lagoon,

and, all-trusting,

wonder how closely my feet

swallowed.

stride over their heads,

This morning I woke

if their perfect round eyes ever open

to car doors slamming productively,
people puttering through their day.

if I could I'd walk barefoot over the tufts
of icy wet leaves

I sat on the edge of the bed

to hear them now,
to let them up

listing
the reasons I exist.

into the soles
of my feet

so that I could sleep,
draping the untucked covers over
straight legs

where once a calloused heel, instep,
toes, now

bubbles water's edge, gummy reeds,
drifting gelatinous color into alveoli

a frothy soled watch
of shiny lids and elastic throats,

and the song
all night

while she sleeps
all night
and the song

Joshua Corey (b. 1970)

Four Corners

Land stunned into flatness + veil. Catastrophic invitation. Those are not the same stars over the Mojave glimpsed through gravebranches of the Schwarzwald. Giant steps cross the secretaries of the interior. An apple shot off of a head of salt. We live in the chaos of the BIA.

Out there in the desert night the century was born. Navajo codetalkers hunched in Nissen huts to protect it. Duke Ellington lived in a limousine receiving signals from Southern roads. Jewish physicists built it in one place + another.

As the buffalo jump turns bison into weapons against themselves.

The native self was carved from a code of tears. Before the cross after the cross: civitas deus, derelinquo deus. The heart's anonymous water on the tip of another's tongue. Before the cross alters the cross alter the silence of the Lord.

The lost tribes were immune to bullets. They dreamed up a shirt to clothe their nakedness.

Now we are living in harmony.

Kazim Ali (b. 1971)

Ramadan

you wanted to break into branches, be wooden,
spin a knot of hunger –

you are not to know when revelation poured,
so you have to choose between the starving month's

nineteenth, twenty-first, and twenty-third evenings –
the liturgy begins to echo itself

and you can wonder why does it matter –
if the ground-water is too scarce

one can stretch nets into the air to harvest fog –
hunger opens you to illiteracy,

thirst making clearer the starving pattern,
the thick night is so quiet,

the spinning spider pauses,
the angel stops whispering for a moment listening –

the secret night could already be over –
you will have to listen very carefully –

you will never know which night's mouth is sacredly reciting
and which night's recitation is secretly mere wind

Elizabeth Bradfield (b. 1971)

Butch Poem 8: A Countertenor Sings Handel's Messiah

Seven verses in, he has stepped out from the tuxed
and taffetaed quartet of soloists. He has begun to sing:
*Behold, a virgin shall conceive, and bear a son, and shall call
his son Emmanuel.* Amplified by good acoustics, the hall
is rustling accompaniment to the countertenor's solo:

*Lift up thy voice with strength; lift it up, be not afraid.
Arise, shine; for thy light is come.* From my seat
next to my parents, high in the mezzanine,

I can see heads turning, bending toward each other,

toward the program, small lights coming on
above the paper. My parents restrain
themselves. But the rest of the hall
is turning to the biography. Is lifting
opera glasses. Is straining ears to hear him:

Then shall the eyes of the blind be opened,
and the ears of the deaf unstopped. He is singing
the alto's part in her key, his voice light and clear.

Whispering underscores the music:
    What is this high, sweet voice in a tuxedo?
I am transfixed. I want to reach under his starched
shirtfront and find a different sex. Listen to him –

He was despised and rejected of men; a man
of sorrows, and acquainted with grief.
He's singing the score and another story alongside it:

He hid not his face from shame. Through
these old words, he is making song
of the drag queen and the bulldyke.
Let him sing without the accompaniment

of rustle. Let him sing without any doubt
between body and voice: high but not shrill,
more lovely than the wide-skirted soprano,
the chunky tenor, the dapper bass. I watch
his shine-parted hair, his weight shift at key change.

Thou art gone up on high, thou hast led captivity
captive, and received gifts for men.

Afterwards, in the bar, where anemones
splay open and salmon flick through
canals designed for our wonder, no one
mentions the countertenor. My parents,
I think, are trying to navigate the appropriate
path of the moment, as am I. But he's all
I can think of, his rolled rs, adam's apple
lifting his tie at crescendo. Onstage,

Then shall be brought to pass the saying
that is written, Death is swallowed up in victory.

billed as high culture, this unsettlement,
this beauty applauded at last.

Susan Maxwell (b. 1971)

El Jaleo

(1882, J.S. Sargent)

There is the sentence bent back on its knee,
the dancer's neck pealing open
toward her theatred skirts, crinoline upturned,
skull of the bell rung to a call

knotted in creams and consumptions,
the humming wasp of belief forced now far
up our throats in this white-limed ringing, this wish
to remain thick in the vanishing, held in the wrap

of some hackled enormity which will not
call a hue up out of its material.
Though it is *paint,*
not light. Within the skirts of her circular

seal the guitarists and the girls
and the tiny dry seeds of our steps
popping then gone, flayed
and patched back in the brawling

scuffle of glasses
and spit.

(As an already recognized type of pilgrim
the Sargent family arrived in the Old World)

The lack spidering through our sockets
which will not get the light, do not get the light,
and she there, stopped like a knife
in her fortune.

(Americans but not provincial. No
claim to high birth, yet irreproachably proper)

Do you hear? Gilt slid
down the chairback.
Not her heel counting out what

happened here
but the blank bud she may not undo.

(Above all, could be counted on to understand the means
by which the status quo
was –) Cannot sit down.

Light smeared along its leash
to the strange black swell
that has risen as a fist behind her.

Risen as a fist, the repetition of it.
My face the station, your face the arrival.
Mine a point of light, yours the price of sky.
Beauty sits down in a box *(what shall I say)*

and there is an argument about suffering
rusted already and set in motion in the room around her.
The light presents itself to me with such unity –
(and the fickle ending bright enough)

– that one tone is sufficient to render it, so it is preferable, even

if it seems brutal,
to pass brusquely from light to dark
rather than accumulate things
the eye cannot see.

The dancer shouts back *I am a last*
known passage. Is it true? Neither light nor dark?
Forestalled? (*it looks like life,* said X)
The enormous machinery of the performance

broken into bits (*but also like a perversion of life*)

and shared out equally as fibrillating fist-gold bread.

"But the supreme moment is one of twelve hours wherein we must make
a finished drawing of the human form divine..."
wherein we shall be, by the hand of history, *here*.
Bird song, trees readying themselves beneath.

Each color crying like a doorway
against the other while the dancer goes in,
hand and heel, to eat her fine maker.
And what is the fire

of that pattern, the law that breaks
a wall into frame and knob so that history
may slaver over it, spitting divisions and arcades,
delays and lumbering slats. What

is the pattern that waits while the birds fly straight
at the door and are crushed, two by two?
Green-white and green-black, seen and singed?
Heart, traveling bag, lump of flips,

the slam at the pane (*will you not try again?*) was only one
thrown into the sharp rules of another.
A stone let go over the lit end of a well
become the decision to remain useful until

the cold oath pushes one's gaze up and out
into the sky that has lost the bodies now, irretrievably,
lost them, the two birds, to the smack
of material.

Even if it seems brutal. The rhythm
streaming gold from the guitar.

The wall sifts down in papillon
browns, powdering her skirt.

She is a penny on the tracks,
a form unshelled to the last remove
and we lower our heads, glances sloughing
off the table's edge, a man in history

announcing he has predicted her freight
her hummingbird maze and *yes yes*
he has, *yes,* as she is fed
like a key into the backdrop

though in the sentence that springs
from her palm as she exits, turning back
on the meridian light, there is some other thing to say,
flame standing there, to stop.

Aaron McCollough (b. 1971)

Adam Naming the Diseases

for Michael Schoenfeldt

from the mountain between jerusalem
I see them   kreutsfeldt   jakob   lou gehrig
before [my] *eyes sad noysom dark*   in which
the bandage "reeks"   the landscape has no term*

there is no time   deluge of biting flies
ezek'l in the valley cries the hand
*determination   frenzy   no   demand
in living   death   in dying living lies

the name   the signature that dies   is both
clinic window   clinic cage   ("pathologos")

the wet within the dark THAT LIVES FOR LIGHT
bacterial infection (also, "life")

the double adam (panacea) (bane)
the ransom cultures stands above the name

Arielle Greenberg (b. 1972)

Exodus 1:6-11

A king went down like the sun behind a hill,
slipping in his golden throne, and a king arose
and the third time a charm: that king
did not know my name.
Did not know our names, how they end
in mountains of stone.

We mean to say he did not know any promise ever made,
or the dream of wheat, or of stars.
A hundred years could have passed
between the first book and these next four
for all he did not know of us.
He was unlike any relation, this new king.

And here we live in the dead city,
winding our favored corpses in dry cloth,
wanting what wants us back
and so do not eat with other wanting.

We reckon with sand. We build the pyramids.
There's a story that goes
in every generation there will be only eleven
who are any good. Another goes
in every generation there will be one who may destroy you.
We suppose the rest stand in corners.

We are getting good at corners.
We miter bricks and have this dull hymn
as our grace:
God are the things we do not control.

Joshua Moses (b. 1972)

Request

O God   not the snow
or the clouds   mud   my heart
God   not any of this
the   people   the people   walking
not this   or the 365 days in the calendar year
the 73 years of average male life
not any of it   Please
do I think matters   But only
one day   grant me
to be in Love   and not doubt
O God   only this

Andrew Prall (b. 1972)

from ~~No~~ *Thoroughfare*

III.
"Let us dream of evanescence, and linger in the beautiful foolishness of things." Kakuzo Okakura, *The Book of Tea*

Thoughts of fleeing from these mettlesome things, flicking the fly from the cup. Tea teaches: 'selfing' results in smaller seed with reduced germeability or no seeds at all. The framed black and white pictures as grounds or ghosts.

Interrelated assemblages of flora and fauna–most of the landscape already modified, so what is left? What is good? Our nose leads us to the vendor of spices, and we want to ask him, his hair wiry and awry. But he is too busy lacerating seeds of morning glories to help them germinate in guesses.

On the corner with a sign:
Help me, I do not know–
who are my philosophers?
Mother bush selection, a bud break
on a pruned stick. This song; I hear
the lovely familiar without warning,
a place transient like all others but
one that has chosen to linger
for which I am thankful.
There are places that would
give buckets for this bounty
of rain.

> "But let's go on to say
> There's nothing wonderful about the fact
> that voices pass through spaces where the eyes
> Can see no object plain." Lucretius

Something about how a voice can wend its way
along a winding path, diffuse in all directions.

> "No sheets of glass to swim through."

Extreme heterogeneity in the existing seedling population.

See one way–I do not know what to say, but sip. The untuned engine slips into talk of salvation and newly paved bypasses. The mettle of a slow rattle, the toy train still chugs into the station, monsoon notwithstanding.

Tell me the secret landslide, the how and whys of it, short circuit a lifetime of study. Instantaneous conferral, transfer states to kingdoms, to want nothing of what is surveyed. The confectioner's sweet smell, the heaps of trash. To be fluent in contradictions, to not speak a damn word of it and speak it over and never again.

Dan Beachy-Quick (b. 1973)

Sonnet

Must I anger and must my anger pearl,
My anger pearl, must I pearl, must I polish
Madness daily, rub nacre into a world
Perfect, round, what in my hand should finish

As wound deepened by wound? Not jewel, not gem,
Not beauty, not gem. I am this anger.
Must each note aria I mean as requiem,
I mean requiem, mean dirge, must one finger

Bear the weight of every word, set in gold,
Hand held so the pearl catches the angle
Of light, and glowing, says, "I am betrothed."
Betrothed? I am small terror wed to wild

Rhyme. We must climb inside the world to live.
A sand-grain in the mind tells us: survive.

Sam White (b. 1973)

God, Numero Uno

Black window. Hard fall
into the manure pile. Straw steaming
spoil of dark coins. I'm on my knees
hammering fence along the line.
Black window. The apple trees
waste roadside. A basketball thuds
to sullen fruit. You know, I had something,
for a while in my hands, not a word,
but a tool for the ages. I had

a shafted fork, the drop of a spade.
In this rut there were bearings. Hammer.
Hammer. The pasture breaks
to a grid. The weeds to my knees.
Black window. Black window.
Something ecstatic in the elms.
All the branches are one picture.

Brian Teare (b. 1974)

from *Transcendental Grammar Crown*

•

This book can't be sung
(Reading Walden)

– solitude   self-definition   :   pure

nationalism!   beans in a row   & a year

to hoe them   heroic vatic stance struck mock

epic   all ironic to trick the mind   into seeing

America   a masculine parable   a second-growth

forest   to walk there   an easy wilderness   vernacular

apples   your grammar so declarative   it *is*

a government   – prophetic voice   come

closer   bring your certitude   so we can pinch

it to pith   force it   to the far wrong side

of moribund bachelorhood   we are stunned blood

we are inherited citizen dualism   we must begin

to ring   must in your ears   rebuttal   stuffed

with spirit   your whole ruddy skin   stung with it

•

Inherited citizen dualism
(*Field Poetics*)

doubt   entered the field

in the form of a body

always   grass at edge

calf-high   then rising

as heat   midday does

waist-length

– transcendent   reason   :   mind forsaking

matter it finds   impossible questions

to consider   – roots

cool   green   below

browning stems   it

didn't want to   eat

our mouth   intended

to tangle   is not

mind   it's never

wanted   for order

•

Our mouth is not mind
(E.D.)

you will never forgive us

for we never visit   sick

with god-longing   livid

fever   reeling   bestial

need sends us on all fours   in the field   where heat

ends mid-stem   spectrum's very heaven   boils above

hawkweed & birdsfoot   trefoil & a roil   of inflorescence

– doubt   a terrible field

to live in   whose laws

are made by a god

without cause or qualities

were we to cry out   lord   our voice   the wrong season

for milkweed   it's the only thing   to come home to is

what scatters   what's always going away

•

What's
(–)

as saint

is slant

to pain

storm   norm numb null

thorn   pressed to thumb

as wait

is pain's

time's

plait

in all's

stall   what becomes

of becoming

fear

nadir of feeling

Oni Buchanan (b. 1975)

The Return

A man – from the snowy corridor
of a mountain of pines, from the heart
of that wilderness – a man

walks toward me. And the ravens fly out
from behind him. He has disturbed their roost,
their silent motionless perch and now they rage

past him like a funnel widening out,
cawing, beating their wings, a deafening funnel of black, he
at its center, walking toward me.

He has come back for me. He calls my name
through the hole in his throat. His head is held on
by a white bandage knotted tightly about the wound.

After the birds subside, he unbuttons
his filthy tartan shirt. With both hands,
he grasps his sternum and wrenches, by the bone,

his chest open like a glass cabinet before me.
For a second, nothing happens. I look in,
holding up my miniature binoculars.

I want to see the menagerie of animals I had
put there, so many beautiful animals
painted with the finest brush tips,

down to a single horse hair flecked
with a bead of paint: winsor green,
cadmium yellow, manganese violet,

quinacridone rose red deep – The animals themselves
of glass and clay and jade and pewter.
Wood and china.

Some blown while liquid, some sculpted out from
their blocked materials, some dug up from the earth,
and one I found on the wooded path –

And from his chest, instead,
from its deep center, first
the raucous cries roused from sleep, then

the beating of wings, like the whole earth
quaked against me, and then the ravens pouring
outward from the source.

What do you want, I ask.

Are more ravens in those ravens' hearts?

Danielle Dutton (b. 1975)

Sprung

Once upon hard-pressed twiggy stuff, under spectacles of small trees, a gorgeous modern promiscuity made a pretty, rare bird. "With respect to your work," said the congregation of men at a useless festival under a hard-to-think sky, "Hey, death shaves me sideways, under an anarchy root. Just pull a thread so the world can worship the dictatorship of the warblers." Humming by the side of the cocooned road, the only familiar formulas were clear as all-at-once. All at once we shot the doctor in the back, his genius spinning and my triangulating heart, clear as compositions of nothing, but stunning. We are rooms rotting and dragged roots on concrete. My magnificent confession of nameless confusion and already quoted ideology, synonymous with slatternly houses, greenish in the back room. Both sides sway toward an edge. The line begins in the thematic pine-drift. There are manifestoes hiding under tables, but summer pavement breathes beneath the feet of giants failing. Dividing sermons hornlike at the river-edge, we tell where whispers melted and never never grew up. Come night the clouds bundle above the rest, past knowing just for me, to bear witness if only to a textured faith – voice or His voice, a felt performance or break-you-apart. In favor of a sermon I cover an elder Egyptian woman's limbs in the black orchard of river. She'd asked about failure, barrels of explosions of melancholy, material details, and what I might call "a loyal lightening around the eyes." I disappear and let go the light, await under white-oak skies.

Karla Kelsey (b. 1975)

from *Iteration Nets*

4

Left in the ground it, rooted, grows
so that the roses glow forth in a higher red
cleft. Tin of sound, excluded, goes.
Go at a Moses flow, mirth tins and tires, says
stand in the desert near them. On the sand
the interval/ between moments that are more/ than thinking
and wind, are weather. Hear. And gone the land
we entered, called/ obscene torments at our shore,/ then thanking,
the water began to fall quite quietly,
substance. The spending (loss) and accumulation of force,
the matter at hand, recalled might riot the
hub's dance, the pending toss, sand's illumination of course
gone down of a Morning Land.
Songs found, shove, raise warning. Span

4.02

for left in the ground it, rooted. The original asked for and the flourishing of syllables repeated, the word or words formed by leaving off in the midst of uttering grow murky in thought: what was said? *Parison? Comparison* uttered after a silence dampening off the com? *Par a son. Par y son. Pare the sun* so that the roses glow forth. *Bad this son. Pad a song. Sad too long* in a higher red. Ineffectual, the being in the bar, asking to thank, to atone, to bask the centuries away. The word cleft showing up lately, today in his grandparents' house, his grandfather minutes hours days weeks months from/towards death. We are. *Tin of sound.* He is more than most. Excluded. You do not get a second life though you are sick of hearing it.

The word goes. Showing up: atone. Thank. Pray. Go at a Moses flow expending energy not held in the palm in the heart in the lung over children hardly blessed. Awakened in the midst of a bad dream, mirth tins and tires, going on for generations as the images were said to go on before we destroyed them.
To skink the one that killed you, Hollywood style. Says: we thank. Says: stand in the desert near them. Atone. To save the one who bore you. *Pad a son. So sad he's gone.* On the sand, the children threatened with a knife, a life, a gun, several, several generations jailed, this is nothing new, nothing informative, the interval dramatic between moments that are no more than. For the sake of. But here, thinking, there, rather, the dining room table, wipe-able tablecloth, plastic roses, rose you were my. And the pictures and wind careening in are weather. Here. And the of of it, my taking him away, the golden son, my mind, in my mind, caught in the tiger's tooth, a parody if for the sake of. But real. And keening.
And bad. And a son. And gone the land

So sad he's gone, we entered. I wanted to go, mid sentence. I wanted to go and squeezed the sides of my chair, called obscene torments at our shore, but externally I was quiet. Plastic and metal. Reassuring. To stay, for you do not get a. Then thanking. And laughter punctuating, the water began to fall quite quietly proving the theory that it does not always matter what you want for generally it is trivial: you do not get a second life. That this is more about your life, *pare the song,* we are a we and woven into the bowels of *he is gone,* or *perception* slurred. Perception, accent on the *Per: Pare: Pare the sun,* substance adding up to near similar final syllables. *Comparison. Perception. Compassion.* The spending (loss) and then death, gentian, you will not like this. And the accumulation of force

We do not get a second life, the matter at hand, different from we will not, from form, from the blue gladiolas, the wedding pictures, the foreseen funeral, image of a sign. As if I could help it. You do not. They inject you with it. Any uttered of false wings and occlusion recalled might riot the hub's dance. We thank.
We atone the pending toss, the sand's illumination of course. For that we have taken of what we have not received. Earned. Forgiveness gone down of a Morning Land. For the image over-muscular and adopted easily into the vocabulary of repetition, *spare the son,* spare another, the father relinquished, renounced, I only met him once and he flattered me. A poet. I could tell.
And you resemble your son. And what to die for. Tiger's tooth, costume done in peacock feathers and Venetian lace, the song found moaning you do not get or where's the life, happy valley where these things do not dream of. As in the Bar-B-Q, the yard of cars, the uttering, squirrels, birds, coke cans, a variety, generous of what I cannot consider taking. Shove and raise warning: we are a sinking and we do not get, we do not have, we do not will. Yet it is and we span

Catherine Meng (b. 1975)

Ode to One in One Thousand

How you are prayerful
from conception.
How your coat
is chosen: red
poppy of wedding day,
white as fine
china at a wake,
blue as both
directionless extremes,
a green wheel turning.
Your perfect square
slid from the rice paper stack
belly exposed.
You are not folded
but measured & creased,
triangle, triangle, open mouth
diamond same
to each side,
thin kite ribbing
the shape of the sky.
I love you when
you are pronged
& prone as if
to expose
your quick needle wit
before your neck
is chosen,
before your wings
are turned down
like banana skin
& arched against the brace
of the index finger
& the flat pressure of thumb.
I love you best
when you are two

erect tails with
two broad wings,
two ends to the same story
both ready to take flight,
when you are about to be
bird, self
before it is I,
slender sadness,
the tears of things going on
without pause,
the moment
before you
are inevitable!
A thought becomes prayer
only when released
from the mind.
The head is a tail
unbent until
the tail is recognized.
This is your one decision:
how one end
is always perfect
by comparison,
your one flaw
tucked into your sturdy neck
& pinched
into your frontlet.
You've known
from the first alignment,
the first horizon
dividing earth from sky,
that holiness is
folded into you,
the shape of it
alighting in the hand.

Jennifer Murphy (b. 1975)

Stories Off the Earth

I call my grandmother at the nursing home in south-
west Bakersfield to tell her I survived the World
Trade Center falling, fire blooming like hot, neon
petals of Iceland poppies in the backyard of my childhood
house on Christmas Tree Lane. Do you remember
that house? I say. "Oh of course I do, for Chrissake –
how old to you think I am? Do you remember?
Do you remember your mother? When are you going
to move back home?" I tell her Nancy saw men
in three-piece suits leap from windows eighty
stories off the earth. She says, "Courage comes like faith
comes to those who need it first, and then to those who work;
that stranger things have happened than seeing humans fly.
And why don't you get a job, by the way? You're too old
to be floundering. You do realize that, don't you?
That you're too old to be floundering?" I tell her the air
I breathe contains dirt and ash and burns the back
of my throat and may contain asbestos.
She says, "Well your high-school had asbestos,
and your mother's house had asbestos, and your Aunt
Donna's house had asbestos too, so I wouldn't worry
about that too much. Plus," my grandmother says,
"you already had cancer and survived that. Do you really
think God would give you the same lesson twice?"

Ethan Paquin (b. 1975)

Persona Resuscitata

I let her touch me in a way I will not let God touch me. God
will occasionally wake to wrestle with. I spit on his fires I

will not let them transport me. I will overlook the fire,
pain on my little toe. My left foot hurts, foot of the devil. My
hurt a pet apen to nurture. My pet tells me nature to discard.
If I discard the jewels I found I will not make it to heaven.
If I keep the hurt I can trawl it, yo-yo it, dawdle it, dangle it,
make it mine and your own. Make it mine again in a way it
was before it lacked its suffer. It was an empty little animal
trolling a yard made my own by my mere presence. I will
bottle my presence; they will have to buy it. They can not stand
to live the way other bottles tell them. They make so many
demands. They are pages to flip and ideas to catch and think
everything or nothing of. When they put their ears to the bottle
bottle hole as it were
they hear oceans of suffering. We will not stand for suffering. We
will stand for something other than the vast silence. But God will lose
if he spins a fire for I am more wretched than fire. Water is more wretched
than fire; so, fire is killed by water. Silences are filled with pets strutting
in the yard. I have made the continents my yard. I have to admit the feat
was unthinkable. I was spurred by some aching brightness. It was the colour
of coral's forehead. It was the colour of cliffs and her beach house stood
out would not stand without the emptiness of the ocean. Me it writes, I write

Chris Dombrowski (b. 1976)

The Flu, the Bath

Maybe it was the fencepost-perched Meadowlark
splashing its song through the evening air just after Torey's
shot in *Shane*, tiny gouts of blood blooming
in the rain-filled wagon tracks; or the way the doctor
met my eyes, only in the mirror, as I coughed up
what felt like needles, bits of glass; or Kurosawa's bandit
swordsman itching, a moment before he strikes
the final blow, a mosquito bite:
I don't know what
assured me my death would be so forgettable, just

as we can't know the exact cause of a flu, walking
pneumonia. I drew the bath I thought I might
and knew I wouldn't die in – outside waxwings
had vanished from the branches, no one to knell
for me – and after some time had to pee, tried
with wet palms to lift myself from the tub, quavering
shoulders. From inside the hair shining like seaweed,
it breached the water's surface: its little eye or mouth
releasing a thin invisible fluid that rippled the bath,
breath blown over a cup of tea to cool it.
                                                                Where does
prayer come from. Warbled notes, glance, cold hand
reaching down to clasp a shoulder in the bath –
                                                                remind me I am here.

Ilya Kaminsky (b. 1977)

Author's Prayer

If I speak for the dead, I must
leave this animal of my body,

I must write the same poem over and over
for the empty page is a white flag of their surrender.

If I speak of them, I must walk
on the edge of myself, I must live as a blind man

who runs through the rooms without
touching the furniture.

Yes, I live. I can cross the streets asking "What year is it?"
I can dance in my sleep and laugh

in front of the mirror.
Even sleep is a prayer, Lord,

I will praise your madness, and
in a language not mine, speak

of music that wakes us, music
in which we move. For whatever I say

is a kind of petition and the darkest days
must I praise.

Nicole Collen (b. 1984)

Layer,
Loosefall.

lights
line
our runway veins

the fasten-seatbelt sign...flotation/
                                        refreshments...

and from such a seat, survey
      the shows
      that the air provides
I was
wrapped around Bjork and the NYTimes
      while the big man
      with the Blackberry belt
      faded   on the floor
of the airplane aisle, his bread belly risen and still.

      I thought:
            he is trapped in this steel bullet, face mashed against cool window
            or:
            he is waving, a gremlin on the wing

At first
the thrust seemed scarring, but to be true I hoped him gone.

Pictured clouds to meld a woeful waking, the way

fog coats a hangover and hides.

Lightanddarkness,   darkness/light
in/out   of loves known
touched/not touched
pinned in, and peeled
from flesh.

There are ghosts of happenings,
galaxies in double-helix,
glimpses of divine elbows
through cotton-weave.

There is the branching of live oaks under-head,
and thoughts believed
that leave us while we sleep. Unknown,
they stroll the sidewalks
of the landed towns,
having one another in hand
all the time.

Acknowledgments

All copyrighted works are used by permission of the authors, in addition to the following:

"A Physics of Sudden Light" from *The Smallest Muscle in the Human Body* © 2002 by Alberto Ríos, reprinted with the permission of Copper Canyon Press, P.O. Box 271, Port Townsend, WA 98368-0271. "A Way of Speaking" is from *The Other Life* © 2001 by Andrea Hollander Budy, reprinted by permission of Story Line Press. "A word made flesh is seldom" and "It was not saint, it was too large" reprinted by permission of the publishers and the Trustees of Amherst College from *The Poems of Emily Dickinson: Reading Edition*, edited by Ralph W. Franklin, Mass.: The Belknap Press of Harvard University Press, © 1998, 1999 by the President and Fellows of Harvard College, © 1951, 1955, 1979, 1983 by the President and Fellows of Harvard College. "All Saints" reprinted with permission from *Matter*, by Bin Ramke, published by the University of Iowa Press. "Amaryllis" © 2004 by Mark Wunderlich, reprinted from *Voluntary Servitude* with the permission of Graywolf Press, Saint Paul, Minnesota. "American Heaven", from *American Sonnets* by Gerald Stern © 2002 by Gerald Stern, used by permission of W. W. Norton & Company, Inc. "Argument to Love as a Person," "Letter to Eve," "On Gaining a Soul," and "On the Inter-Relatedness of the Universe" from *Poems Seven: New and Complete Poetry* © 2001 by Alan Dugan, used by permission of Seven Stories Press, www.sevenstories.com. "Blesséd Being" reprinted by permission of Scott Cairns and Paraclete Press. "Boy at Paterson Falls" from *Captivity*, by Toi Derricotte, 1989, reprinted by permission of the University of Pittsburgh Press. "Christmas" from *Mulroney & Others* © 2000 by Baron Wormser, used with permission of Sarabande Books, Inc., www.sarabandebooks.org. All rights reserved. "Earthstar" from *Quipu* © 2005 by Arthur Sze, reprinted with the permission of Copper Canyon Press, P.O. Box 271, Port Townsend, WA 98368-0271. "Faithless" from *Some Are Drowning*, by Reginald Shepherd, 1994, reprinted by permission of the University of Pittsburgh Press. "God", from *Rooms Are Never Finished* by Agha Shahid Ali © 2002 by Agha Shahid Ali, used by permission of W. W. Norton & Company, Inc. "God, Numero Uno" by Sam White reprinted by permission of Slope Editions. *John Brown's Body* (selections) by Stephen Vincent Benet © 1927, 1928 by Stephen Vincent Benet, © renewed 1955 by Rosemary Carr Benet, reprinted with permission of Brandt & Hochman Literary Agents, Inc. "Magic Psalm" and "Psalm IV" from *Collected Poems 1947-1980* by Allen Ginsberg, © 1984 by Allen Ginsberg, reprinted by permission of HarperCollins Publishers. "Mantra" reprinted by permission of Anne Waldman from *Structure of the World Compared to a Bubble* (Penguin). "Nocturne" reprinted with permission from *Such Rich Hour*, by Cole Swensen, published by the University of Iowa Press. "Patterns of Paint in Certain Small Missions," by Brenda Hillman from *Cascadia* (Wesleyan University Press, 2001) © 2001 by Brenda Hillman and reprinted with permission of Wesleyan University Press, www.wesleyan.edu/wespress. "Poem" from *Collected Poems* by Frank O'Hara © 1971 by Maureen Granville-Smith, Administratrix of the Estate of Frank O'Hara, used by permission of Alfred A. Knopf, a division of Random House, Inc. "Prayer Rug" from *The Half-Inch Himalayas* © 1987 by Agha Shahid Ali and reprinted by permission of Wesleyan University Press. "Four Psalms" from *The Volcano Sequence*, by Alicia Suskin

Ostriker © 2002, reprinted by permission of the University of Pittsburgh Press. "Signs and Self Prophecy and Such" from *A Carnage in the Lovetrees* by Richard Greenfield © 2003 The Regents of the University of California, University of California Press. *Songs of Gold Mountain* (selections 30, 21, 59, 123, 162) by Marlon K. Hom © 1992 The Regents of the University of California, University of California Press. "Soul Song", from *Aspects of Eve* by Linda Pastan © 1970, 1971, 1972, 1973, 1974, 1975 by Linda Pastan, used by permission of Liveright Publishing Corporation. "Stylite (fragment #10)" © 2000 by Nick Flynn, reprinted from *Some Ether* with the permission of Graywolf Press, Saint Paul, Minnesota. "Sunday" from *Awake* © 1995 by Dorianne Laux, reprinted with permission of BOA Editions, Ltd. "The Deposition", from *Early Occult Memory Systems of the Lower Midwest: Poems* by B. H. Fairchild © by B. H. Fairchild, used by permission of W. W. Norton & Company, Inc. "The Foreskin" from *The Orchard* © 2004 by Brigit Pegeen Kelly. Reprinted with permission of BOA Editions, Ltd. "The Night House" from *Picnic, Lightning* by Billy Collins, 1998, reprinted by permission of the University of Pittsburgh Press. "The War Prayer" (401 words) by Mark Twain © 1923, 1951 by The Mark Twain Co., reprinted by permission of HarperCollins Publishers. "To The Lord Protector" from *There Are Three* © 1998 by Donald Revell and reprinted by permission of Wesleyan University Press. "Where Any of Us", from *Jack and Other New Poems* by Maxine Kumin © 2005 by Maxine Kumin. Used by permission of W. W. Norton & Company, Inc.

Used by permission of the Massachusetts Historical Society: William Adams, Account of his conversion experience, MHS; Samuel Sewall diary, *Collections of the Massachusetts Historical Society*, Volume V, fifth series, MHS; Thomas Tillam, "Upon the First Sight of New England," John Davis Papers, MHS.

Used by permission of the New England Historic Genealogical Society: John Stansby conversion narrative from Thomas Shepard's Confessions (Mss 553).

Used by permission of the Rare Book & Manuscript Library, University of Pennsylvania: "[Thy Garden, Orchard, Fields]" and "[Most Weeds, Whilst Young]" from the Pastorius Beehive.

The following authors gratefully acknowledge the publications where their work first appeared:

Dan Beachy-Quick: "Sonnet" appeared in *Poetry.* Bruce Beasley: "Lord's Prayer" appeared in *Image.* Robert Cording: "Parable of the Moth" appeared in *Image.* Chris Dombrowski: "The Flu, The Bath" appeared in *The Louisville Review.* Timothy Donnelly: "Chapter for Being Transformed into a Sparrow" appeared in *The Literary Review.* Denise Duhamel: "Fall" first appeared in *5 a.m.* Frank X. Gaspar: "Bodhidharma Preaches *The Wake-Up Sermon*" appeared in *Prairie Schooner* and *Night of a Thousand Blossoms* (Alice James Books). Sydney Lea: "Recovery" appeared in *The Georgia Review.* Stephen Murabito: "Benediction: How to Winter Out" appeared in *Pitt Magazine.* Ethan Pacquin: "Persona Resuscitata" appeared in *The Violence* (Ahsahta Press). Liz Waldner: "(What Virginia Woolf Means to Me, by Egress Altner)" appeared in *Denver Quarterly.* G.C. Waldrep: "What is a Hymn" and "What is Selah" appeared in *Octopus* and *Salt Hill.*

Contributors

Listed by first name

Aaron McCollough is the author of *Welkin, Double Venus*, and *Little Ease*.

Abram Joseph Ryan was a priest in the Vincentian order who served as chaplain in the Confederate army.

Agha Shahid Ali was the author of many books, including *The Half-Inch Himalayas*.

Alan Dugan's last book was *Poems Seven: New and Complete Poems*.

Albert Glover is the author of four books of poetry and *Charles Olson: Letters for Origin*

Alberto Ríos is the author of *The Smallest Muscle in the Human Body*.

Alicia Suskin Ostriker is the author of many books, including *No Heaven*.

Allen Ginsberg was the author of *Howl*.

Amos Bronson Alcott, father to Louisa May, was a leading Transcendentalist and founder of a utopian community.

Amy Lowell's first book was *A Dome of Many-Coloured Glass*.

Andrea Hollander Budy is the author of three books of poetry, including *Woman in the Painting*.

Andrew Prall's *No Thoroughfare* is based on research of the tea industry conducted in Darjeeling, India.

Anne Bradstreet's first book of poems, *The Tenth Muse*, was published without her knowledge.

Anne Marie Macari is the author of *Ivory Cradle* and *Gloryland*.

Anne Waldman is the author of many books, including *In the Room of Never Grieve: New and Selected Poems 1985-2003*.

Anthony Butts is the author of *Little Low Heaven* and *Fifth Season*.

Arielle Greenberg is the author of many books, including *My Kafka Century*.

Arthur Sze is the author of many books, including *Quipu*.

B. G. De Sylva was a popular songwriter.

B.H. Fairchild is the author of many books, including *Early Occult Memory Systems of the Lower Midwest*.

Baron Wormser is the author of six books of poetry, including *Subject Matter* and *Mulroney and Others*.

Benjamin Franklin King's work was collected, shortly after his death, in *Ben King's Verse*.

Billy Collins is the author of many books, including *The Trouble with Poetry and Other Poems*. He served as U.S. Poet Laureate for 2001–03.

Bin Ramke is the author of many books, including *Matter*.

Bob Hicok is the author of many books, including *Insomnia Diary*.

Brenda Hillman is the author of many books, including *Pieces of Air in the Epic*.

Brian Teare is the author of *The Room Where I Was Born*.

Brigit Pegeen Kelly is the author of *The Orchard, Song*, and *To the Place of the Trumpets*.

Bruce Beasley is the author of many books, including *The Corpse Flower: New and Selected Poems*.

C. D. Martin was a popular lyricist.

Carl Sandburg was the author of many volumes of poetry, including *Chicago Poems*.

Catherine Barnett is the author of *Into Perfect Spheres Such Holes Are Pierced*.

Catherine Meng's first book is entitled *Tonight's the Night*.

Charles Anderson Dana lived at the Transcendentalist community at Brook Farm before becoming an editor and journalist.

Charles Timothy Brooks was a poet, Unitarian minister, translator of German poets, and biographer to Channing.

Chris Dombrowski is originally from Michigan.

Christopher Noyes was ordained at Salem in 1683 and took part in the witchcraft trials.

Christopher Pearse Cranch was author of *The Bird and the Bell with Other Poems.*

Cole Swensen is the author of ten books of poetry, including *Goest* and *The Book of a Hundred Hands*.

Conrad Aiken was granted exemption from service in WWI by claiming his work as a poet made him "essential industry."

Cotton Mather was author of *Magnalia Christi Americana.*

Dale Hobson is the author of two chapbooks: *Nickelodeon* and *Second Growth*.

Dan Beachy-Quick is the author of the collections *North True South Bright, Spell,* and *Mulberry*.

Dana Curtis is the author of *The Body's Response to Famine* and *Pyromythology*. She is the founder and editor of Elixir Press.

Daniel Bliss is lost to history.

Danielle Dutton is the author of *S P R A W L*.

Deborah Slicer is the author of *The White Calf Kicks*.

Denise Duhamel is the author of many books, including *Two and Two, Mille et un Sentiments*, and *Queen for a Day: Selected and New Poems.*

Donald Revell is the author of many books, including *Pennyweight Windows: New and Selected Poems*.

Dorianne Laux is the author of four books of poetry, including *Facts About the Moon*.

Duriel E. Harris is the author of *Drag* and poetry editor of *Obsidian III*.

Edgar Allan Poe was author of "The Raven."

Edith Wharton was author of *The Age of Innocence.*

Edmund Hamilton Sears was a Unitarian minister.

Edna St. Vincent Millay wrote plays and poems, including the volume *Wine from These Grapes.*

Edward Johnson was the author of *Wonder-Working Providence of Sions Saviour in New England.*

Edward Rowland Sill published *The Hermitage and Other Poems* and *The Venus of Milo and Other Poems* in his lifetime.

Edward Taylor attended Harvard, became minister at Westfield, MA., and did not publish poetry during his lifetime.

Edwin Markham's first book of poems was *The Man with the Hoe and Other Poems.*

Eleni Sikelianos is the author of many books, including *The California Poem* and *The Book of Jon.*

Elizabeth Bradfield works as a naturalist in Anchorage, Alaska. She is founder and editor of www.broadsidedpress.org

Elizabeth Kirschner is the author of three books of poetry, including *Slow Risen Among the Smoke Trees.*

Elizabeth Robinson is the author of many books, including *Apostrophe.*

Ellen McGrath Smith's poetry and criticism have appeared in *Diner, Sentence, The Chiron Review*, and elsewhere.

Ellen Sturgis Hooper was admired in the Transcendentalist circle; she died at the age of 36.

Elton Glaser is the author of many books, including *Here and Hereafter*.

Emily Dickinson wrote more than 1500 poems in her lifetime and published seven.

Emily Pauline Johnson (Tekahionwake) was the author of *Flint and Feather.*

Emma Lazarus's words from "The New Colossus" grace the Statue of Liberty.

Eric Pankey is the author of seven collections of poetry, including *Reliquaries.*

Ethan Paquin is the author of *The Makeshift, The Violence,* and *The Thieves*. He is founder and editor of Slope Editions.

Ezra Pound was author of *The Cantos* and many other works, including translations and essays.

Fenton Johnson was the author of three poetry collections: *A Little Dreaming, Visions in the Dark,* and *Songs of the Soul.*

Frances Ellen Watkins Harper was born to free black parents in Baltimore. Her first book was *Forest Leaves.*

Frances Richard is the author of *See Through.*

Francis Daniel Pastorius founded the village of Germantown, PA.

Frank O'Hara published six collections of poems in his lifetime, including *Lunch Poems.*

Frank X. Gaspar is the author of many books, including *Night of a Thousand Blossoms*.

Frederic Henry Hedge was an early Transcendentalist and German scholar.

Frederick Goddard Tuckerman was the author of "The Cricket."

G.C. Waldrep is the author of *Goldbeather's Skin* and *Disclamor*. His is a member of the Old Order River Brethren.

Gail Mazur is the author of five books of poetry, including *Zeppo's Wife: New and Selected Poems*.

Gary Margolis is the author of many books, including *Fire in the Orchard.*

George Bennard was a minister and hymnist in Michigan.

George Santayana was a professor at Harvard whose students included T.S. Eliot and Wallace Stevens.

George Shepard Burleigh was the author of *AntiSlavery Hymns.*

Gerald Stern is the author of many books, including *Everything Is Burning.*

Gertrude Stein was a prolific writer of poems, plays, novels, and other works, including *The Autobiography of Alice B. Toklas.*

Greg Rappleye's second book of poems is entitled *A Path Between Houses.*

H. D. (Hilda Doolittle) was a translator and author of novels, memoirs, and poetry, including *Trilogy.*

Helen Hunt Jackson was the author of many poems and novels, including *Ramona.*

Henry David Thoreau was the author of many works, including *Walden.*

Henry Wadsworth Longfellow was the most famous American poet of the late 19th and early 20th centuries.

Herman Melville's most well-known book today is *Moby Dick.*

Horace Logo Traubel was friend and literary executor to Walt Whitman. His books include *Chants Communal* and *Optimos.*

Ilya Kaminsky is the author of *Dancing in Odessa.*

Jack Collom is the author of *Red Car Goes By.*

Jack Myers is the author of 17 books of poetry, including *Routine Heaven* and *The Portable Poetry Workshop*.

James Russell Lowell was a critic and poet. Among his books are *Poems, A Fable for Critics,* and *The Biglow Papers.*

James Weldon Johnson was author of *Autobiography of an Ex-Colored Man.*

Jane Augustine is the author of many books, including *Night Lights.*

Jane Dunlap is lost to history.

Jane Hirshfield has written many books and is editor of *Women in Praise of the*

Sacred: 43 Centuries of Spiritual Poetry by Women.

Jane Mead is the author of *The Lord and the General Din of the World* and *House of Poured-Out Waters*.

Jennifer Murphy is the author of *Remain.*

Jim Daniels is the author of many books, including *Show and Tell: New and Selected Poems.*

Jo McDougall is the author of five books of poetry, including *Satisfied with Havoc*.

Joaquin Miller, who was known as a poet of the American West, published *Specimens* and *Joaquin et al.*

Joel Barlow was a lawyer and prolific poet whose work included the mock-heroic *Hasty Pudding.*

John Banister Tabb was born in Virginia and published nine books of poems, including *The Rosary in Rhyme.*

John Greenleaf Whittier was a prolific Quaker poet.

John Jea was author of *The Life, History, and Unparalleled Sufferings of John Jea, African Preacher.*

John Newton was a ship's captain before experiencing conversion during a sea storm in 1748.

John Rolfe was a member of the Jamestown colony.

John Stansby was a member of Thomas Shepard's congregation at Newtown, MA.

John Stephenson's hymns became popular folk material.

John Weiss was a minister and member of the Transcendentalist Club.

John White Chadwick was a minister, theologian, and poet whose books included *A Daring Faith* and *Belief and Life.*

Jonathan Edwards wrote and preached the sermon *Sinners in the Hands of An Angry God.*

Jonathan Winthrop was the first governor of Massachusetts Bay Colony.

Jones Very wrote over 800 poems in his lifetime; he was minister at Salem for his whole career.

Joseph Scriven wrote "What a Friend We Have in Jesus" upon the death of his fiancée.

Joseph Smith was led by an angel to buried golden tablets, which Smith translated into *The Book of Mormon.*

Joshua Corey is the author of two collections of poetry, *Selah* and *Fourier Series*.

Joshua Moses lives in Brooklyn, NY. He studies anthropology at CUNY and Buddhism at the Village Zendo.

Josiah Gilbert Holland was a critic of (and more famous than) Walt Whitman; his wife was a friend of Emily Dickinson.

Joyce Kilmer was killed in action in WWI.

Julia Ward Howe was a prolific poet and songwriter. Her first published book was *Passionflowers.*

Julie Suk is the author of four books of poetry, including *The Dark Takes Aim.*

Jupiter Hammon was the first published African American poet.

Karla Kelsey is the author of *Knowledge, Forms, the Aviary* and the chapbook *Little Dividing Doors of the Mind*.

Kazim Ali is the author of *The Far Mosque* and publisher of Nightboat Books.

Koshin Paley Ellison is a poet, psychotherapist, Soto Zen Buddhist priest, and the editor of *Enso: Buddhist Arts Journal*.

Langston Hughes was a prolific author of drama, prose, and poetry, including *Shakespeare in Harlem*.

Leonard Gontarek coordinates Peace/Works: Poets and Writers for Peace in Philadelphia. He is the author of *Déjà Vu Diner*.

Linda Pastan has published 11 volumes of poetry, including *Carnival Evening: New and Selected Poems 1968-1998*.

Liz Waldner is the author of many books, including *Saving the Appearances.*

Lizette Woodworth Reese published ten volumes of poetry, including *White April.*

Louise Imogen Guiney was the daughter of Irish Catholic immigrants. Her books include *Martyr's Idyl and Shorter Poems.*

Lynn Stanley is a visual artist and writer living in Provincetown, MA. She is author of the chapbook *Gravity Claims Us.*

Madison Cawein was known as The Kentucky Poet. He published *Blooms of the Berry* and five other books of poems.

Margaret Fuller's *Woman in the Nineteenth Century* was a major influence on the early women's rights movement.

Mark Doty is the author of many books, including *School of the Arts*.

Mark Jarman is the author of many books, including *Epistles*.

Mark Twain is most famous for his novels *Tom Sawyer* and *Huckleberry Finn*.

Mark Wunderlich is the author of *Voluntary Servitude* and *The Anchorage.*

Maurice Kilwein Guevara's books include *Postmortem, Poems of the River Spirit,* and *Autobiography of So-and-so*.

Maxine Kumin is the author of many books, including *Jack and Other New Poems.*

Maxwell King's poetry has appeared in *5am, Tar River Poetry, The American Poetry Review,* and elsewhere.

Melanie Braverman, the author of *East Justice* and *Red*, lives in Provincetown, MA.

Michael Fortune's piece was performed during the January 1, 1808 sermon at the African Episcopal Church in Philadelphia.

Michael Poage has published five books of poetry, including *Abundance.*

Michael Wigglesworth's *Day of Doom* was a bestseller in 17th-century colonial New England.

Nathaniel Hawthorne was author of *The Scarlet Letter* and many other novels.

Nick Flynn's books of poems are *Some Ether* and *Blind Huber.*

Nicole Collen is from Rochester, NY.

Norah Pollard is the author of *Leaning In* and *Report from the Banana Hospital.*

Olaudah Equiano, also known as Gustavas Vassa, was the author of a well-known slave narrative.

Olena Kalytiak Davis is the author of *shattered sonnets love cards and other off and back handed importunities* and *And Her Soul Out of Nothing*.

Oni Buchanan is the author of *What Animal*. She is on the piano faculty at the New School of Music in Cambridge.

Ottiwell Heginbothom was a minister in Sudbury, Suffolk, England whose hymns became American folk material.

Paul Hamilton Hayne was born in Charleston and moved to Georgia after the Civil War.

Paul Laurence Dunbar, the son of Kentucky slaves, became nationally known when his *Majors and Minors* appeared.

Peter Blair is the author of *The Divine Salt.*

Peter Williams, Jr. delivered the hymns reprinted here to commemorate the outlawing of the slave trade.

Philip Freneau was a sea captain, journalist, friend to Thomas Jefferson, and widely known as "the poet of the revolution."

Philip Terman is the author of *Book of the Unbroken Days* and *The House of Sages.*

Phillips Brooks attended Harvard and became an Episcopal priest who supported abolition.

Phillis Wheatley achieved international fame as an African-American poet in the 1700s.

Ralph Waldo Emerson is most well-known for his essays, including his *Divinity School Address.*

Rebecca Wolff is the author of *Manderley* and *Figment.*

Reginald Shepherd is the author of many books, including *Otherhood.*

Rennie McQuilkin is the author of *Learning the Angels.*

Richard Allen was founder of the African Methodist Episcopal church.

Richard Greenfield is the author of *Carnage in the Lovetrees.*

Richard Hovey's first book was *Songs of Vagabondia.*

Robert Cording is the author of many books, including *Common Life.*

Robert Frost read at President Kennedy's inauguration.

Roger Williams founded Rhode Island.

Romella D. Kitchens is the author of the chapbook *Hip Hop Warrior.*

Ruth L. Schwartz is the author of many books, including *Dear Good Naked Morning.*

Sam White is the author of *The Goddess of the Hunt is Not Herself.*

Samson Occom was a Mohegan minister.

Samuel Danforth's *Errand into the Wilderness* was the election sermon for Massachusetts in 1670.

Samuel Gray Ward, financier and poet, was one of the founders of the Metropolitan Museum of Art.

Samuel Hazo is the author of *A Flight to Elsewhere* and *Just Once.*

Samuel Longfellow was the author, with Samuel Johnson, of *The Book of Hymns.*

Samuel Sewall was a judge at the Salem witchcraft trials and Chief Justice of Massachusetts.

Sara Teasdale's books included *Rivers to the Sea, Love Songs,* and *Strange Victory.*

Scott Cairns is the author of many books, including *Compass of Affection: Poems Selected and New.*

Sidney Lanier was the author of travel books, novels, poems, and literary theory, including *The Science of English Verse.*

Sidney Wade is the author of four collections of poetry, most recently *Celestial Bodies.*

Stephen Dunn is the author of 14 collections of poetry, including *Different Hours.*

Stephen Murabito is the author of *Communion of Asiago* and *The Oswego Fugues.*

Stephen Vincent Benét's *John Brown's Body* was written as an epic, booklength poem.

Steven Cramer is the author of four books of poetry, including *Goodbye to the Orchard.*

Susan Maxwell is the author of *Passenger.*

Sydney Lea is the author of many books, including *Ghost Pain.*

T. S. Eliot was author of many books or criticism and poetry, including *The Waste Land.*

Tara Moyle's poems have appeared in journals such as *Brilliant Corners, Diagram, Margie,* and *Yemassee.*

Thomas Morton was expelled from Massachusetts and wrote *New English Canaan.*

Thomas Tillam escaped to New England just before the English Civil War.

Timothy Donnelly is the author of *Twenty-seven Props for a Production of Eine Lebenszeit.*

Toi Derricotte is the author of five books of poetry, including *The Black Notebooks* and *Natural Birth.*

Trumbull Stickney published only one volume, *Dramatic Verses,* during his lifetime.

W. E. B. Du Bois wrote extensively on race in America. Among his books is *The Souls of Black Folk.*

Wallace Stevens' first book was entitled *Harmonium.*

Walt Whitman was the author of *Leaves of Grass.*

William Adams died in 1659. His son and grandson attended Harvard and became ministers.

William Billings was one of America's first significant composers and author of *The New-England Psalm-Singer.*

William Bradford was the first governor of the colony of Massachusetts.

William Carlos Williams was the author of many volumes of poetry, including *Paterson.*

William Cullen Bryant was an editor, lawyer, and poet. Bryant Park in Manhattan is named for him.

William Ellery Channing was minister of the Federal Street Church in Boston and a leading Unitarian theologian.

William Ellery Channing II dropped out of Harvard, married Margaret Fuller's sister Ellen, and settled in Concord to write.

William Everson became the Catholic priest Brother Antoninus and wrote many books, including *The Veritable Years.*

William Hamilton delivered the oration reprinted here at the African Zion Church in New York City, July 4, 1828.

William Henry Furness was a Unitarian pastor in Philadelphia.

William Vaughn Moody wrote many works of verse and prose drama, including *The Fire-Bringer.*

Witter Bynner was Harvard's Phi Beta Kappa poet for 1907; his last book, *New Poems,* was published in 1960.

Index of Authors and Titles

Index of First Lines

Design and Production

Text and cover design by Kathy Boykowycz
Cover photo: evening on a Wyoming river, by S. A. Neff, Jr.

Text set in ITC Giovanni, designed in 1989 by Robert Slimbach

Printed by Thomson-Shore of Dexter, Michigan
on Nature's Natural, a 50% recycled paper